LEARNING MY LINES

LEARNING MY LINES

From *Cathy Come Home* to *EastEnders*

Ray Brooks

Book Guild Publishing
Sussex, England

First published in Great Britain in 2009 by
The Book Guild Ltd
Pavilion View
19 New Road
Brighton, BN1 1UF

Typesetting in Garamond by
Keyboard Services, Luton, Bedfordshire

Printed and bound in Great Britain by
CPI Antony Rowe

A catalogue record for this book is available from
The British Library

ISBN 978 1 84624 371 4

Contents

Prologue

I had my hand over Dot Cotton's mouth ('Don't get your thumb up my nose, Ray'), the door is thrown open – Jim, Dot's husband, shocked: 'Dorothy!' He rushes towards us, I stumble away into the window and crash through it down into Albert Square. Dead as the dodo.

John Steed in *The Avengers* killed me. Again I fell from a height but this time with a knife in my chest. I was killed by a giant octopus under the Aegean sea when searching for a nuclear warhead while working at Butlin's holiday camp. My throat was cut by a pirate when our galleon was attacked five miles off the Spanish Coast. Alec Guiness and Dirk Bogarde survived. The film, *HMS Defiant*, didn't. I think I had my head chopped off when I was eight, doing *The Mikado*.

I saw Julius Caesar killed when I was wet behind the ears; I was Brutus' young servant. It was horrible. BBC Children's Television shouldn't show such things.

I *nearly* died in *Casualty*. I read the signs. Toast in the morning, arguing with the kids, rushing to work, a stressful car journey, the traffic terrible. I park at work; on leaving the car, I stagger and clutch my chest. Next scene in emergency, tubes out of every orifice. I never opened my eyes again. But I'd read the signs, so I decided not to do it. That was just a 'nearly'.

Of course, there is a different kind of dying and I've done that plenty of times. But then it's the critics who do the killing.

As a mad pathologist, in *Death of an Expert Witness*, I killed Geoffrey Palmer, Brenda Blethyn and a couple of others before not finishing off Adam Dalgliesh. Had I done so it would have stopped

P.D. James in her tracks. I've killed people in *Z Cars*, *Dixon of Dock Green*, *The Saint*, *Danger Man* and in Agatha Christie plays all over the country. I've finished off pirates and, with Peter Cushing as Doctor Who, I shot Daleks and Cybermen – also the occasional wife, wife's lover and mother-in-law. In fact, it seems that in fifty years it's been a hell of a blood bath. I threatened to kill Michael Crawford during the filming of *The Knack*.

The scene is Brighton, The Theatre Royal, an amateur production of *The Happiest Days Of Your Life*, half an hour before the curtain goes up. It's Thursday. I, aged ten, enter the stage door with a bag of bulls eyes (liquorice tasting boiled sweets) and proceed to a dressing room under the stage to wish luck to the boy who will be playing my part for the rest of the week. What's in that bag? he says. I tell him. Can I have one? he says.

It must have been at that moment, between the bulls eye bag and that boy who popped one in his mouth, that I realised that I wanted to be an actor.

At the same time I discovered that most important nugget of knowledge which the frippery of theatricality hides under its munificent frocks: for all its giggles, it's a cut throat business.

Incidentally, for those of a sensitive disposition, the bulls eye boy subsequently recovered magnificently from his choking fit and now has six children and a season ticket at Brighton and Hove Albion.

But I suppose my most famous murder was recently, in 2006 – yes, another wife: *The Death of Pauline Fowler*. There have been many famous deaths in history but none matches the enormity of this shock and horror that rocked millions around the world – the tragedy that occurred in snowbound Albert Square on Christmas night. Mouths opened, children cried, grandmas dropped their sherry in disbelief and even dogs ran into corners and yelped their hearts out. Yes, she was dead. And I had ended her life with a frying pan. But, sadly, this scene was never even shot. They didn't trust me with a frying pan. What a pity! Dum, dum, dum.

In Plaistow, in 2001, a little old lady stopped and stared at me. 'Weren't you in *The Knack*? I thought you were dead.'

The Knack was a film that starred Rita Tushingham, Michael Crawford, Donal Donnelley and me, directed by Dick Lester in 1965.

It won the Cannes Film Festival in the summer of 1966. Its premier in London was attended by Princess Margaret, Lord Snowdon, The Beatles and every tight-trousered and mini-skirted air head that strutted their stuff all over Carnaby Street and the covers of every 'Look At Me' magazine. Photographers everywhere. We were all over the papers.

In 1966 this film was big but in 2001 who's left to remember it, apart from the lady in Plaistow? The rest of them – those who might still be around – can't even remember whether they've put their socks on or not.

But there's always a flip side.

'They're here! They're here!'

Yes, Liam Gallagher's minder was coming over to my table outside a pub. This giant of a man seemed to shrink as he came towards me.

'Aren't you Mr Benn?' he squeaked. 'Liam would like to meet you.'

Mr Benn, also in the sixties, was a job that was going to pay our rent of four pounds ten shillings a week for a year and a half. Sadie, my wife, and little Emma were struggling on all fronts. But our rent was our biggest worry. We had to keep a roof over our heads. My work was patchy, always waiting for the phone to ring. So, Mr Benn was handy. Very.

The Mr Benn cartoons became the second longest running children's programme after *Blue Peter*. There were only thirteen of them but they have been repeated and repeated on the BBC (and are currently on Sky) from the sixties until today. By the way, I haven't made any more money with all these repeats; nor has Dave Mckee who wrote it. Only Duncan Lamont who wrote the music has. The only extra money Mr Benn has earned me is when I did the voice-over on an R. Whites Lemonade commercial. Mr Benn leapt out of a fridge. I can't remember what the words were but you can guarantee that 'Suddenly, as if by magic…' came into it somewhere.

He has glued me, tenuously, to the past. In this mad world of shout, scream, spin, rush, fast forward, instant gratification, celebrity, image, fear, grunt; where smoking is banned but you can drink twenty-four hours a day, millions are starving, the baked potato takes too long in the oven, the pencil is an antique and four million CCTV cameras watch us breathe, the only private place is inside our heads.

And childhood memories can be a comforting place to rest: that innocence, the sun that always seemed to shine, the tab cards, the marbles, the certainty of everything, the seagulls, the sea, the slot machines, when running was easy, trees were there to be climbed, where Mr Benn could go into a costume shop, put on knight's armour, go through another door, and save a dragon without being arrested for ingesting LSD.

Big men wilt, massive rugby supporters go misty eyed – not everybody, of course, that would be silly, but enough to have peppered my life in the most joyous and surprising ways.

It doesn't matter what I've done or what I'll do. That little bowler hatted man strides through the years leaving everything else in his wake. Bless him!

*   *   *

It's dark. Six o'clock in the morning, March the fourteenth, 2006.

The car starts. It didn't yesterday. The AA man had lifted the bonnet and said: 'It's either something disastrous or something simple.'

He stared at the the monster, touched and turned things. Then took something out of his pocket and disappeared into the gleaming heart of the beast. He finally reappeared. 'Try it now.' I did. It started.

He held up a piece of sandpaper. 'This weather, dirt kicks up off the road and fucks up the starter motor.' I gave him a fiver – probably just enough to replace the sandpaper.

It's cold outside but the car is warm, I start my journey on the South Circular. I pass Dino's shop. The lights are on and I can see him marking up the newspapers for the delivery boy.

Fifty-five years ago Dino would have been growing up in India and I would have been humping my paper round bag through the dark streets snaking off The Seven Dials in Brighton delivering *The Star*, *The Sketch*, *The Mirror* and the heavy broadsheets to the snoring residents of Vernon Terrace, Davigdor Road and other roads long gone. And on March the fourteenth 1951 it would have been cold as well.

It's a long way and a long time since then. Now I'm driving a car to work. I didn't even own a bike in those days. When I was very

x

young, two or three, my mum used to go up to kids riding tricycles and offer them a penny to 'let me have a go'.

Gunnersbury Lane, Hanger Lane, North Circular, A41, turn right A1, left at the first roundabout, turn right into Boreham Wood High Street, first left into Clarendon Road, first right and here we are: Elstree Studios.

The Security Guard at the gate looks tired. 'Morning.' Takes my card and swipes it. Gate opens. 'Have a good day.'

I had a call from my agent in May of the previous year. 'I've had a phone call from *EastEnders*. They'd like like to meet you. There's a couple of other people they're talking to. But they're very keen on you.'

It was a big moment. Out of the blue!

Let me put it into context. In the last thirteen years the only acting work I had done was six episodes in *2000 Acres of Sky* with Michelle Collins and the ubiquitous Paul Kaye.

In the old acting parlance it was just 'a spit and cough', but I had found it stressful. I was out of practice, I had doubts about my ability to learn lines. So, in preparation for *Sky*, I had learnt the first eighteen pages of *Vile Bodies*. But that turned out to have been a waste of time, because Waugh's language was so colourful, bright words a mile high that stuck to my memory like glue whereas modern dialogue is dull as ditch water and instantly forgettable. But, by the skin of my teeth, I got through it.

And here was *EastEnders* – big, four episodes a week. No *Vile Bodies* certainly, so the same problem loomed large. Nervy to contemplate, but here was a chance to get back into the swim. If you're not on television you're dead and buried. Newspapers would be fascinated surely–' The bloke that was in *The Knack, Cathy Come Home*, Stoppard at The National Theatre, *Big Deal*, the voice of Mr Benn!' Yes, here was a big opportunity to make things happen. I'd be resurrected. Just one problem: learning the lines.

The car park here is massive. Virtually empty at this time, but in another hour or so it will be packed. It's still dark.

Everyone seems to have a car. I park in my usual spot, get my bag out of the back, plod twenty yards or so and go in through the door to Stage One.

I pass the deserted Help Desk, mount the stairs, turn left and here is my dressing room, E110, and on the door a brass plaque – 'Ray Brooks, London Borough of Walford E20'. There should be four screws securing it. It has two.

1

Through the Magic Door with Two Screws Missing

It's not a bad dressing room: a sink, a toilet and shower, a fold up bed which closed up on me like a toaster in December and it took them until early February to get a new one. And this is the BBC's flag ship show!

I've showered at home; here I just wash and shave. I have my thermos of coffee – the café doesn't open till seven – I light my second roll up of the day and look at the script.

A few weeks ago, I brought in a box of old photographs to put in a natty picture-holding display that Sadie had bought me for Valentine's Day. It holds eleven snaps of various loved ones, many gone.

Looking at pictures – maybe I'm going mad, maybe it's the Old Holborn I'm smoking – I feel if I stare at them hard enough I'll be able, in some small way, to go into that world, go past the edges of the picture and see what's happening there, almost live within it.

There's one of Brighton sea front, black and white, my mum and me (I think!) sitting on what looks like a stuffed donkey of the sort seaside photographers use. Smudgers, they used to call them. In the background I can see the Albion Hotel and lots of people walking along the sea front.

The little boy must be me because my mum looks so young and her dress is very forties. But I can't be sure. That's why I would like to go in. Search around.

My mum was a bus conductress; she worked through the war. She was the eldest of seven children, five of whom were called up. My mum, because of two months old me, and my aunt Vera, who was thirteen, stayed behind.

It must have been terrible for my grandmother and grandfather to

1

have seen five of their children going off to war. They all came back, apart from my uncle Billy. I have his photo in front of me now, a proud young man in his navy uniform, serious faced, perhaps hiding a deep fear. But maybe you can read too much into a photo, knowing what you know now. He died in his submarine off the coast of Ireland, leaving Rosie his wife. I was so young I wasn't aware of the Ministry of Defence who sent out telegrams telling the parents and wives about the fate of their loved ones. On the Whitehawk Estate it must have happened almost daily.

Sitting here in my dressing room, it all seems like a dream. But everybody, even those ghosts in the black and white photographs, lived in 'the now', like serious faced Billy. *Then* was 'now' to them. The fear, the fleeting happiness, all that pathetic hope that we know now came to nothing.

After that seaside photo of my mum and me had been taken, the people frozen in the background would have walked away and got on with their lives.

They'd have gone for a cup of tea, talked about the war, the hardships or the weather, made love, slept, got up, had more tea and laughed. I always remember laughter.

The making love wasn't quite so obvious then as it is now. Babies seemed just to arrive, brought by storks and left under gooseberry bushes. Now you can't avoid it; most of the population seems to have its tongue down somebody's throat. But then, because of the threat of war, they must have been at it like rabbits. Imagine a young man with his trousers round his ankles. 'Adelaide,' he whispers, 'please. I might never see you again. They say they send the young ones first, up to the front line. Cannon fodder it's called.' So what does Adelaide do? Yes, you're right – she does. That's how I came into the world. Adelaide Roach was my mother.

Although, I don't think it was a young soldier. I was led to believe that it was John Brooks – anyway, he gave me his name. He was a poster artist, later cinema manager, much older than Adelaide.

I remember him well. He lived with his real wife at the other end of Montpelier Crescent from us. I called him Daddy. I was so young – three or four – it never crossed my mind why he didn't live with us. Maybe it did, but I can't remember. It's so long ago.

I used to stand at the front gate of number 37. One day when he was passing he gave me a balloon. It had bicycle repair kit patches all over it. I'd never seen a balloon before so I thought it was fantastic, magical.

Over the years, I have been interviewed a number of times by newspapers. Inevitably, they have asked me about my past and, as a result, I have had a lot of letters from people who remember the old days in Brighton. They're the usual stuff: remembering my mum on the buses, me as a little boy, how she'd give them a free ride, help little old ladies on and off the bus; nice, but when you get a lot of them the same, although I don't throw them away, I don't have time to reply to them all.

Anyway, clearing stuff out the other day I came across this one from a Mrs Joyce Woodhouse.

I am the niece of Miss Edith Jones who was your father's common law wife until he died. I have decided at last to write to you regarding your father, John Lewis Brooks, as I remember him.

[I never knew his middle name was Lewis.]

Your father was married with three children although he had separated from his wife, who would not divorce him, when he met my aunt in 1928. My aunt and your father set up home together and had a daughter Pamela in 1930.

[Three children and Pamela! All related to me! Why hadn't I paid any attention to this letter before?]

During the 1930s your father and my uncle Leslie were in business together as Commercial Artists with a studio in Brighton. I'm not sure when their business folded but it was near the beginning of the war.

My uncle went to work at Alan & West and your father joined the ABC Cinema circuit. My aunt went into hospital during that time with a bad leg and it was while she was in there that a relationship developed between your father and

3

mother. This relationship finished when my aunt came out of hospital having been in there a considerable time. The children you say that you saw playing in [the] garden at Montpelier Crescent was [*sic*] probably your half sister Pam and myself, although Pam and I were mainly staying with our grandmother in May Road, we visited my aunt and your father several times a week throughout the war years. When the war finished, I went back to my parents in London, but visited Brighton as often as I could and every Christmas was spent at Montpelier Crescent. Your half sister Pam did not know of your father's history and thought that my aunt and your father were married and I am able to write this to you as Pam died of cancer last September.

I have a picture of flowers painted by your father and a cartoon drawing by him when I was expecting our first child. If you are interested you may have the painting, which is signed by your father, as a keepsake.

Sent in 1989! Why hadn't I done something about it at the time? I should have chased it up. The detail is fantastic. Yes, I know he lived at the other end of Montpelier Crescent. But the woman he lived with wasn't his wife. I'd always assumed that she was. What made me think that? I suppose I thought that if a man and a woman lived together they had to be married. That's the way it was in those days.

There's a phone number on the letter. I'm going to have to call her.

The code has changed. There is no reply. No answer phone. I'll try another time.

Now I'm called down to Studio B to do a scene in The Vic that will be watched by eleven and a half million viewers.

I watch my fellow actors walking around zombie like, egos bubbling on their shoulders; chippies whistling and hammering doors; cameramen tripping over cables; set designers fiddling with curtains; the assistant director shouting for 'line runs' – and in all this chaos and noise, of course, you're not allowed to smoke. I tell you, if you'd never smoked, this place would soon kick you off.

Days here are long, with very few laughs. And, of course, The Vic is the most dangerous place on earth, even celebrations there are accompanied by fights, bottles being smashed, screaming rows, fornication in the toilets, mysterious calls on the mobile, Peggy screaming 'Get out of my pub!', Phil throwing somebody through a window and, contract permitting, the occasional death. But, socially you have to watch your back too. Things are not always what they seem. Yes, the days are very long.

2

12th May, 2005: The Audition

My first meeting at Elstree is with Kate Harwood (executive producer), Julia Crampsie (casting) and another lady (casting?) who might have been Beth, Kate's secretary.

I took a taxi there which cost £35. Sadie was using our clapped out VW. When the taxi arrived at the security gate, I had to collect a visitor's card.

'Er ... Ray Brooks. I'm expected.'

'Oh, Yeah, *EastEnders*. You're for casting, right?'

A bit humiliating as I'd told the taxi driver that I was having lunch with friends! That old ego again!

I'm early for the appointment. Can't find the building, walk around for ages, find *EastEnders* entrance, not the right place. Very tatty. Portakabins. Not quite what I'd expected. Where's the glitz? A car park littered with dog ends and where most of the cars would look out of place even on a back street lot. It's bleak.

Eventually I find the proper entrance. I'm given an envelope at the desk. It contains three scenes – one with Jim Branning – dear John Bardon ('Alright, son?') a joy – and Wendy Richard, whom I've never met. Of course, not exactly *with* them; someone will read in.

I notice sitting opposite me a man reading the same scripts. I don't recognise him. 'They're only seeing a few people,' my agent had said. Seeing a bunch of non-entities: that's more like it – me included. Shit. Back at the bottom of the ladder.

I read through the scenes a couple of times. A salsa dancer, mid-fifties. Me? No chance.

I go outside to have a cigarette. You can't smoke inside anywhere these days. It's a sunny day. If it'd been raining I think I might well have gone home. Any excuse I was very nervous, you see.

Suddenly, here's Steven Grief, an actor I've known for a few years, saw a lot of him during my commercial voice-over days.

'What are you doing here,' he says?

'*EastEnders.*'

'Oh, are you up for the salsa dancing part?'

'I don't know,' I reply, panicking.

I don't want to share my fears with him.

'I've just been up for it,' he continues. 'It's supposed to be a happy character, but I'm down so I couldn't brighten up. Bit tired, you know, I've been so busy.'

(Lucky bugger!)

'I know you're up for it,' he says. 'Come on, you *must* be – and you'll get it. You're real, I'm a bit theatrical.'

You can say that again! I thought. He pushes off.

I go in. Second floor. A woman comes rushing up the corridor towards me. 'Ray!' she shouts, full of enthusiasm. I don't know her from Adam, but it makes me feel good.

I enter the office, trying to walk like a dancer, holding my stomach in, attempting to give the impression that I'm in my mid-fifties. I must have looked like a constipated duck.

I have my pages with me. I notice that one of the ladies has a video camera under a cushion on her lap.

What have I been doing? they ask.

I could have said, 'Well, I get up, clear up the mess made by incontinent cats, make breakfast, take it upstairs to Sadie, wash up, maybe do some ironing or hoovering, around lunchtime I'll go the pub, when I get back I'll watch a bit of *Countdown* or *Deal or No Deal*, then fall asleep; Sadie'll come back from work, cook, we'll watch television and then go to bed.' But, of course, I didn't. I didn't want to seem like a complete slob.

Then one of them says, 'We've tried to get you lots of times.'

'Just once that I know of,' I say. (Shut up, just smile.)

Kate Harwood says that she was working front of house when I was doing *On the Razzle* at The National. Amazing!

I say, 'Salsa dancing? I can't dance.' Tell them the story, I think, about *Lie Down, I Think I Love You* and two left feet. And that I'm sixty-six and the character is supposed to be mid-fifties.

'We can change that,' says Kate.

What? Change it?

Then I have to read (the three scenes). Totally forgetting about Grief's remark that I am 'real', I plough on like Max Miller on roller blades, roaring and overacting like mad. It's all about being nervous.

When it's all over Kate says that I have a twinkle in my eyes. She must be very imaginative to spot a twinkle in my blood-shot pin-prick eyes.

Back at reception, more people are going up for interviews. Mostly girls now. Like a factory. Well, I'd got through it but I'd let myself down, being in a rush, saying silly childish things, making stupid jokes. Why can't I be more mature? Maybe because I'm not.

I ask for a cab at the desk and am told it will take an hour. So I walk out into Boreham Wood High Street and make my way to the station. Get taxi. £40. Home.

I hear nothing. I'd assumed that if they'd liked my Max Miller – if they remembered who he was – they'd have been on the phone lickety-spit. But no.

Did I want to do *EastEnders*? Yes ... no ... yes, no, yes ... no ... I didn't know. I couldn't be sure. I didn't know if I was up to it. Could I keep my head above water or would I be wheeled away a gibbering wreck?

But what if, in the misguided belief that I was just the ticket, they offered it to me? Could I, would I, take it? Could I live with the ignominy of turning down a job most actors would give their eye teeth for? It's the old thing about wanting to be wanted.

I didn't have long to wait.

It's Thursday 19th – a week later. I'm coming back from The Coach and Horses after a few drinks. Steven Grief – he doesn't live round here – comes leaping out on me.

'Just having a meeting with Robert Young (a TV director),' he says. 'We're developing a script.'

'Have you got it?' he roars. 'Everyone I've spoken to says you're perfect.'

'It's been over a week,' I reply. 'No chance.'

'When I went up for one scene in *Judge Dredd*, he says, 'I had to wait for at least a week. They have to show your test to the head of series.'

9

Well, next day I get it! Spooky. Roger, agent Ken's partner, tells me. He sounds as if he's talking under water, or maybe it's my ears that are submerged.

What do I do now? If I take it. Terrifying. If I turn it down I could live to regret it.

Why am I scared? It's about learning lines. My memory is on the blink. Names? Forget it. Tell me something, the next minute – it's out the window. Four episodes a week. Oh, God! I must, I must, I must. Pull yourself together – deep breath.

So, with great trepidation, I do take it. The biggest soap in Britain. Me? But it could change my life. Actor/novelist, rich, Booker prize winner, celebrity – the world will be my oyster. In this business, everything is possible.

3

An Actor Prepares

I have blood test to make sure I won't drop down dead before I hit the heights. I go to Barry Gatoff and have my teeth polished – got to look as good as possible.

On 2nd June there's another meeting with Kate Harwood. She seems very pleased that I've said 'yes'. Then she tells me the restrictions: no recording commercials while under contract; any interviews have to be agreed with the BBC; nothing on ITV, unless special circumstances. I tell her about books I've written and that Dave Mckee might want me to record some more *Mr Benn*. She says she'll check but that it should be fine.

The character I play is called Joe. I didn't pick up on that when I went for the reading. But it's incredible. That's the name of Emma's son. It's almost as if sweet Emma had organised it all.

I rabbit on. Eventually, Kate says that she has a meeting to go to. She seems slightly relieved. I was rabbiting on too much, I expect – as usual.

Another taxi home. Roger phones. They've done the deal already: £1,500 per episode; a guarantee of sixty-five shows in the first year at least. The bonus is 80% on repeats which, because of the omnibus on Sundays, puts the total at around £190,000 a year. Better than a smack on the bum with a banjo!

They want an option for a further year. The increase in salary would be three per cent. So done and dusted. Ten per cent to the agent, and of course the tax man will want his pound of flesh – but not bad. The incontinent cats will have to clean up their own mess.

I organise salsa lessons with Robert Pierre under the arches near the house. It's called 'homework'. Ha, ha! Here we go again. In 1965,

I was about to film *The Knack*. In a sequence behind the credits, I'm supposed to be playing the drums. What do Woodfall Films do when they hear I can't play the drums? They send me a full drum kit and an album by Gene Krupa, one of the best drummers in the world. Needless to say, when the scene's shot, I just swished the brushes over the skins. Lesson? You can be a bit too worried about this so called 'homework'.

Elstree. June 6th

Julia Crampsie to show me around. Straight to the nub. Wendy Richard. Introduction. Kissed her on the cheek. Bit of practice, I say. (Over the top again.) Then Gary Hobbs (Ricky). 'Do you want a cup of tea,' he says?

'Thanks.'

Then wardrobe. 'What kind of trousers are you comfortable with?'

'These,' I say, indicating the ones I'm wearing.

'Well, get about four pairs.'

'They're about £100 each,' I say.

'That's all right, get a receipt.'

They're the best trousers I've got. Maybe they think they're typical *EastEnders* tat. Says a lot for my taste, doesn't it?

Introduced to the smoking room. Wendy puffing away. Laurie (Jane), Natalie and James (Sonia and Martin) and David Spinx (Keith). I squeeze onto the couch and light up. In come Jessie (Kat) and Kacey (Little Mo) to be introduced. Smiles all round. Then Adam (Ian); he seems thrilled to bits to see me 'after all these years'.

'Still got the broom that you gave me in *On the Razzle*.'

(I didn't give it to him, Felicity Kendal did. But it doesn't matter. He seems pleased.) Then Gerry Cowper. She is bubbling over big time — she recalls the seventies when we did a series at LWT. Then I meet a director. Not the one doing my first episode. Everybody's smiling. They all seem really pleased I'm coming in. Good start!

The director tags along with Julia and me to the stages to look at the sets. Then he says, 'I'm going to the bar. See you later.'

Go to see publicity people — all sorts. One says, 'Got your character biography here but you can't have it yet, Kate's got to approve it. Oh, have you got any things hidden? Better tell us now.'

'I'm illegitimate,' I tell them. 'Don't worry about that,' they say, 'most of them are.'

Julia takes me to Albert Square. All built, but nothing behind. Smaller than I thought but the usual stuff. Very impressive, all the same. Trees, bushes, grass, birds – oh, they just happen to fly in; they are not contracted. Not a stupid thing to say, as I find out later that all animals on the show, which includes two budgerigars, cost £300 a day each.

In 1971, I had a small part in *The Cherry Orchard* for the BBC. Celia Johnson, Edward Woodward (Noel Coward: 'Sounds like a fart in the bath'), Charles Gray, Gemma Jones, Jenny Agutter and my mucker in another 'spit and cough' part, Adrienne Posta.

Now, that same BBC had four horses on standby for the three days we were in the studio, and never used them. That's where a lot of your licence money goes, but if you love animals that's fine.

Back to the 6th. Julia Cramsie and I go to the bar and there's this director who's almost finished a bottle of wine when we get there.

She has one glass. I get another bottle. Julia's off to Glasgow, so she goes. The director prattles on worse than me.

Tracy-Ann Oberman (Chrissie) comes to the table. I say, 'Still here?' (Meaning, as you're a killer, haven't they rumbled you yet?)

'Have you heard something?' she says in a panicky voice?

'No,' I say, trying to calm her nerves. I must be careful. They're all scared. And rightly so.

Then Robert Powell looms over. Of course I couldn't remember his name till later but it didn't seem to affect his rattling on.

'What you doing here?'

'*EastEnders*. You?'

'*Holby City*. Two year contract.'

He seems happy about it. 'What you playing?'

'A nurse.' He opens his jacket and he's wearing a blue uniform with a name tag on it and an upside down watch.

'A nurse?' I say. 'Shouldn't you want to be a doctor? After all, you did play Jesus. All that healing the sick!'

He says smugly, 'All those medical terms? All I have to do is say, "Would you a like a cup of tea, Mrs Whatever?" Easy.'

He goes, then David Spinx arrives. Nice bloke. Honest about it, how it's changed his life. 'All sunglasses and base ball caps,' he says, but not swanking, just a bit overwhelmed by it all.

Two bottles of wine, then the director offers to give me a lift back to Chiswick. Saves forty quid, but doesn't save on the nerves.

7th. Salsa lesson

Exhausting. Not easy. Keep chasing this famous Joe Macer biography. 'Soon,' they say.

8th. Doctor

Blood test result. OK cholesterol. Hooray!

Into Twickenham to Volvo garage. Got to get a car for the drive to Elstree. Four second hand Volvos. Two blue, one muddy red and one silver. The first three no good: don't a get a blue one – Sadie doesn't like blue; didn't like the sludge one. So silver. Diesel, and almost £17,000! But I'm going to be a soap star. I'll get the money back, Mr Barclays. I sign cheque and get back on the train.

Phone rings in transit. Will, eldest son. Tell him about car and price. 'What!' he says. 'Why didn't you get something knocked off? Haggle.' 'Done now,' I say. He sounds disappointed. Like I'm stupid or something. I sometimes think that I am. The way he talks makes me think I might have got it for £1,700, not £17,000. Anyway, another cock up.

Biography arrives by e-mail. It's all over the shop. So many inconsistencies.

Born 1940 on the back of a bus. (What are they talking about?) A sister eight years younger. My parents let me think of a name for her. I come up with Bobbie because I've read *The Railway Children*. (Eight years old, born on the back of a bus! Am I a likely candidate to read *The Railway Children*?)

Eventually I get married and have two children. In 1984, my wife gets cancer, doesn't tell me, I get angry, she falls downstairs and dies. Youngest daughter, eight, (they seem to love that number) sees this. I go to prison for manslaughter. Released in 2001. Seventeen years for manslaughter!

This is really sloppy, and these writers get paid for this! They've just come out of university, they read *War and Peace* while hanging

14

off mummy's teat. Days in the sun being pushed around by Norland Nannies. Grandparents and uncles and aunts, having fallen out of the tree, before they let go their grip, signed over their accounts in a Swiss bank to the little darlings. Oh yes, these pampered little sweethearts were just born to write for *EastEnders*. Bless them!

Monday 13th
Collect car. A bit odd to drive. Got out of the habit of Volvos.

Salsa afternoon. Seem to have forgotten all that he taught me last week. Need a flashy move in my armoury. Get one, but straight out of my head an hour later.

Tuesday 14th
Go to see Brid Hendon in Harley Street. Will's recommendation. She helped him with his confidence about meeting potential money men for his projects. I need to get my confidence built up. The approach to learning lines. So I go.

Lovely lady. Obviously, she took a lot of notes when Will went, so she had a bit of knowledge about me. So, a few steps ahead. She asks me what my fears are. I say, 'Learning lines, overweight, going bald, generally being a bit of an old fart.'

She says I have all the experience, the background, all the values I've got from my career.

'Picture what you want from *Eastenders*. I say, 'Books published.'

She says, 'Well look ahead and imagine what it will be like when you can get these things.' I do what she says: it's a pretty picture.

'It's your duty to do this. You know you can. With your history it's all there.'

That cost £120 – but I felt better.

Take Joe, our grandson, to Brighton for a couple of days, I break the news to him that I'm going to be in *Eastenders*. He's very excited. He disappears for a couple of minutes and comes back with a piece of paper. He's written down all the characters he wants me to kill! Out of the mouths, or biros, of babes, you see. Significantly the ones not ticked are June Brown, John Bardon, Barbara Windsor, Derek Martin and, strangely, Minty, Cliff Parisi. When I told Cliff about Joe's reprieve he smiled and gave the 'house style' grunt.

15th. Wardrobe, Elstree

Deliver trousers and receipt. Cash immediately. Took in some of my stuff and a few jackets to supplement the stock. Most of the tops I tried on were too small. 'Don't worry, we'll get a larger size.' All very friendly.

Smoking room. Wendy puffing away. In come Charlie and Jim (Derek Martin and John Bardon) both enthusiastic and welcoming.

'Any chance of scripts?' I ask.

'Always late,' they say.

Wednesday 16th

I phone Julia about scripts.

'Nearly ready but we'll bike them over to you.'

Kate phones. I talk about biog. Tell her about the mess that it is. She denies having ever read it. Whoops! Interesting, bearing in mind more recent developments. Anyway, she brushes it under the carpet. She was only phoning about the scripts.

Not quite ready but just one script, about three short scenes. Salsa? 'We thought we'd ease you in,' she says.

So, no parachuting into The Square making a big entrance. I'm being 'eased in'.

Friday 17th

The script arrives. Yes, three scenes in The Community Centre. Eight lines and a lot of dancing. Help!

Then, a phone call later that day from the Production Office. Next Thursday, the 23rd, is to be my first day.

Monday 20th

Norwich to narrate last three episodes *The Way We Were*. It's sad really. Such smashing people, made me so welcome. Ali and Jane have been so nice to me. Every time I've been there they've taken me to a different pub at lunchtime. They love lunches and I love beer, so it was a splendid arrangement.

I've enjoyed doing these and they want me to do more but I can't because of *EE*. It's also been a bit of a financial life line. Nice people.

But I'm going to be a soap star and even stars have to make sacrifices!

16

4

Thursday 23rd: First Day

Drive in early. Scared shitless. Three cigarettes in the car. The PC Volvo has got no cigarette lighter, no ashtray. It's a no smoking car. But it's mine and I'll do what I like because I'm stressed and I need to.

Have I learnt my eight lines? One of which is 'Pleased to meet you.' – not to be found in *Vile Bodies*.

It is strange being there. *This is the reality*. This is where the hard work starts.

The weird thing is, maybe it's getting old, but I'm constantly thinking back, making comparisons. What would my mum have thought? What would all my aunts and uncles have thought?

Could they even have imagined way back then anything like a soap? I suppose there was *The Archers*. Radio was very big when I was a kid. *The Billy Cotton Band Show* on a Sunday was a must, and *Ray's a Laugh* – Raymond Glendenning commentating on football matches. It all seems so long ago. And I feel so long ago.

'You're in *The Sun* already.' Shane Richie, playing Alfie Moon, a big hit in the show, tells me about Ron Moody who came into *EE* for a few weeks. 'He said to me it changed his life.'

I see *The Sun* newspaper article. Yes, I'm in it. But the picture of me (circa 1966) is the size of a pin head. There are, however, big pictures of Mr Benn in the Queen Vic pub with all the favourites of *EastEnders* staring at him and smiling. No mention of *The Knack*, *Cathy Come Home* or *Big Deal* – just that I'm famous for the voice of Mr Benn. Wherever I go, he's still with me. Well, it's early days.

But now I've got to do my lines and my twizzles on the dance floor.

Wendy Richard really is looking after me – introducing me to people, a sort of guide to the mechanics of the place.

And it is vast. Three large studios the size of aircraft hangers, a golf buggy to transfer you from one studio to the next. 'You sometimes have scenes from different episodes back to back.' Not something I wanted to hear. And then the Square itself. The Minute Mart is big enough to film in; Fargo's, the restaurant, is the same – and The Community Centre.

And that's where my first three scenes are going to be filmed. Wendy takes me there.

I have been working on my lines – eight over the three scenes – ever since I got the script. Joe is someone who turns up in the Square, is lonely, living on his own, a widower.

Then he sees Pauline Fowler and fancies her. It's going to be a very long courtship – very, very long – with lots of 'soap' twists and extended 'will she? won't she? situations.

I have planned how I'm going to play the 'part'. I'm going to be shy, withdrawn, deep but somehow mysterious and fascinating. Different – you know what I mean.

Anyway, led by the hand by 'Brown Owl' Wendy to the set, I'm confronted by a place full of lights, a crane (a camera on a swinging arm that can go high and low amongst the dancers), two other cameras static and our director, John Greening.

'Hello...? he says, extending a hand.

'Ray,' I say, a bit quietly over the hubbub of the extremely fit race horse types who are going to join in the Salsa.

He obviously doesn't hear me. 'Joe,' he says in triumph.

'No, it's Ray,' growls Brown Owl.

'Right ... Ray,' he says. 'When Mo comes over and says that stuff about Rudolf Nureyev and Margot Fonteyn and you say your line...'

'"Pleased to meet you",' I say in triumph, thrilled that I've remembered it, in my shy, withdrawn but somehow mysterious and fascinating way.

He looks distracted.

'...give a bit more volume. We've got the music to put over it later in the dub. And get a bit more energy in to it er ... Ray.'

So, that's roughly how my 'three scenes' went: loud and quick.

Nowhere like shy, withdrawn, deep but somehow mysterious and fascinating. In short, just get on with it, the clock's ticking.

I drove home disappointed; it was going to more difficult than I thought. But the car glided smoothly and gently through the traffic on the North Circular. The air conditioning cooled me, Barbra Streisand sang 'Putting It Together' by Stephen Sondheim on the CD; I felt calmed. I sang along with her. I couldn't reach the notes. I never could.

5

My Career in Music

That's the trick, I used to think years ago: write a song, a big hit, become famous! Easy. It isn't. I know because I tried.

When I worked at Butlins in Clacton (The Playhouse Theatre in 1957), my second job, I learnt to play three chords on a Spanish guitar. The digs I had were in a guest house annex. In that same annex were a husband and his wife who were a part of an adagio act at the local Variety theatre. An adagio act, for those who haven't a clue, is where two men throw, in a fight, a woman, whom they both love, all over the stage. Bizarre, eh? But it originated in France, so makes sense (to the French).

Anyway he teaches me the three chords that might lead me to success.

I buy a £3.00 Spanish guitar.

In 1958 I get a summer season at the Alhambra Theatre, Ilfracombe. Me ASM and small parts, Richard Davies stage manager, his wife Jill, painting the sets.

Dickie played the guitar and was Welsh (apparently they can sing). We teamed up and when Jack Warner (Dixon of Dock Green) came down to do a charity concert in the town, we leapt at the chance to appear on the same bill.

We did well, felt good – a little comic patter and The Everly Brothers song 'Dream', then off. At the end of the season everyone went back to London and Dickie and I ploughed on with our 'act'. Up and down Charing Cross Road we went, visiting all the agents, auditioning for the BBC at the Aeolian Hall. It was a small theatre with a raised platform stage; the auditorium had no seats, just a bleak concrete floor. At the back was a booth with a glass window, behind which sat, presumably, the BBC.

We had developed the act. I'm now a pop singer and Dickie wanders on as a tipsy back stage cleaner. We indulge in a 'Pinteresque' chat and then launch into, you've guessed, 'Dream', then off. No reaction from behind the glass window – so we went home.

Another time we went for an audition at Ronnie Scott's Club. All the greats had been there – Ella Fitzgerald, Louis Armstrong, Ray Charles – so why not a bus conductress' son and Welsh miner's son who weren't funny, couldn't play guitars and couldn't sing?

I wasn't wearing my glasses, so fell over the cable of a lamp and knocked my guitar out of tune. We went home without even a 'we'll let you know'.

Eventually we got a booking. Julius Dalwalski, a Charing Cross agent, offered us a job on a variety bill starting at the Sunderland Empire, starring Tommy Steele ('Rock with the Caveman') who was doing his first UK tour.

You wouldn't have seen us because we didn't do it. Dickie got an acting job on television, so that was it. Our variety career was over.

But there was a future, wasn't there? If only I'd known then what I know now, what would I have felt? All the ups and downs, the waiting, then the phone call. But how could I have known? And would it have helped if I had? That gift isn't allowed us and I'm glad. Now I look just a few months ahead; in those days years and years that stretched ahead. Better eye sight when you're young, I suppose.

But we're still friends. Dickie went on to achieve fame in *Please, Sir*. Dickie's one of the best actors I've ever met. He could play anything. If he'd had a different face, he could have been a big star. If he'd looked like Brad Pitt he'd have been away, but then if I'd looked like Elizabeth Taylor so would I ... I'd have married Richard Burton, also Welsh, then Dickie and I would have been related. This is a fine example of our very unimpressive humour.

Those three chords – G, E7 and C – stayed with me over the years. In 1962 I was doing a television series called *Taxi* with Sid James and Bill Owen. One day I was on the tube going to rehearsals and I noticed a young bloke with dark glasses staring at me. I got off at Baker Street, went over the bridge to another platform and this bloke followed me. He was as thin as a pencil, with a smart, trendy suit and blonde floppy hair.

He introduced himself as Andrew Loog Oldham, manager of The Rolling Stones. Would I like to make a record? Would I like to make a record! He gave me his card.

It was a mad time the sixties. Oldham was one of a bunch of people – good education, smart, a bit of push and sell – who would rise up and disappear without a trace. He happened to be in at the beginning of what was to become one of the biggest groups in the world. They weren't that then and, to be honest, most people at the time had their doubts as to whether they would survive. Oldham flowered for a while, but then he was gone. A lot of sweet talking, sharp sharks were hovering about smelling profit. And when they went in for the kill, you stayed killed. It was tough. A lot of those groups didn't survive; royalties were lost, money disappeared and those spotty, guitar playing teenagers are now middle-aged men crying into their beer.

I didn't know much about it in 1962, but I went along to Oldham's office, just off Regent Street. Parked on double yellow lines outside was an open topped American car the size of an ocean liner, with a driver dressed to the nines, peaked capped and sporting the fashionable dark shades. I climbed the stairs to the second floor. The door was open.

Oldham was on the phone, with what looked like a rum and coke in one hand, in his mouth a cigarette (which I assume contained an illegal substance). The record player blared out deafeningly; young girls flopped around in mini skirts up to their armpits.

Tiffany lamps proliferated and the carpet was so thick that you sank in it up to your knees. I stood there for what seemed like five minutes. Nobody took any notice. I smiled. I coughed. I think Oldham looked at me for a moment, but obviously didn't recognise me. So I left. Well out of it. Who wants Tiffany lamps and wall to wall girls?

In 1961, before The Rolling Stones and Andrew Loog Oldham were ever thought of, I did a live television drama from Manchester playing a pop singer, a part that Adam Faith had turned down. It was called *Girl on a Roof* and was about a mad young fan who had got on to the theatre roof and was threatening to commit suicide if she couldn't meet her pop star. Me! Now Faith had turned it down because it might have sullied his reputation. But as it had been written for him, it was decided that I would have to dye my hair blond. The bonus of the whole thing was that I was going to have to sing, live; the band behind me was The John Barry Seven. That was big news for me. Barry and the boys were the powerhouse sound behind Adam Faith and they had a massive reputation.

But things never turn out the way you expect them to, do they? John Barry will feature later in the sixties. He won't go away.

After *Girl on the Roof* I got a call from my agent, who wanted me to audition for the first West End production of Rogers and Hammerstein's *The Sound of Music*, which was a big, big hit on Broadway.

They'd seen me singing in *Girl on the Roof* and wanted me for the German postboy. Such imagination! There's me on television with blond hair. Ah, he looks German! But they were shrewd enough to realise I couldn't sing, so they would give me lessons.

Try and imagine the situation: Sadie and I are living in Kilburn, in one room with 6ft 6in Michael Kilgarriff, paying £4.00 a week rent. Killy and I had been at the same school in Brighton, Xaverian College. He was in the year above me so we never really knew each other then. After school he had worked in a bank, I had worked in the accounts department of the bus company. He became an actor and that's how we met again.

Sadie's working at Lisson Grove Labour Exchange. I'm spasmodically working, not earning much. Poor Sadie's paying the rent and there's not much over for wining and dining in The West End. So *The Sound of Music*, if I got it, could mean about £60 a week for a year or more. You don't have to be an accountant to see how much would be left over from my wages after we'd paid the rent. We'd be in clover.

But I couldn't sing; that was the pimple on the nose. The only song for the post boy was 'You Are Sixteen, Going On Seventeen'. It's not a big number. They should have cut it but they didn't, more's the pity.

I was coached, week after week. It was very good of them; it was my blond hair, of course.

There were two very high notes I couldn't reach but with practice, they assured me, I would.

The auditions were at The Palace Theatre. There must have been upwards of 100 potential post boys. I auditioned. Waited. Then I was recalled. More singing lessons. I was getting through by the skin of my teeth. Maybe I was reaching those impossible notes that even Maria Callas would have found difficult.

Actually, I suppose, after every successful audition, my confidence grew. I was beginning to think I had a chance of getting the part. It was a very exciting time.

Finally, it got down to two of us. Just one more hurdle.

I didn't know the other boy – Peter something his name was. I was going on second. I hid away in the depths backstage, where I couldn't hear anything; I didn't want to hear anything. I knew that Rogers and Hammerstein, together with the director, were in the stalls watching. It was terrifying.

I waited and waited. Then this Peter boy suddenly appeared. 'They want you to go on now. But you won't get it. They've given it to me.'

I was stunned. I walked onto the stage.

They didn't even want me to sing. 'Sorry, Ray. You're a good actor but it's a musical.'

Those two notes. I walked out of the stage door, thinking my life was over. I'd blown my big chance. Where was I ever going to get sixty quid a week?

I remember that bleak ride home on the 65 bus. But it's only writing about it here that brings all the horror back to me. Twenty-two and thinking 'It's all over'. I feel sorry for young people. Well, I was young once. Hard to believe, as I clip my nasal hairs into the sink, in my bleak dressing room at *EE*, that I was ever young.

6

Back From the Front

The Volvo gets me home. I'm a hero. That 65 bus back to Kilburn forty-three years ago is in sharp contrast. I have done my first day on *EastEnders*. I put my toe in the water. Whichever way I think about it, I am pleased. It's got me out of my domestic and sloppy routines; I'm actually working and hopeful that I might be able to crack the 'learning lines problem'.

Everyone is excited. In my local, everyone's asking me how it went and who I met. I gossip a bit which seems to raise the temperature. Everyone laps it up. It is extraordinary that, even in 2005, people are thrilled by television. Ever since I got the job, it seems it's impossible to stop people talking about it.

Could it go on? In my naivety I suppose I believed that it would. After all, it's a massive soap: eleven and half million viewers for every episode. It would surely do for me all that I hoped.

But I've been in this business for nearly fifty years. I should have known the truth: that nothing is ever what it seems to be.

Wednesday 29th June
My second day. Episode 851. Oh dear. Why am I thinking that? Second day, biggest soap in the country, and I'm thinking: oh dear. It's because I'm lazy, I suppose, and there is that powerful undercurrent of fear that I'm going to to make a mess of it.

Why do I have these doubts? I suppose I've always had them.

For instance, in 1947 my mother had enrolled me for elocution lessons. Speaking well for a working class person was an enormous lift up the the ladder. Nobody I knew had ever been to university. If you wanted to work in a bank, a fantastic job, a cut glass accent meant that you were trustworthy. So off I was sent to The Sutton School of Dramatic Art to be taught how to speak properly by a Miss Pat Donavon. Yes, the famous Miss Donavon. Sister of Terry, who's married to the great Barry Cryer. More of them later – if I remember.

With all my mother's interest in cinema and the theatre, I suppose it was inevitable that she would steer me vaguely in that direction.

But, first of all, she sent me to dancing classes. The Molly Ball School of Dancing. Down an alley way, up three flights of stairs, past a club, which I would get to know later, and into this world of giggling girls and Molly. I was only about eight or so and not really at the stage of being interested in legs and pretty faces, so I thought it was awful, added to which I was the only boy in the class.

I remember all the girls had to pirouette across the room – more a stumble I suppose it must have been – but I didn't have a clue, so Molly threw me.

It was embarrassing, I'd only just joined – me in my plimsolls and shorts, with all these snotty nosed girls pulling faces and laughing. I learnt then that girls become women early and at no stage do they take prisoners. If you seem vulnerable, watch it. Dancing wasn't my forte, so I left Molly and her sniggering maidens. Maybe my doubts started there.

Miss Donavon, my elocution teacher, was terrific. She was pretty, enthusiastic and made me feel comfortable. I enjoyed my weekly lessons. I have a certificate in front of me now; it had been shoved, with all sorts of memorabilia, into an old cardboard suitcase that seems to have followed me about over the years. It's dated 17th of July 1948, time 3.45. An elocution exam. And the elements that they judged you on were fantastic: 'Facial Expression', 'Deportment and Gesture', 'Technique' and 'Test Reading' – I got only five out of ten for that.

The upshot was that I learnt I could speak well when I had to, then switch back to normal with my friends.

Every year there was The Brighton and Hove Music Festival. I was entered in Elocution Class 211, 'Boys nine and under ten' in June 1949.

At the Royal Pavilion on a sunny afternoon, the big hall crowded with parents of the entrants and a frightening table in front of the podium where the adjudicators sat, I had to recite 'Bob has Blown a Hundred Eggs'. I can only remember the title of the poem, but the occasion is branded in my memory.

I came first. But I wasn't worrying about that, I was hoping to get through it all without letting Miss Donavon down. My mother was there and she was very happy. Everyone was happy. It was a suprise to me because I'd never got a first in anything. Apparently, after my triumph, Miss Donavon had had a chat with my mother and said that I looked nervous and maybe I should do some acting classes to build up my confidence.

There's the start of it all: '. . . should do some acting classes and build up confidence'. Acting and confidence are strange bedfellows in my book.

Confidence. We all know what it means but it's a tricky skill to hang on to. The 'fuck up' factor sees to that.

The following December I was entered straight into Stage Technique examinations. Here the categories for marking were even more extraordinary: 'Timing', 'Movement', and (here it comes) 'Staying Power and Repose'.

Hell's teeth! Stage Technique has got to mean preparing you for a life in the business. But 'Staying Power'. How can you stay when you don't get any work?

And how can you 'Stay' in 'Repose' when the landlord wants the rent and you're broke? Who thinks up these categories? Why do they fill kids' heads with such nonsense?

Much better categories might be 'Learning Lines', 'Keeping Your Back To The Wall When Someone With A Beard Wearing Earrings Comes Towards You' or 'Learning How To Survive On Plumrose Ham On Toast'.

The word 'Repose' in the dictionary is defined as 'a peaceful or quiescent state'. If you've ever stumbled across an actor, quiescent is not a description that readily comes to mind.

All this 'quiescence' led to amateur dramatics and 'at the same time' the elocution lessons led to competing in the Festival. No wonder my education went to pot. (Miriam Margolyes once told me, 'The trouble with you, Ray, is that you don't like yourself and you're ill educated.')

Thanks!

So here I am at my second day on *EastEnders*. Where's the confidence, or this magical quiescent state? I certainly ain't got it.

Three scenes in 851 but shooting only one today. I can't understand all this. Why not shoot them all? They're all in the same location and the time difference is minimal. But, in a way, I'm happy not to have too much pressure. So, just two lines coming out of the launderette. A bit easier than the eight last week. And no dancing.

Had to take a plug in for my wash basin. Still got to pinch a chair from somewhere.

Make-up at 9.10, then to smoking room. Brown Owl insists on watching *I Love Raymond* on the dodgy television. More fags, television blaring out – can hardly hear myself think. I learn over the coming months that Brown Owl loves watching television. And smoking.

Then to Albert Square, Brown Owl almost leading me by the hand. 'There's a short cut out there. Go through the gents. It leads you right back to the dressing rooms.'

She introduces me to a couple of technicians. I had worked with them years ago; they knew me. 'Fuck! I won't bother anymore. You seem to know everyone,' she says.

Aussie director, Graham Hattrick, still has trouble with my name – unlike the technicians. He is young and obviously wasn't born when I last had a job.

Rush, rush, rush as usual. Line run, get the cameras in, one run for them, then shoot. 'Check it.' 'Clear.' And it's time to go home. 10.15.

'I've got three hours to kill. You lucky bugger!' Wendy chirps.

She tells me about a row she had with a director the previous week about a line she wanted to change. It had generated a heated debate but she still had to say the line. She was so pissed off that when John, her partner, came to pick her up, she told him she wanted to leave *EE*. But... 'Oh, fuck! I can't. Ray's here for a year.' However things will change. Oh, yes.

Even in those early days, I had a niggling feeling that *EE* wasn't all it was cracked up to be. It was just an itch back then.

It's certainly a powerhouse in some ways. For instance, if the BBC wants a new show to get good ratings, they stick it either side of *EE* because it will get a spill over of *EE*'s viewers.

But who are these viewers? My first fan letter: 'So pleased you've joined the biggest and best soap in Britain. I have been watching Coronation Street for years...'

I send her the standard *EE* photo of me leaning over the fence above the Albert Square sign. 'You've got the wrong soap.'

She writes back. 'I'm sorry. I'm getting old and I get confused.'

Yes, who are these viewers? Of the eleven and a half million who watch, how many of them are confused and think they're watching '*Corrie*' or *Emmerdale* or *Casualty* – or even *Bill and Ben*?

Joe Swash (Mickey Miller) gets photos of young women wearing next to nothing, lounging around on beds with their legs akimbo. Jessie Wallace (Kat) gets photographers with telephoto lenses smack up against her bedroom window, hoping for a flash of her knockers. Shane Richie (Alfie) gets invited to Manchester United to sit in the Director's Box. Did Laurence Oliver get fan letters congratulating him for his performance in *Carry On Abroad*, or photographers sticking lenses through his bathroom window? I don't think so.

Show business is a circus now. Funny noses and handstands is what they want. It's certainly nothing to do with 'Stage Technique', 'Timing', 'Movement' or 'Staying Power and Repose'.

Maybe 'Staying Power' makes sense. Stickability, hanging on: these are the kind of techniques required.

An eager young actor once asked Olivier how he did it. The great man said, 'A lot of hard work.' Walked away, then turned, winked, and added, 'And a little magic.'

We're not talking Paul Daniels here. It's about imagination – something that makes the audience gasp in wonder. A great performer doing something that takes your breath away. That quality has disappeared with the dinosaurs. It's 'as rare as hen's teeth'.

Therefore, in this subterranean world of soap, this dark world of deception, where wonder and magic have lost their meaning, the starship Celebrity trundles into outer space.

And at its hub, its engine room, is the smoking room, where on one side sit the miseries and on the other the squeaking, giggling air-heads, the whole thing fuelled by the the cacophony of screeching from the television where Jerry Springer berates a single black mum about her crack addiction.

And upstairs, in the mysterious, air-conditioned offices of the tall, elegant puppet masters, the plans are laid for more drivel to put into the gaping mouths of the greedy space travellers, to be regurgitated and fed to a public who doesn't seem to know its arse from a hole in the ground.

Not that I'm bitter, of course, but you might get the impression from the above that *EE* is losing its glitter for me. It's true. It didn't happen overnight but this job gives you a lot of time to think – and to watch.

Learning the lines was always going to be a problem but once I'd realised that they all cock up constantly, I hung on and dealt with it. But spending so much time here, just listening and watching, I began to realise that all was not what it seemed to be.

In the beginning I stuttered along, keeping my nose clean, lapping up the smiles and little jokes. I felt that I was being embraced by the company.

My 'working days' became more frequent as my character, Joe Macer, the 'secret burglar' (they'd scrubbed the prison spell for manslaughter idea) began courting the famous soap grump, Pauline Fowler: in the launderette, at the salsa classes, occasionally in The Vic, until finally I take her out to dinner in Fargo's.

A whole afternoon was spent on three dinner scenes. Pauline and Joe talk about their different backgrounds; Joe doesn't mention his burgling past, but they discuss their fears for the future, their loneliness, never quite reaching the conclusion that the answer might be that they share their lives together. That was left hanging in the air. And there it hung for weeks and weeks.

Then there is the start of things to come. I phone Martha, the line producer for the next block. I have a problem with the dialogue in a couple of scenes. I get the voice mail.

On Tuesday the 16th of August there is a message that Martha wants to meet Wendy and me at lunchtime. Wendy has some problem as well.

'Wendy, what do you want to ask Martha?'

'No, you go first, Ray.'

I tell her my problems. She agrees with me and accepts my changes. 'Anything you find awkward or difficult, Ray, change it.'

Now it's Wendy's turn. It seems that the only time she can get her hair re-coloured is on Saturday.

'And if you want to do that pick up shot on Monday, then I'm going to have to go through the next block with my roots showing. If I do get them done, my hair won't match up with the stuff already shot. So what are you going to do?'

Martha suggests that Pauline wears a hat or a headscarf.

'I never wear hats or headscarfs. I haven't worn them in the twenty years I've been in the show.'

Martha looks blank and mutters, 'Well, you'll have to do something.'

Wendy thunders back, 'You're like a fucking man. You just don't understand, do you?'

Martha slinks out of the smoking room.

Wendy turns to me. 'You see. They'll do anything for *you*, they'll bend over backwards for *you*, do anything to make you happy. But they don't give a fuck about me.'

I tell her the truth. 'I think they're frightened of you.'

She grunts. End of conversation.

She's good at the job, but there's no doubt that she'd get a better response if she just smiled. But, as I come to realise over time, smiling is something that Pauline Fowler doesn't do – except to Betty, her £300 a day screen dog.

I suppose Betty has a real name but I've never heard her called it. All soap people seemed to be called by their character names. In fact, the actors *become* their characters. The Fowlers are the Fowlers; anyone who's been in a soap for a good number of years disappears. It's *The Invasion of the Body Snatchers*. Scary.

But I don't want to disappear. I don't want to be Joe Macer for the rest of my life, having to spend my days living in the Fowlers' house, drinking in The Vic, walking in the fake snow on Christmas day in The Square. It'd be spookily like the British version of Jim Carrey's *The Truman Show*. I was determined to keep my head down and hang on to my identity.

I think I'd better dive back into my past, before Joe Macer gets me by the throat and I disappear for ever. But even going back to my comforting past can reveal clues about my current 'headaches'.

For instance in 1963 with Sid James in *Taxi*. Here we are knocking on a door. We want to know the whereabouts of some character in a plot that I've long forgotten. The door opens and there stands a little old man. It's a short scene. The old actor, shorter than us, delivers his lines. But we become aware that he seems to have his left hand cupped and up in front of his chest.

Then the scene is over. Simple.

As we walked away, I asked him for a light and he waved the previously cupped hand up dismissively to indicate that he didn't smoke. I noticed then that he had his three lines written on the palm of his hand. It made me smile. Why would anybody need to write their lines down? A crib!

Silly young me, so full of myself – done a film, done television, been in the business for all of seven years. Writing lines down! Ha, ha.

That man's face haunts me now, wagging his finger at me and shaking his head. We all get there in the end. I remember once being on the book (the prompter) when the leading lady couldn't remember a single line. I sneered. Young, spotty, I could climb Everest, I was a wow with the girls. Learning lines? Ha! She was shaking with fear and I had no sympathy. That poor, ashen faced, desperate woman haunts me too.

When I did Juke Box Jury in 1966, I saw the make-up girl darkening David Jacob's bald spot. I sneered. But I've had that done. Yes, we all get there in the end.

So here I am in *EastEnders*, surrounded by the finger wagging ghosts of my past, ashen faced, bald and writing my lines down on bits of paper, beer mats, serviettes, anywhere that's close enough, just out of shot, so that my tired, old, myopic eyes can read them.

7

Marriage?

I get called up to Kate Harwood's office.

'We'd like you and Wendy to get married. It'd be a great story for the 21st anniversary of the show. It would bring more interest into Pauline's life, stretch her character – it was getting into a rut. Don't tell Wendy. We'll tell her soon.'

I didn't think much about the fact that they hadn't told Wendy, though I was rather pleased that they'd told me first. It made me feel they thought fairly highly of me. A bit of respect – and quite right too. (Get in the drawer, you stupid, redundant ego.)

Friday, the 19th of August
My first appearance on screen in *EastEnders*.

Everyone's excited. The Greyhound pub puts up a notice telling all the punters.

'We'll be full in here tonight, Ray.'

Shane Richie had said it would change my life. There was certainly a big build up. I couldn't believe it, but I hoped it would be true. Maybe it would be the rocket that would zoom me to success.

At eight o'clock, Sadie and I sat down to watch it.

The Community Centre pops up. All the salsa dancers are bobbing about. Somewhere a voice says, 'Pleased to meet you.'

It's a bald, fat, triple-chinned, ugly old man with my voice. Have they put another actor in and stuck my voice in his mouth? It can't be me!

At 8.30 it finishes. Sadie smiles at me. 'Well, done. You were so natural, real.'

Real! Has Steven Grief turned into my wife?

35

Will and Tom phone. 'Well done, Dad.'

I have a sleepless night. That apparition was me? How could it be me? I don't look like that surely? But I know that it was. Oh, where has that young man gone? The one that sneered at David Jacobs having his bald patch painted in. Yes, that one. You'd have to pour the entire contents of a Dulux factory over my head now to dull the glare.

Next morning I walk down the street. A neighbour sees me. 'Saw you last night. Doesn't television put weight on.'

I'm seriously thinking of calling Kate Harwood on Monday and asking her if I can kill anyone in the show and get sent to prison. I must find Joe's list. But, deep down, I know I'm stuck with it. Wendy and I are going to get married. The fat man and Brown Owl will live happily ever after.

I have the following week off. At Victoria Station, on the way to Brighton, while having a coffee, an old lady turns round and stares at me, then says something to her companion. Whisper, whisper – a quick glance back at me. It must have been *EastEnders*. I check my nostrils – no bogies.

But, of course, she could have been saying, 'There's that fat bugger who's fucking up my favourite soap.' In my current state, I'm convinced it's the latter.

In the old days, coming out of Brighton Station, looking down Queen's Road, almost seeing the sea, seagulls squawking, it felt like home. It is my real home. There are memories everywhere, just across the road from the bus terminus where my mum's bus used to stop is Divell's, the greasy spoon where she'd have a cup of tea. It's still there. And on the corner here is the Queen's Head pub, where Mike Dolling and I used to pore over our roulette cards, trying to find a 'system' to break the bank in the now defunct Sergeant York's Casino across from the pub. Further down was a shop called Rocko's. It was an Aladdin's cave for us kids after the war. The windows were stuffed to bursting with delights: pea shooters, catapults, see-back-scopes, detective outfits, indian headresses, cap guns, potato guns, cap bombs, indoor fireworks, 'the highest bouncing balls in the world', masks, McGill postcards and, best of all, stink bombs labelled 'the biggest stink since Hitler'.

36

Rocko's is now a pub. And through those dusty windows I now see the early morning drinkers.

To the left, down North Road, where now there is a multi-storey carpark, was a poster artist's studio where I had my first job after leaving school. My 'dad' got me the job. Two pounds ten shillings a week. I learnt about silk screening and ran around delivering posters to shops. The famous shot of Marilyn Monroe in *The Seven Year Itch*, her skirt billowing up when she's standing over an air vent in the street, was the sort of thing. There was a man who worked there called Dave. He kept himself to himself. His job was humping around sheets of hardboard, cutting them to length, tapering them to the right shape to be used for backing. One weekend he followed his customary practice of sleeping, a bit of cooking (he wasn't married) and a lot of drinking. This particular weekend, after a lunchtime skinful, he went home for a sleep and dropped off while he still had a fag on and set fire to himself.

And here is the clock tower. To the left of it is Boots, the chemist. That used to be The Regency Cinema and Ballroom. My grandfather was the doorman in a military smart green uniform, peaked hat, epaulettes, frogging and the shiniest black shoes I'd ever seen, then or since. He had been in the Irish Guards in the First World War, where you took care of your boots.

He used to get me in for free, I'd sit in the back row and during the film he'd ruffle my hair and drop a bag of sweets into my lap. In that same cinema, my mum and I had watched *A Song to Remember*, with Cornel Wilde playing Chopin and Merle Oberon as George Sand. We saw that film thirty-seven times, sitting there through the afternoons and evenings, with a blanket over our knees and eating sandwiches.

All the streets seem to hold memories for me. I glimpse ghosts round almost every corner. People are noisier now but even buildings that have been altered to burger bars and phone shops seem recognisable to my nostalgic eyes. I had a happy childhood. I miss those days. And they've certainly gone.

Back to The Factory
I suppose I must have let it slip, although I couldn't remember doing

it. There had been a general rumour about the place that marriage was inevitable. I expect I assumed that Wendy had been told the news.

Anyway, Brown Owl didn't like the idea. 'Why couldn't we just live together? Like me and Ian Lavender?'

'Ian Lavender's character was gay and I'm heterosexual. It wouldn't work.'

She wasn't happy. I tried, in my mature way, to ease her around. But she wasn't having it.

'I'm furious that they told you first. The minute you told me, I went up to see Kate and gave her a piece of my mind. It's not fair. I've been in this show for twenty-one years. And they told you first.'

Oh, dear! Did I mean to tell her? I don't remember, but maybe I did – the chatterbox, desperate, fat, bald man.

EE has made me realise that women have been very important in my life. Here currently, there's Wendy 'Brown Owl' Richard, MBE. She's been helping, guiding. But if she's going to switch off, it could be a rocky year. We might have been mates; it could have worked. But the will has to be there on both sides and now it was sliding away. Would Pauline forgive me?

But there is Kate Harwood. She's given me the job. Kisses me on the cheek. There's an ally – but for how long? I'm not good at recognising the signs. Never have been.

Oh yes, all those important ladies. But you need them on your side. I remember those little girl dancers at Molly Ball's. I saw the danger there. It didn't take long for them to turn. And they always turn. I suppose men do as well, but when a pretty smiling face changes the cold North wind chills you to the bone in the wink of an eye.

Chloe Gibbon gave me my first television part in 1960. Figgins, in *The Secret Kingdom*. The BBC, the same *EE* BBC. Five episodes but they paid me for six. I never told them. That extra 12 guineas bought me my first suit. She gave me another couple of jobs, but then it all changed.

Then there was Val James, Sid James' wife, who pushed to get me into *Taxi*. Val Wood, wife of Charles Wood the writer, who suggested me for *The Knack*. When John Hurt heard that I'd got the part of

Tolen, which he'd gone up for, he apparently said, 'Well, if they've given it to *him*!' But he's done all right.

Yes, they all changed. Maybe it was me as well. It's difficult to tell after all these years.

At the Sutton School of Dramatic Art, at the age of about eleven or twelve, I fell in love for the first time. It was infatuation really, but it felt like love at the time.

Her name was Ann Thompson. She was a dancer and an actress. Her mum and dad owned a guest house, Redbrick Lodge. She had an elder sister called Janet. They seemed rich.

We went out to the pictures, held hands, occasionally kissed, had coffee and dreamed. But all the time she seemed out of my league.

At the top of the stairs from the basement area where they lived, I first experienced sex. Fumbling, searching – not like sex now. My memories are of my handkerchiefs (we had those in the old days) becoming stiff as crumpled up cardboard. Coitus interruptus? I don't think I need to go into detail.

It's horrible when I look back, but I was ashamed of our poverty compared to everything the Thompsons had. The car, the big house, nice clothes and holidays abroad. We had none of those things. Instead I had a mother who worked on the buses, no father, a rented flat, poor old Rysie, my godmother, and a cat.

There were other bits and pieces around that relationship that hurt me. They were going skiing in Switzerland. Ann hinted that I might be invited. But no – I saw them off at Brighton Station. I was only fourteen.

But we carried on going out. Then her mother, an ambitious woman, decided that Ann should go and study at The Royal Academy of Dramatic Art. When she came back from her daily trips to RADA, so enthusiastic about how wonderful they all were, jealousy churned me up.

I was working now in the wages office of the local bus company. I got two tickets for us to see Johnny Ray, her favourite singer, in London.

I waited for her outside RADA. It was summer and the windows were wide open. I could see aspiring thespians walking around with books on their heads. *These* are 'wonderful'? *This* is about acting? James Dean and Marlon Brando didn't bother with books on their heads. They were actors. Great actors. They had studied at The Actors Studio in New York.

I was an avid reader of *Picturegoer* and there one day I found an article about a branch of The Actors Studio soon to be opening in London. It was going be run by an American actor call Al Mulock. Somehow I found out where he lived in London – I must have phoned the magazine. This was going to be my big chance. Bugger all these drawing room comedies. I was going to scratch, slouch and mumble like the big boys.

It was a mews flat – very swish. I rang the bell. An American voice answered. It wasn't Al, it was a woman. Her name was Dorinda Stevens and she was pissed out of her mind. I'd got my handkerchief, but I loved Ann and I wanted to be an actor. I don't suppose anything would have happened anyway, although she was very floppy and silly. I was a boy smelling of seagull poo and hardly in her hamburger munching, gum chewing, sophisticated league.

The audition for The Actors Studio was in Baker Street.

The stipulation was for a duologue, so I pulled in a bloke from the amateur circuit. I'd rather have done a couple of speeches from *Rebel Without a Cause* but if that was the way they wanted it, fair enough.

There were five judges, including Al Mulock, and the decision had to be unanimous.

I noticed, as we went up the escalators at Baker Street, that my acting partner had a huge hole in the heel of his sock. I remember thinking, At least I'll shine in the sock department. Anyway, he was only coming along for the ride. He didn't want to be an actor.

The audition went well. We went back to Brighton and we waited – we waited and waited. Except that he wasn't really waiting because he didn't care.

Save the ink, save the eyesight the outcome is obvious. You should know me well enough by now.

They voted for him unanimously and I got one vote. I was gutted. He didn't want to go to the classes and didn't. I was desperate to go but couldn't. Maybe Al had put the mockers on my chances of joining The Actors Studio. He might have worried about me and Dorinda becoming an item. Scenes from *A Streetcar Named Desire* might certainly become handkerchief moments. But maybe not.

40

Holes in socks are good for auditions, I decided, silly bugger that I was. Better that than ending totally down in the dumps.

Many years later, when I was doing voice overs, I met a fellow VO, whom I told about The Actors Studio saga.

'I was one of the five panellists,' he says.

A tense moment. His name was David de Keyser. He was a nice man, too nice to let a fellow actor down.

'I was the one who voted for you.'

With Ann Thompson, from almost the moment I went off to rep., it all went wrong. Nothing was the same again. I was hurt.

And now, there's Pauline, a screen wife who is showing signs – even I'm recognising them – that the game is up.

Anyway we dance on in *EE*, performing an even more stuttering waltz. When I have to console her with a hug when she's upset (as it says in the stage directions) she says, 'No. Pauline Fowler's a strong woman. She wouldn't do that.' So we didn't.

Brown Owl herself is a strong woman. She's gone through two bouts of cancer. It still concerns her, naturally.

Yes, she is strong. I'm back to tough ladies again. They are influential in my life. They have the ability to boost me up or fuck me up. It's one or the other – no compromise.

For example, after some scenes between us in the early days, Wendy tells the director, 'Now, don't you edit any of those scenes between me and Ray. They're fucking good.'

'I won't, Wendy.'

'You'd better not. And don't tell him how to say lines. He's been in the business longer than me.'

Extraordinary – a real outburst. Happy days.

Now it had become awkward. If someone in authority – a director or producer – didn't put their foot down, things were going to go from bad to worse. But nobody does. 'They're frightened of you,' I'd said. Yes, they are. I was right.

I didn't feel in a position to say anything to her. Serious conversations foundered, and if it kicked off there was no telling where it would end. If I spoke up, bridges could be burnt permanently. So I held back. Maybe things would get better.

But, you see, I really wanted to get on with her. It's essential when you have to work closely together. Not to live in each other's pockets, of course, but just discuss scenes, work out how to play them. You have to. It's a pattern that's always seemed to work for me in the past.

In 1979 when I worked with dear Gemma Jones in *A Nightingale Sang*, a play that toured then came into the West End and closed after seven weeks, we worked hard on our stuff. Gemma, however, is a dedicated actress. And if I've learnt anything in this business, especially from people like Gemma, it is that you have to work at it. I've never found it easy but I try.

On the first night of that tour, in Nottingham, a 'Brummie' soldier (me), carrying a kit bag, comes onto the stage to meet Gemma, who's sitting on a bench, head turned away from me. I'm dragging on, not just my kit bag, but thoughts about the shitty digs I've got, worries about the mortgage back in London, Sadie and the three kids, having just put out a fag, the fact that it was just another 'day at the office' for me. I sit on the bench; Gemma turns to me and ... I didn't recognise her! It was the most amazing thing. This great actress was the character; there was no Gemma to be seen. I wanted to be out front watching this. The last place I wanted to be was where I was. I got through the whole play in a daze.

The next day, a local paper wanted to interview me and I told them the story of the night before. My conclusion was that I was second division; there was no way I could ever reach Gemma's level, such people apply themselves to their craft and occasionally have a touch of the Olivier magic. It certainly is an exclusive club and one that I'll never be a member of. I'll just have to get on with what I do and keep the wolf quiet. I don't know whether I ever talked to Gemma about my feelings but I know, if I had, she would have laughed.

The first performance in the West End of *A Nightingale Sang* was at the Queen's Theatre on Tuesday 17th of July, 1979. Two weeks later, on a Wednesday, I think, my mum, Ernie, the bus driver husband, and the landlord and landlady of The Whitehawk pub came up to see the show. It was chaos: a hot summer night, and Ernie pissed, trying to sell programmes in the theatre.

After the show and after visiting two pubs, we went to Rodo's, a

Greek restaurant near Centre Point. I ordered a *meze* for the assembled rabble. Total madness and mystery filled the air: 'What's this?', 'What's this bit sticking out?', 'Is this fish or meat?'

Ernie tucked so hard into the first three courses that when I told him there were another eighteen or so to come, I had to take him out for a walk. Thank God the pubs were closed by this time. I gave him a small sight-seeing tour. 'That's Foyles, the biggest bookshop in the world.' That fell on deaf ears.

A taxi home, the engine drowned out by the raucous singing from the passengers. 'Are we going to have a nightcap?'

Nightcaps were poured. My mum and Ernie were going to sleep on the 'put-u-up' in the front room. Mum, awash with Russian vodka, was standing on the bed getting her clothes off. 'Have you got a tape of *Cathy Come Home*, Raymond?'

They all sat, in various states of undress, on the edge of the bed, and watched the flickering screen through half closed eyes. It seemed the longest television programme there had ever been.

Next morning, when I came down, Ernie was sitting on his own in the kitchen. The sun was streaming through the window. 'Cup of tea, son?' A few minutes later, my Mum came in – very, very slowly. Her eyes seemed waterlogged. Ernie looked at her.

'I tell you what, son. I'm not going to risk your mother on the wing, she'll have to go in goal.'

A week later she had a severe stroke. I heard about it on Friday night and drove straight down to Brighton. They'd put her in a sort of cot. She was unconscious.

Sadie went down to Brighton to see her every Monday. I went only occasionally. I don't know why. I loved my mother. I think my excuse must have been that I had work. As I write these words, I feel I'm trying to wriggle out of telling the truth. Maybe I couldn't stand seeing her so ill. Whatever it was, Sadie went though she wasn't even her mother and I made excuses. It's something that haunts me.

When I did see her it was in a vast, echoey rest room lit by fierce fluorescent lights and a television pumping out *Catweazel* in the corner.

The room was full of old people, seemingly stuck in straight lines parallel to the skirting boards, slumped, sleeping or moaning incomprehensibly in their high-chairs.

The stroke had paralysed her down her left side and, maybe because of her age or the shock of the stroke, her thinking seemed to be muddled.

There were so many things that I wanted to ask her about the past, *her* past, but there was 'always another time', when she's well, next weekend, next visit. The consequence was that I never got round to it. And now it seemed I never would.

She would sit in this 'high-chair' with a tray attached in front of her which seemed to be encrusted with tiny specks of dried up carrots and potatoes. She found it difficult to speak. It was a horrible place, like a mad house.

Ernie turned into a good guy. Every night he would visit, clean her teeth and wash the palm and fingers of her permanently clenched left hand.

A year later she died.

After the cremation, everybody went back to 5, Manor Hill accompanied by crowds of Ernie's drinking pals from The Whitehawk pub, plus the ever present landlord and landlady of that establishment and my Aunt Muriel and her husband John.

Prior to our getting back, a lady drinking pal of Ernie's had volunteered to make the 'sandwiches, etc'. Her 'etc.' included sinking bottles of booze to help stave off her tears for 'poor Adie'. When we got back, she was legless and we quickly packed her off with a few expletives.

The crowd tucked into everything on offer with gusto. The landlord was sent back to the pub for replacements. He returned accompanied by more drinkers wanting to toast 'the memory of dear old Adie', their sentiments fuelled, no doubt, by the offer of free booze. The afternoon roared on with more people pouring in and pouring down. Old feuds were revived and people began being pushed around. Aunt Muriel and Uncle John had gone out into the garden. I could hear them screaming drunkenly at each other.

There are no louder ghosts in my past than those sweaty, alcohol induced, stumbling, nostalgic, almost childlike images that fill my mind when I opened that door, closed for so many years. In that trembling house at 5, Manor Hill, her friends gathered to celebrate the life of Adelaide Elizabeth Whittingham, née Roach, born 1914, died 1980.

My mum was 25 in 1939, when I was born. Six months before the start of the Second World War. I can't imagine what it must have been like to be the eldest of seven children of a Catholic family in those days, to be unmarried, and suddenly have a bun in the oven. I never heard anything about disgrace but it must have been a very tense time for Adelaide Elizabeth Roach.

But it didn't seem to slow her down according to my Aunt Muriel. The whole family lived at 35, Manor Hill. I was always left upstairs in my cot when she went out. 'You used to cry and cry up there, Raymond,' Muriel told me. 'We were on strict instructions to leave you. One night, we felt so sorry for you we brought you downstairs. When your mother came back she kicked up such a stink. But your grandad said, "you leave that boy up there all the time he'll get bunions on his bum".'

I've relied on Aunt Muriel for all the history of my family. When my mother died, I took Edie and George Bishop out to lunch in Rottingdean. My main reason was to find out about my mother's background. After all, Edie had worked with my mother when they were nineteen in the cigarette kiosk on The Palace Pier. After lunch, I broached the subject.

'Your mother was a very secretive woman.' That was all Edie had to say on the subject.

Secretive! It made me think that if I'd tried to prise information out of my mother maybe I'd have hit a brick wall.

Now the only person left who could shed some light on the mystery is Aunt Muriel. But, whatever she tells me, there is no-one to corroborate her story.

That's why, when I looked at that photograph of me and Mum, taken by some sea front smudger, I desperately want to get into the picture and get back there. And the more I look at it – and I do every day I'm in that dreary dressing room – I find my imagination taking over. Now even that is being coloured by what Aunt Muriel has told me.

When I look at the photos in that same frame of Sadie, Emma,

Will and Tom, I can recall the world around it, the before and after. But even though I'm in that photo with my mum and I push my brain as hard as I can, I can't do the same with that picture. Something tells me that it shouldn't be, but I'm going to keep on trying.

Muriel's never said anything to me about my mum during the pregnancy. I sometimes wonder why she didn't consider an abortion. Maybe she did, but something got in the way. In those days, I suppose, it was in some back street two-up-two-down with an outside toilet, a load of gin, kettles of hot water and a douche. Not hygienic and not always successful.

But there's no doubt she carried a lot of guilt around with her. She didn't tell me I was illegitimate until I was twenty. She must have thought I was thick. I suppose she needed to get it off her chest. It must have been eating her up.

In *EastEnders*, Stacey, Lacey Turner, multi-award winner, gets pregnant. After a few emotional scenes ('Will she? Won't she?' stuff) she's off to the clinic and, Bob's your uncle, back to market slagging people off as if nothing had happened. That's soap for you – but is it? Maybe it mirrors life. But not so sixty-seven years ago. Vera Drake country. Prison and humiliation, even though they were all at it, or knew somebody who was. That was in the black and white days, just like the photographs.

I finally get through to Mrs Joyce Woodhouse. Her knowledge of my background is more or less what she had written in the letter. Her mother, who might have been able to tell me more, is dead. She agrees to send me my dad's painting. A new piece of my past, another piece of the jigsaw. Maybe.

8

Six Months Down the Line: October 5th, 2005

Bad day yesterday. Scenes in the Vic. Cliff, Ricky, David, Mo, Hilda Braid, Shane and Barbara. Mo in a whisper, not like her, 'Do you like Shane?'

'He's fine.'

'Naah, he's a bit full of himself.'

Joe Swash is in hospital. Schedule changed. Lots of phone calls but nobody can find out what's happened to him. Somebody upstairs must know but they won't tell us.

'Learn your lines and do your job ... fast!'

Barbara Windsor says, 'Have you heard Phil Daniels is coming in?'

'Yeah.'

'We've got him and you now. Good actors.'

That's a laugh.

The director, Clive Arnold, a bit like a traffic warden, drives us forward. He gives the impression that he hasn't read the script and is suspicious of anyone (including the actors) who has.

We hurry through the scenes.

'Keep up the pace!'

He's intent on getting everything done as quickly as possible. Doesn't want to get behind, get the sack. What with him and the mob messing around, the scenes go out of the window.

Wednesday 6th

In make-up. 'Saw yesterday's scenes in The Vic with you, Cliff and Ricky. So good. You're such a refreshing, cheerful character. It's what we need in *EastEnders.*'

What's going on? Are people blind?

47

The *EE* juggernaught rolls on, I do a recorded interview on Radio Two with Steve Wright. Waiting outside the studio with an *EE* press lady – they're always there to brief you – she says to me, 'Here's a chance to talk about the books you've written. There could be publishers and agents listening.'

A lady comes over, also waiting. 'I represent George Galloway; he'll be here in a minute. I heard what you said about getting books published. I might be able to help. I'm a big fan of *EastEnders*, by the way.'

Wendy Bailey, for that's the lady's name, was as good as her word. On her recommendation, I sent a few chapters of my books to a Ivan Mulcahy, literary agent.

Everything takes longer than you think in this crazy business. You assume the people who matter are going to drop everything and recognise that this work of genius has got to be given. But life isn't like that; even geniuses are screwed from pillar to post. I go in to see him.

'You're a good writer, not a great writer. A good voice – but to pull what you've shown me around, into some shape, will take a lot of work. And you haven't got time.' A slight nod towards *EE* here. 'I think you should write something closer to the sort of job you do, acting. The bookshops love trying to unravel fiction and fact. Could you be slagging off someone you worked with for instance? Set the tongues wagging. Give it a try.'

Here is my attempt.

Smoke and Mirrors

Mickey and six of the others were waiting around as usual. Three of them were already installed in Madame Tussaud's, the other three were gagging to be exhibited. Didi Wells was already in the final stages of mummification, so when she popped her clogs, all they'd have to do would be to cart her off to Marylebone Road and prop her up with the rest of them.

It looked like rain, not that they ever stopped for rain. Snow ... yes. Christmas only came when they wanted it, always on Christmas Day. The rest of the country never seemed to get it but in West Street, whoops there it was, courtesy of the snow machines to welcome some disaster or other, suicide, murder or an alien invasion.

Still, it was Friday and the weekend was coming into focus.

The wind whistled round the corner of the pub, posters flapped on the bill boards, the fake trees in The Square stood unmoving on cement bases, polystyrene cups cartwheeled down the street and the seven of them wrapped in anoraks, hand warmers gripped tightly – some, the female thespians, had them stuffed down their bras – thermals from head to toe, still shivered violently.

'Fuck this for a game of soldiers.' Didi Wells muttered, dragging on a fag.

You can see the similarity to my current employment, can't you? Writing about acting, dipping into my (carefully disguised) weirdo wall-to-wall job. On the button, wouldn't you say?

So I sent Ivan a few chapters of this.

'A bit confusing,' he said.

Oh, dear.

Hence this new project, encouraged by Will and Tom, our sons. 'Do it, Dad,' they say. Maybe it's because they want to know about me, not find themselves in a similar pickle to the one I'm in about my mother. All the mysteries, almost too complicated to unravel. And, funnily enough, mysteries that seem to get more and more important as I get older. You'd think they'd matter less but they don't.

The painting from Joyce Woodhouse arrives. It's a watercolour, a bit 'Van Gogh' but signed J. Lewis Brooks. I'll put it up in Brighton.

October 6th 2005

Not called in till 3.45. Leaving Ian's party. June Brown, Brown Owl and me walking across The Square. June funny and eccentric. A real joy in the gloom and doom.

There had been a phone call from Kate saying, 'Wendy's all right about the marriage.' You could have fooled me! But you have to learn that about producers. I have, but I always stupidly think that 'this one' is going to be different. They always avoid the truth or, to put it another way, they are consummate liars, trying to keep everybody happy – until the day you get tipped the 'black spot', of course.

Brown Owl must have gone home, thought about 'marrying me' and decided that she hated the idea. Maybe she would rather have maintained her status as a widow. Slippers in front of the fire with Betty on her lap and Ian Lavender putting his knitting down and the kettle on. She'd stopped short of making a wax effigy of me to stick pins into and opted instead for giving me the cold shoulder.

The walk across The Square is completed and June, sadly for me, is released.

Brown Owl and I now have to do a scene outside the Fowlers' back gate. Another night, another episode. Usual chaos. I've been in The Vic, in the studio, which we did over a week ago, drinking loads of beer to find the courage to schmooze Pauline.

Now, a week later, I come out of The Vic and start singing, 'They can't take that away from me' outside her gate. I give a poor impression of the great music hall comedian, Jimmy James, slurring and staggering around. We rehearse this, Pauline coming out of the gate to 'shhh' me, the two of us having a bit of chat and that's it. The producer tells me that I should cut the drunkenness back a bit.

'But, when we did the scene inside the Vic, you told me that I had to keep downing pints. And I did. It won't match up if I stop slurring and staggering about.'

(An actor's got to keep his end up, the thespian's art is a mystery and it's got to be protected at all costs.)

'Well, just pull it back. It's getting a bit National Theatre. We can cut round it. This is *EastEnders*.'

'All right.'

I'm being pathetic, I'm too tired to argue and the clock is ticking. So much for the thespian's art: mumble and keep your head down – it's *EastEnders*, for God's sake! 'We can cut round it.'

It's tricky but I do my best. Brown Owl stops the scene.

'What happens after this?'

'You go into the launderette and ... er Joe fixes the machine for you, Wendy.'

(Still struggling with the name, you see.)

'He couldn't fix a machine. He's playing it too pissed!'

She's talking about me. I may as well not have been there. She could having been talking about an old relative suffering from

Alzheimer's. So I have to pull back the 'tipsy' even more; now I'm almost as sober as a judge.

I try and try and try. Then dry and dry and dry. Brown Owl's eyes are watching my every move. It's unnerving. But I get through it.

'Let's try one more.'

Shit!

'Good. Check it.'

'There was a cable in shot.'

Shit, shit!

'Take six.'

Finally, it's over. No goodbyes. Another day at the factory. I trudge back to my dressing room, get changed and drive back home in a daze. I know it's going to get worse, the clouds will gather, a chill wind will come in from the North and I'll be blown away. I'm not happy.

The only other time that I have had this empty feeling was when I was doing *Growing Pains* – twenty episodes, over two years, also with the BBC. Again, I started with such optimism. Steve Wetton, a supply teacher in Derby, had written a pilot for a potential radio series. He was a great fan of *Big Deal* and thought that Sharon Duce and I would be good as a couple with three children, who decide to foster. Sharon and I recorded the pilot. We waited to see whether it would be picked up for a series. It was and we did six programmes.

I took out an option on *Growing Pains*. I approached David Cregeen, head of series and serials at BBC Television. He commissioned one script. Steve Wetton almost wet himself with excitement. I went up and down to Derby to help him shape the script. We submitted it.

They came back very quickly and commissioned another two scripts. Before these were finished, however, David Cregeen phoned and said could we do ten! Amazing!

We shot on location, the interiors being filmed in Bristol. It should have been perfect. Sharon and I had got on well during *Big Deal*. But things had changed, as things always seem to do. It became bleak and miserable.

You might think that I'm being self pitying but when you feel that nobody's on your side it can get a bit lonely. It's a struggle to get

51

out of bed in the morning. I'd only been in *EastEnders* for just over six months and already I was losing heart. Maybe, it's that I wanted praise. I suppose that, deep down, I do, though that need is something I despise in others. All I can say in my defence is that in fifty years in this business, *Growing Pains* and *EastEnders* have been the only shows on which I have felt this desperate. Maybe it's all to do with getting older, less tolerant; just being a grumpy, bald, old, fat bastard. Which, of course, I am – in spades.

I read a lot of book reviews, *Saturday Times* and *Guardian*, buy a lot of books but never seem to have time to read them. I suppose it helps sales, and the author may get his ten per cent. I also read *The Guardian Film & Music Supplement*. All these publications throw up snippets of ideas, introduce you to new writers, dig up forgotten ones.

Today I read an article by John Patterson about Oscar Micheaux, a pioneering black artist who lurked in the shadows for most of the fifty-five years since his death. He was one of the most prolific film-makers of the 1920s and 30s making some forty 'race pictures'.

When he died it seemed that all his efforts had died with him: his six novels were out of print and his movies were scattered to the wind, to the furnace and the foreclosure auction. In 1951 he vanished into a pauper's grave. There is a biography of Oscar by Patrick McGilligan.

With next to no money he made his films, using amateur actors, then peddled them across the country. Thirty-two years later he was dead and for fifty-five years his legacy was almost entirely wiped away.

Why am I telling you this? Because men like that – dedicated, creative believers – make today's puffed up, television fed, money grabbing inheritors seem shallow and vacuous. It's a different world and I'm a part of it. It's all a bit shoddy. I get angry with myself for being upset by silly spats. How would Oscar have dealt with *EastEnders*? He'd probably have thought he was in Valhalla, got on with it and said, 'Fuck 'em all! They won't get me down.' Good old Oscar.

The 7th of October
The 'famous' scenes in the restaurant are being aired. It seems a lifetime ago that we did them.

52

This is my take on what should have been written in the Radio Times or some other TV Listings magazine:

The Fat Man returns to your screens tonight!!! Fatty takes Brown Owl to Fargo's for three exciting scenes where Fatty talks about Salsa Dancing! Depression!! Loneliness!!! AND the Death of his Wife!!!! Will Fatty pay the bill? Will Fatty kiss Brown Owl? Join in the fun and thrills with F and BO tonight and find out!

It was about as 'Exciting' and offered as many 'thrills' as watching a salamander trying to tap dance. She didn't know about the marriage plans then because we shoot about seven or eight weeks ahead of transmission, so the shit was yet to hit the fan. Metaphorically speaking, of course. Dum, dum, dum!

9

An Allegory

Say that you had just taken over a flat, an old flat with bits and pieces of old fashioned furniture scattered about – what they used to call in those ancient days 'a furnished flat' – bits of old tat really, but the landlord can charge you 'key money', like a deposit. That's what used to happen.

When Killy, Sadie and I moved into 9, Dunster Gardens in Kilburn, in 1961, the stuff they'd 'furnished' it with must have come out of the Ark. The flat comprised two bedrooms, which was sophisticated for us. Having shared just one bedroom in Camden Town with the gentle giant Killy for six months already, it was getting a bit claustrophobic. It was not unusual to wake up with his size sixteen plates of meat underneath your pillow – and his bed was on the other side of the room. Now we had two bedrooms, a tiny front room leading to an even tinier kitchen and, off that, a garden we shared with two other flats. The shared bathroom was on the first floor landing. This flat contained an armchair and a dining-room table that would comfortably seat twenty people for dinner. The only way to get through the front room to the kitchen was to climb over this monstrosity – just to get a glass of water. We dumped it pretty damn quick. So it was bye, bye, deposit.

But just suppose, you've moved into a flat with 'left behind furniture' and there, in your front room, is an old chest of drawers. It's not to your taste but it might be useful just for the moment.

When you open the drawers, you find they are full of rubbish. You start clearing them out. One of them contains letters and postcards; the postmarks are faded. You empty them onto the floor.

It's a rainy Sunday afternoon; there's nothing on television; you're bored, so you sit down and pick a letter out of the pile next to you on the floor. You become interested, and then intrigued. You pick another one. 'What are these?' you might say to yourself. There's no logic: one is dated '1967', the other '2007'. The handwriting is similar. You pick up another: 1977. Another: 1939. Then 1956. Say you were about to embark on writing the biography of Ray Brooks. What a mystery!

This is how my memory works: a lot of postcards and letters, thoughts jumbled up, shuffled randomly, that can be animated by something that happens now, or might happen in a couple of minutes, sending me rocketing back to a conker I had in 1951, or Brian Cobb on a Xaverian sports day, or even the yawning comfort blanket of a television with the sound turned down.

No, I'm not maligning the trusty goggle box, for a lot of people it's their only friend. It certainly can offer up some tasty fodder if you search.

Talking about nothing on television, here's something.

9.00. BBC1. *Just the Two of Us*. 'Tess Daly and Vernon Kay watch as Janet Ellis, Julia Bradbury, Greg Wallace and Mark Butcher team up with Russell Watson, Natasha Atomic Kitten, Jocelyn Brown, Beverly Knight, Alexander O'Neill, Tony Christie and Marti Pellow.'

Now, what's this all about? It's like *Celebrity Come Dancing*, except this programme is *Celebrity Singing*. Why would I be watching this? One of the names they have left off the list is John Bardon, Jim 'all right, son' Branning from *EastEnders*, and he certainly is a good reason for turning the sound up!

'It'll show the punters that I can do something else.'

That's what he told me and the millions of viewers.

'Sing?'

''course I can, son.'

It seems that John can do almost everything. He was a tailor and can still stitch and sew, or cut out patterns; he is a big D.I.Y man; he had his own one man show in the West End, a tribute to the great comedian Max Miller; and he can design.

I can't remember what he sang or who his singing partner was, just that he was riveting. All the others were spinning around, boogying, twisting their faces all over the place. John's no Engelbert Humperdinck, thank God – can you imagine 'Please Release Me' coming out of John's face? Of course you can't, and more importantly wouldn't want to – but there he was, smiling, giggling, strutting around in a suit that looked a bit big, wowing them.

And there in the front row of the audience were June Brown and Barbara Windsor, applauding wildly, Denis Waterman supporting his daughter Hannah – also warbling away in the contest – and Ricky Groves, her husband. John was terrific.

I don't love John, though I admire him enormously. He's one month younger than me and with him what you see is what you get. He's had a bumpy career – fill in jobs, a spit and cough in this and that – until he had a couple of auditions for *EastEnders*. At the time he was driving mini-cabs to and from Heathrow Airport. It was when he was taking some obnoxious customers to Heathrow that he got the call offering him a contract in *Eastenders*. 'I nearly threw the fucking bastards out the cab, but we were going down the M4 at the time, so I thought better of it.'

I think *Just the Two of Us* as a concept for television is a pretty mediocre idea. It's a cloned show of a cloned show, and if you go back where you came from and round the corner, you might see, in the far distance, the original idea playing a mouthorgan trying to scratch a living. I suppose nothing's new. To liven tired formats up, they introduced, a few years ago, the idea of using 'celebrities' instead of punters to behave like prats. But, I must admit, a few of them glitter gloriously in their new personae. And Mr John Bardon is up there twinkling away.

My dream mix in *Just the Two of Us* would be John and Beverly Brown, June Brown and Paul Robson, Barbara Windsor and Marie Lloyd, Derek Martin (more about him later with affection) and Two Ton Tessie O'Shea, Ricky Groves and Frank Ifield, Kellie Shirley and Edith Piaf, Phil Daniels and Screaming Lord Sutch, and some others doing duets with their egos. All a fantasy, but Fix It, Jim, please.

Barbara Windsor is bubbly, flirtatious, funny and has a bone structure to die for. When I see her I always think of a remark made about Sammy Davis Junior, 'When he opens the fridge and the light goes on, he goes into his act.' That's Babs in a nutshell – show-biz to her fingertips. During her early years working in London clubs, she used to go home on the bus.

'Weren't you scared, only seventeen, at that time of night?'

'No, darlin'. All the petty crooks and the tarts, we got on like a house on fire.'

Then she worked with the legendary Joan Littlewood of Stratford East fame. Joan Littlewood was a giant in the theatre. Brendan Behan's *The Hostage, Oh, What A Lovely War, Sparrows Can't Sing*, of which the acerbic critic Bernard Levin wrote: 'A hit, a hit, a palpable hit.' I remember seeing that pasted outside The Garrick Theatre in Charing Cross Road. Little did I realise that Barbara 'Where Do Little Birds Go in Winter?' Windsor and I would cross paths in the years to come. She was also in Lionel Bart's ill fated *Twang*, playing Maid Marion. Somebody said, 'When you come out of the theatre you're humming the sets.' Sean Kenny *was* a great theatre designer. His sets for Bart's *Oliver* were staggering.

I first met Barbara in 1967–8 when I did six days' work on *Carry on Abroad*. I'd worked with Sid James on *Taxi* doing two series of twelve episodes each in 1962 and '63, as I've told you before.

Sid had treated me like a son. He organised my first car, a Fiat 600, from a mate of his in Wandsworth.

'It's got rust under the bonnet.'

'Well, it's been out in the car lot, hasn't it? That's normal.' Then, 'When's Sadie's birthday?'

'April the 8th.'

'I can get her a 24 carat bracelet. It's got a nice trinket of St Paul's Cathedral on it. Mate of mine in Hatton Garden. Eighty quid.'

And then, before we started the second series of *Taxi* I had a phone call from Sid. 'How much do you want for the second series?'

'Well, I got a £100 an episode for the first one. I was thinking £125.'

'No, I think £110. That'll be all right, won't it?'

Of course, I had to take it. It was Sid, after all, who was looking after my interests. Can you imagine that happening with the BBC today? Did Sid know the budget for the programme? How much there was to spread around? Or was he making sure that he was getting everybody on the cheapest deal so that he could have more for himself? I'll never know, but that's how it was.

When we were rehearsing in Hammersmith, at lunchtime we'd go to the nearest pub. He'd have bought a Racing Standard; he'd have a gin and tonic and he'd let me have a brown ale. One day an actor I'd seen somewhere before came into the pub: Paul Carpenter, a Canadian or American, who had come here after the War and settled to work in films.

Actors from America, North or South, were employed in cheap British movies. The producers hoped that an actor who sounded vaguely American might help to sell their midget budgeted, third rate movies across the pond.

Paul Carpenter says, 'Hello, Sid!'

Sid knew him, of course, but didn't like getting lumbered with people when he wanted to immerse himself in the racing paper. It turned out that Paul was on his uppers. His next port of call was The Hammersmith Palais where '...I can pick up some old widowed bird and give her one.' The mind boggles. These days he'd probably be shoed into *I'm a Celebrity, Get Me Out of Here*. I think on the whole, if it were me, I'd shoot into The Palais, have another brown ale and shoot out again. Poor old Paul, poor old silly widow.

Sid treated me very kindly. Silly thing, driving me in his flash Rover towards Chiswick roundabout, he had to brake suddenly, so he put his arm across my chest to stop me crashing into the dashboard – this was before seat belts.

Val, his wife, and Sid took Sadie and me to The Pickwick Club, opened after the great success of *Pickwick*, which starred Harry Secombe (book by Wolf Mankowitz, music by Cyril Ornadel). It was a really trendy place. Sid ordered a bottle of red wine. It was £12.00, a staggering amount of money to me, and then ordered the food. Sadie had lobster. She looked aghast at this monster on her plate. She'd never had lobster before in her life. The waiter slapped down a pair of crackers. Sid looked at the shuddering Sadie. 'Pick it up and break it with your hands,' he said, 'that's what I do.'

The relief on her face was a picture.

Sid's my mate; sorts out my first car, sorts out Sadie's birthday present, takes me to the pub, organises my salary, makes sure I don't bang my head, trusts me to write down what shots they're taking in the studio during rehearsals, because they don't want him to see a monitor – 'I did that for Hancock.' Then I used to take my jottings to him in his dressing room and he'd call the director in and give him a bollocking. Why he didn't insist on having a monitor so that he could see, heaven knows, but that's the way it was. Everyone's mad.

Four or five years later, my first day on *Carry On Abroad* at Pinewood Studios, Sid is walking towards me down the main corridor. 'Hello, Sid!' I'm happy to see a familiar face.

'Hello, mate,' he says and walks on past. He never spoke to me again all the time I was there.

I told Barbara that story and she said, 'Well, that was Sid, wasn't it.'

Not quite the answer I was looking for. I couldn't understand it and I was hurt. Not anymore, of course, but it's funny revisiting these moments. You can still recall the taste of those old times.

One early morning at Pinewood, I was in the make-up room (I was supposed to be a Spanish waiter, so tons of dusky make-up). Everyone was there: Sid, Kenneth Williams, Joan Sims, Bernard Bresslaw, Barbara, Kenneth Connor, Peter Butterworth, Jimmy Logan, June Whitfield and Hattie Jaques. Imagine, all these funny people at seven in the morning looking as miserable as sin. Everyone seemed to be smoking, drinking cups of coffee, bleak faces staring into the mirrors in front of them. A room full of zombies. The door flies open and Charlie Hawtrey bounces through with a young man on his arm.

'Hello, darlings,' he shrieks. 'Too much R. Whites lemonade last night. Bit pissed.'

And then, as one, all of them without looking up shout, 'Shut up, Charlie!'

The director of all the *Carry On* movies was Gerald Thomas. He always came to work wearing silk shirts; indeed, his general ensemble gave the impression that he was just about to board his yacht for a few weeks' sailing in the Med. After every take, he had a habit of shouting, 'Cut. Print.' with a 'God! That was so wonderful' tone in his voice, but only if one or more of the 'regular' *Carry On* team were involved. If it was us ordinary mortals, his tone was one of abject boredom and 'why the fuck did I employ this rubbish?'

Gerald was on a percentage of the films, no wonder his clothes were the best and he could drive to Pinewood in a different car every day: E Type, Bentley, Roller – if it was the best he'd have it. The stars, on the other hand, never got more than £5,000 a picture.

There was a rumour that a well known name did a *Carry On*, made a bit of a hit, was asked to make the next picture, then made the mistake of asking for £7,000 – he never worked for them again. It was a tight ship. Very.

June Brown is extraordinary. Scenes with her are a master class. Her concentration, her intensity, her timing, blow me away. Scenes between her and John Bardon crack me up.

She's been in this business for ages and her work has covered every aspect. Maybe she hasn't done underwater paper tearing yet, but if an offer cropped up she'd be in there like a shot, bathing cap and waterproof fags at the ready.

She told me a story a few months ago about somebody in *EE*, but when she heard on the grapevine that I was writing a regular diary of my time in the soap, she got very twitchy.

'Please don't put that down in your book, Ray, it was in confidence.'

Her eyes wide and voice trembling, how could I let down the mighty June! In fact, she's a bit of a chatter box, and she often launches into a story and then realises that she's talking to me, whom she now thinks of as a Nigel Dempster clone, whereupon her eyes open in horror and her mouth shuts like a mouse trap.

She has honed her skills to such a degree that very few actors can match up to her. It's not that she tries to out-act them, it's just that she hits such a high standard. I keep my eyes open (metaphorically) in scenes with her: watch, listen, knowing that I haven't got a snowball's chance in hell of keeping up with her and, even though I've been in the business since the world was black and white, I realise that my standards are pretty skimpy. But I don't care. I just get enormous joy just being there with her. Without her *EastEnders* would wither and die.

Derek Martin is a different kettle of fish. When he came through the Fowlers' kitchen door carrying a box of veg, Dave Hill, my mate in the series, turned to me after it was over and said, 'Bloody hell, how does he do it? He plays it so natural and simple. There's something to learn there.'

I had first worked with Derek and John in *Big Deal*. I'd heard of Derek, of course, but never met him before. He had a reputation as a bit of a gambler, and I must say when he shuffled a pack of cards in a scene it was obvious he'd been round a card table plenty of times before. Latterly, he's knocked gambling on the head, apart from the odd gee-gee race. I think what really summed Derek up was an interview in *The Walford Gazette*, which is an internal paper that guest members of staff edit.

He said, 'When I was a kid I loved playing cowboys and indians. Now I'm getting paid for it.'

The attitude of both John Bardon and Derek Martin was put most succinctly by John: 'This is my bloody pension, mate.' They both deserve it.

Wendy Richard is another truly extraordinary person. She has concentration in spades. Her parents ran a pub just behind where the Hilton Hotel is now. I believe she went to a boarding school. One of her first jobs on television was *The Grove Family*; she was also in *Dad's Army*. She did one play, a tour of *Blithe Spirit*, which she said she hated. She never did another play again.

Most of her career has been on television. *Are You Being Served* ran for almost twenty years, and that was followed by over twenty years in *EastEnders*.

I said to her once that it was a pity that she hadn't, during those forty years, done more varied work. 'Think of the different doors that would have opened for you.' (I'm great with advice, me.) She was non-committal. I didn't know whether she thought I was right or wrong. I just thought that she could have been a more versatile actress because she certainly had the ability, but she was channelling herself into such a narrow field.

I was trying to be friendly but she is a difficult person to get know. Maybe she just didn't like me.

I remember very clearly one occasion when she showed her vulnerability. We were on location and had four scenes in a café; just the two of us, and all day to shoot them. Towards the end of the afternoon she was, understandably, getting very tired. She was having trouble with a longish speech and kept breaking down. I heard her mutter to herself, 'Don't lose it now.' It seemed like a fear, weakness;

it was very sad. I wanted to comfort her but I didn't want to be rebuked. It's been a funny old relationship.

I feel closer to these people because they are all about my age. They've been round the block a good few times and get the best out of what's thrown up; most of them are grateful to work.

Of the younger members of the cast Kara Tointon, Amanda Drew (Doctor Drew), Stuart Laing and my little mate Kellie Shirley, whom I first saw in the television adaptation of Patrick Hamilton's *Twenty Thousand Streets Under the Sky*, are my favourites. 'Mr Vibrator', Kellie calls me (nothing naughty – it's just that if I say something during a hug of greeting my voice rattles her ribs). She's quite slim so it wouldn't have far to go. She is a beautiful girl and somebody to watch for in the future.

Natalie Cassidy and James Alexandrou, who have been in *EE* for ten years, are leaving. She has grown so much during this time. Natalie is a stunning actress; like June, her concentration is phenomenal. She hardly needs to get herself 'in the mood' for a scene; she can be gassing away seconds before we begin but when the starting tapes are up she's in the scene up to her eyebrows. James too can switch on and off, his concentration as acute as Nat's.

They are now twenty-one or twenty-two. At their age I had been in repertory theatres up and down the country for four years, doing a different play every week. As an Assistant Stage Manager my job was to go round organising props, playing small parts in the play, living away from home, paying my own bills, paying rent for my digs. I was growing up but doing a job that I really wanted to do.

Natalie and James have done only television; they have no experience in any any other area. I'm not saying that what I did was the right way to start, but what they have to do is go out and start at the beginning – not easy at their age. Famous for playing Sonia and Martin on television, there's no doubt that people will pay money to come in and see them but they can't afford to wobble and falter. But I've got every confidence in them. She *wants* to learn, is keen to find her feet and, with her intelligence, there shouldn't be any problems. She'll be around for a long time. James spent three months studying in New York, learning about film technique. He wants to be a film director. Eventually, he could be one.

63

The cast of *EastEnders* spans almost the full age range. Some are my age and the others are like me when I was young. *EastEnders* resembles one of those giant greenhouses in Kew Gardens, the old plants reaching high up to the roof and the younger ones inching their way into the warm air.

10

My Theatrical Beginings

I never started in a greenhouse. With Ann Thompson ensconced in RADA, bleating on about how wonderful all her fellow students were, I had to do something to prove to her that I was one of the greatest actors in the world. But how could I start?

There was no chance of the great RADA for me but my Aunt Vera knew a juggler in Croydon. Close enough. I expected to meet a man in a spangly suit, but jugglers in Croydon just sit in front of gas fires stroking cats. I think this man's name was Jack.

Jack gave me a list of theatrical agents. I had some photos done. Looking at them now, this stranger from the past, puppy faced, Brylcreemed hair, in a sweater that wouldn't have been out of place whaling in the North Sea and an expression as if someone had put an ice cold suppository up my arse.

I wrote to all these agents, enclosing the amazing photo.

In my letter, I included all my 'credits' *The Pirates of Penzance*, *Peter Pan*, *The Happiest Days of Your Life*, all the other bits and pieces, and ended '... that all these were amateur productions but to a professional standard and therefore I would like to be represented by your agency for further engagements. Yours sincerely, Raymond Brooks.'

I waited and waited, gave up, became suicidal and one day, as I sat in the rain, in one of those sea front shelters, the wind whistling through the broken panes, all the drama enveloping me, out of the blue the 'on and off' love of my life, Ann Thompson, arrived.

'There's a telegram for you.'

It was from the Daphne Vosper Agency. They wanted the puppy faced Brylcreem boy to play John Hunter in *Treasure Island* at

Nottingham Playhouse for four weeks at a salary of four pounds ten shillings a week, starting rehearsals on the 1st of December. It was 1956.

As I was 'unexpectedly available' during that time, I decided to take it. Even the 'on and off' Ann appeared 'on' again. Here was the boy with his cardboard handkerchief, now a *professional* actor. I ran home. My mum and Rysie were even more excited than I was. I was on the ladder. Nottingham, here I come!

It was the furthest north I'd ever been. I didn't have anywhere to stay, I'd been told by someone at the Vosper office just to go the stage door of the theatre and they would give me directions to some digs which would be in keeping for a budding star. That's not exactly what they said to me (forget the 'budding star' bit) but that was the kind of euphoric state I was in.

Another fledgling star, Peter Paul, and I were directed to some desperate back street digs, arriving at what must have been about 10 o'clock at night. The only room left was sharing – not just Peter and me, but with half a dozen others.

The room was dark, though the curtains were open and let in the dim light of a street lamp. Our companions were all asleep and snoring. On the window ledge stood a false leg.

Peter and I left those digs very early, too early to see that limb reunited with its owner. And I got different digs the next day, not being partial to legs that came off at night.

The day to day details of the rehearsals are vague, but two incidents stick out.

On *Treasure Island*, when the Hispaniola arrives with the pirates and they find Ben Gunn, there's a skeleton. One day Kevin, the Stage Manager, dropped a sack at my feet.

'Make a skeleton out of these bones.'

I must have said something about not knowing where to start.

There followed a wink and a cheeky smirk. 'Well, come to my dressing room later and I'll show you what goes where.' Needless to say I didn't go and I kept well out of Kevin's way from then on.

The other humiliation was that I only had two lines in the play. One was in the stockade during the fight between Captain Smollett and the officers against the pirates. During a particularly boisterous

66

rehearsal, the director, John Harrison called a halt and said, 'Raymond, I'm going to have to give your line to Greville. We can't hear you over the gunfire.' So much for elocution lessons.

I shared a dressing room with Willis Hall. It wasn't a dressing room really, more a prop hole containing all the pirates' cutlasses, pieces of eight, peg-legs and, I think, the odd back-up parrot for Long John Silver. There was also a ladder that led up to the trap door in the stage (the deck of *The Hispaniola*), so there was a constant troop of pirates up and down it. It was chaos.

The name of Willis Hall may be largely forgotten today but, with Keith Waterhouse, he co-authored *The Long, The Short And The Tall* and *Billy Liar*.

The Long, The Short And The Tall was on at the Albery Theatre in St Martin's Lane. Peter O'Toole, Robert Shaw and Eddie Judd were members of the cast. Apart from those three, there were another five actors including the Japanese camp commander. The understudy for *all* of them was Michael Caine.

Billy Liar opened with Albert Finney in the lead and when he left to make a film, Tom Courtney, fresh out of RADA, took over. When *Billy Liar* was turned into a musical at The Theatre Royal, Drury Lane, Michael Crawford, my old adversary, played the lead.

So the pirate I shared the prop hole with in 1956 did well for himself.

We had Christmas Day off. The landlady was doing Christmas lunch for her 'guests', but she was charging twelve shillings and sixpence for it. I hadn't got twelve shilling and sixpence.

I bought a half tin of baked beans and ten Park Drive; I had two shillings over for the gas fire. It was cold. My bed had one blanket and a sheet. I'd pinched a large sheet of brown paper from the theatre and I put that between the blanket and the sheet, to help keep me warm. It was a rotten Christmas.

Monday 17th of October

Crematorium. Nana Moon's funeral. Hilda Braid, who played Nana Moon, didn't want to leave *EastEnders*. I had lunch with her on her last day. She wasn't happy.

On the day, everyone's kitted out in their regular burying kit for the latest character to get the chop – except, of course, for lucky buggers who've booked their annual holiday in Barbados.

Shane Richie had a massive speech, pages of it, droning on about his 'dear old Nan'. He did it very well, he'd obviously worked on it. When the coffin was carried in, someone said, 'Bloody hell! You'd just about get a cat in that. Why didn't they measure Hilda up before they ordered it?' The speech continued. The 'congregation' sitting there for Shane's eyeline took no interest at all. Some were doing crosswords, others reading, most of them just scratching themselves. 'He's no actor,' a voice whispered.

The close up on the speech having been recorded, the cameras are turned towards the congregation.

The director, not my favourite, says to Wendy, 'Wendy, when Shane mentions "love" in his speech, I want you to turn to look at ... er, er, Joe.' (No prompt from Brown Owl.)

Wendy says, 'Why? We've only known each other a couple of weeks. My character wouldn't do that.'

The director risks life and limb. 'Well, just a *brief* look.'

Take one.

'Joe, you didn't look. Do more.'

The man is an arse hole.

'I did. Wendy looked round. I gave her a flick. It's not music hall.'

The director, confronted by this vast flock of stars, retreats. 'Oh, well. I wasn't looking at the monitor. I'm sure it was fine.'

Wonderful, isn't it?

I suppose I'm begining to feel detached in a way. I'm here, I can't change anything, so why worry? Easier said than done.

Lunch time.

A fleet of mini buses takes us all over to a park where the chuck wagon is situated. Our dining area comprises two pre–1950 London buses. And it's raining. Also parked there are half a dozen luxury Winnebagos. The television series *Waking The Dead* is on location.

The queue of *EastEnders* actors and technicians, sixty or seventy of them, stretches out in the lunchtime drizzle. Near the back, an afternoon of weeping and sobbing awaiting him, is Shane Richie.

While the *Waking The Dead* mob are lounging around in their caravans, with probably a personal chef for each of them, the BBC's 'flagship show' actors, who command the attention of eleven and half million viewers, are queuing in the rain for today's specials: nut hard steak, carrots and chips or chicken curry and chips. Nobody dares complain because, deep down, all actors are scared.

Tuesday 18th

Albert Square, all following the hearse. Everything's back to front when you film. Both John and June are very funny.

'Fucking fifth funeral this year! Drives you mad!'

There's the usual chaos, you'd think they were shooting the chariot race from *Ben Hur*. Everyone's moaning, the younger mob are screeching and messing about and going missing when they're needed. It's amazing that anything gets done.

Natalie says, 'I don't think that you and Wendy getting married's going to work.' Fuck. 'I mean you can't talk to her. Where would it go?'

I'm still undecided whether I should talk to Kate Harwood or not and try and get out. Maybe I should just let it run for a bit and see what happens. I think of the money; things might perk up.

I'm up and down like a yo-yo. Praise, praise – that's what I want. It's pathetic. I blame it on the fact that I was brought up by two women, my mother and Rysie, who adored me. That's my excuse. I'm sure Jung would have an explanation. But we all need praise.

When I finished *Treasure Island*, fifty years ago, The Nottingham Playhouse did a schools' tour of *Noah's Ark*. I was given the part of The Elephant. I must admit I wouldn't need the padding these days.

Now we come back to praise. Here I am, seventeen years old, fresh as a daisy, cast to play The Elephant. John Jackson, who played Mr Arrow in *Treasure Island* was cast as The Man, a sort of narrator. He couldn't be around to rehearse for the first couple of days, so I was asked to play his part *and* The Elephant. Everyone said I was brilliant ... wasted on The Elephant. I got the impression that people who had seen the original production in London thought I was better than whatever Knight, or Lord, or Olivier, or Richardson who had dared to play it before. Some whispered that if John Jackson didn't turn up I would be the toast of all the schools in Nottingham.

But, of course, Jackson did turn up. I was disappointed, but I basked in that praise as I lumped around in my elephant's head listening to Jackson saying the lines I had 'magically' turned into sheer poetry. Oh, the simplicity of everything then.

When all these dreams and applause drifted away and the tour was over, I went home to Brighton and waited for the phone to ring, picking up dole money and praying for a miracle ... and more praise. Well, another job anyway.

Ann was engaged to a boy called Tony. They're married and now live in Norfolk, I understand, where Tony is a vicar.

I found a letter the other day, in the famous brown suitcase, from a girl called Helen. Now why on earth did I keep that? Very cheerful it was. She talked about her new bikini and couldn't wait to see me again. I can't remember what she looks like; all girls in those days fade in comparison with Redbrick Lodge Ann Thompson. But she was off with the religious-leaning Tony, young thespians have to have some sort of female company to brag to. So Helen must have popped into the frame.

After a few months of cavorting with Helen and pining about the newly converted Ann, I got a call from Daphne Vosper, my agent. She had got me a job with The Forbes Russell Repertory Company as Acting ASM for a season at The Playhouse Theatre in Butlin's Holiday Camp at Clacton on Sea. No accommodation on the camp.

I had the usual trouble finding digs, though this time there were no false legs. It was a sunny house, high above the town with French windows where I sat having my delicious fried breakfast looking out over the lawn. But it was too far away from the action for my liking.

I needed to get down and dirty, suffer, like all actors are supposed to do, live in a world of false legs, live like my heros, James Dean and Marlon Brando: torn jeans, grubby tee shirts, standing in the rain, fag in the corner of their mouths, in the black and grey streets of New York.

But this was Clacton on Sea, and even Brando and Dean would have struggled to be cool there. So, I packed my bags and moved to the hub of the town, the theatrical digs Beach House.

I ended up sharing a room with Mike Vardy, an actor in the Butlin's company, in the annex.

Butlin's in those days was amazing. The cost of going abroad – I think you were only allowed to take twenty-five pounds out of the country – and the parlous state of most destinations made it all a bit daunting. Happy Sunny Butlin's was the holiday destination of the majority of post-war Britons.

They came in their thousands, every Thursday, screaming with excitement through the gates: kids, grannies, aunts, uncles, mums and dads, all determined to have a great time.

Ensconced in chalets, possibly better than the homes some of them came from, with the Redcoats patrolling and a baby-sitting service (via a baby alarm in the chalets) the adults could go out drinking in the 'Pig and Whistle' pubs, dance in the Viennese Ballroom, go mad in the Rock 'n' Roll ballroom, play bingo, play snooker with Ray Reardon, go to The Gaiety Theatre and watch the theatrical Redcoats strutting their stuff, or even go and see a comedy in The Playhouse Theatre.

Days were filled with meals – breakfast, lunch and dinner, plus all the snacks in between – swimming in the pools, playing snooker, slot machines, bingo, glamorous grannie and knobbly knees competitions, bonnie babies competitions, running, jumping, swimming, blowing up balloons, or Miss Butlin's April 15th 1957, with a possibility of becoming Miss Butlin's for that year and a modelling contract.

During all of this The Forbes Russell Repertory Company performed their plays *ad nauseam*: *Gaslight* by Patrick Hamilton, cut to an hour, twice a day between 2 o'clock and 4 o'clock; in the evenings *Hippo Dancing*, *Relations Are Best Apart*, *Gathering Storm*, and a thriller I can't remember that we performed in the Gaiety Theatre, during which young kids would come up on the stage and stand by me dressed as a policeman standing guard at the suspect's door.

'Are you famous, mister?'

'Shut up.'

Three times a week, we did a kids show at ten in the morning – fifteen to twenty yawning kids, held down by hungover Redcoats, watching me searching for a nuclear war head under the Aegean Sea. Behind a scrim cloth, dressed in swimming trunks with an oxygen tank strapped to my back, I give a fair impression of Marcel Marceau's grandmother, miming walking on the bottom of the sea, only to be attacked by a giant octopus cranked down from the flies. On one occasion it separated from its wires and fell on top of me. That morning I wrestled it to death.

71

A couple of other things during that season stick in my mind. Prior to one of the thriller Gaiety performances, I went to the loo, and standing in the cubicle next to me was Russ Hamilton. Now, unless you're as old as me, or a pop chart freak, it's unlikely you would remember him. But he was a Redcoat who made a record that reached number one in the charts. 'We Will Make Love' it was called. It was not surprising that it hit the heights because he was shunted from Butlin's Clacton to all the other Butlin's holiday camps, and there were plenty of them at the time, to sing his song. People bought the record in their thousands, to remind them of their happy week at Butlin's. I bet poor old Russ hardly made a penny out of it.

One day Billy Butlin paid a visit to our camp. He landed in his helicopter on the lawn, by the swimming pool, outside the Playhouse Theatre. For some reason or other the lights fused in the theatre. But did we stop? No, no, no! Candles were found. We all held one, like choir boys, and continued the performance.

The next day I watched him walking around the camp. People were shaking his hand, asking for autographs, taking photos, grannies kissing him – he was like a god. And I suppose he was in way; he was giving these people who had gone through a terrible war the holiday of a lifetime. The ambient style of Butlin's camps derived from the Festival of Britain: plastic, sub G-Plan furniture and everything in bright colours. Everything the dark forties wasn't.

Sunday was our day off. In the sunny annex could be found the adagio guitar playing dancers; Andy Cole, a singer from the local Variety Theatre; his wife and kids; Mike Vardy, our juvenile lead; Gina Potter, the landlady's daughter, who still writes to me, and Ronnie Pember, who was acting in the local repertory theatre. Clacton in the fifties was a vibrant seaside resort, offering wall to wall entertainment.

I got on especially well with Ron Pember. We were both dreamers. We each wanted to be a writer. Ron said you should always carry a notebook with you to jot down ideas. We kept in touch for a while, mostly by letter, talking about the plays we were writing – usually about tragedy and death. After all, John Osborne's first success was *Look Back in Anger*. (What a clunky title!) Others I remember in those old Royal Court days were *The Sport of My Mad Mother* and *Infanticide In The House of Fred Ginger*. Hardly subtle. Ron and I were of that generation, so naturally we wanted to dwell on the dark side of life. Strange, when you think about it – we were young, days were bright and long, we had so much to look forward to ... yet all we wrote about were angry young men, misunderstood by everybody, riddled with acne and stalked by the Grim Reaper.

Ron appeared at The National Theatre, but never really got his name above the title. Many years later (1987 to be precise), I was doing my first sit com. It was for London Weekend Television and was called *Running Wild*. There was a modest amount of outside filming, which was to be slotted into the studio stuff. The situation is that I'm moving out of the family house (running wild! geddit?) and going to look at a potential bachelor pad.

It was snowing, and there was a scene outside with my landlord. I didn't know until I got there that the landlord was Ron Pember. I'd like to say that it was a wonderful reunion but too many years had passed. We were older and I think he'd forgotten the Clacton days and our ambitions to be writers. Maybe the years had chipped away at him the way they did for all of us. His life hadn't been as rosy as mine. He'd been struggling, I suppose, and here was I starring in a big new TV sit com.

I found out later that he and his family had moved to Clacton. A few years ago I read in The Equity Magazine that he had died. I always turn to the obituary columns. That extra dark, funereal print covers a quarter of the inside back page.

I find names of people I knew in television or rep. theatres from years ago, the ones who had never hit the heights – stars' obituaries appear in *The Guardian* or *The Times* – but as long as they kept their Equity subscription up, they were assured of a mention.

Bernard Severn died. He was a friend of Pat Becket's – more about her later. The last time I saw him he was working in the furniture department of Bentall's. When Pat had a first night in rep. somewhere, Bunny once sent her a first night telegram with the message: 'A warm hand on your opening.'

Life was simple in those days, everybody being away from home at some soon-to-be-busy seaside resort – it was great. I was happy but I didn't know it. Nothing was required of me, apart from doing the job I wanted to do. I didn't think about death (apart from in my writing, of course – but that wasn't real). People didn't seem to be bad tempered. It was fun and the sun always shone. Except when it rained, but in those days you didn't mind getting wet.

Obituaries have become a bit of an obsession with me. One I read was about a cartoonist who died at the age of forty six. His wife was extremely ill and they had moved to be near her parents. They were both found dead in bed.

Ivan, the pilot, phoned. 'Had a shock, thought you were dead.'

And there on the obituary page of *The Times* was a large photo of me, Carol White and Sean and Stevie, her kids – the picture they always use from *Cathy Come Home*.

I'm not suprised he thought I'd gone. If I hadn't read it myself that's what I would have thought. It turned out to be an obituary for the Revd Bruce Kendrick, the founder of the housing charity Shelter. A tiny picture of him and a massive one of us. Typical.

Funnily enough, on the same page was the Birthdays column, and there was Michael Crawford. How ironic, I thought, if I were to pop my clogs on Michael Crawford's birthday.

A while ago, Anthony Newley died. He's had a staggering career: many wives, including Joan Collins; starred in films; written two musicals with Leslie Bricusse – *Stop the World, I Want to Get Off* and *The Roar of The Greasepaint, The Smell of The Crowd*; had hit records – 'What Kind Of Fool Am I?', for example; appeared in Las Vegas ... big, big, big. Then something went wrong, and he ended up living with relatives in England. Then he got into *EastEnders*. He didn't stay long and not long after he left he was dead. When I was in the show, I asked about him but nobody seemed very forthcoming. I don't suppose most of them knew who he was.

Ronnie Pember would have been perfect for *EastEnders*, being a true cockney, but he didn't get a sniff.

Life ain't fair, is it? Here I am in it, twiddling my thumbs, shmoozing Pauline Fowler, eventually going to marry her and move into the House Of Doom and Gloom. 'There's never been much laughter in that house,' says Dot Cotton.

The happy Sundays in the courtyard of the annex at Clacton, learning the guitar, surrounded by smashing people, all went by too quickly.

In the winter of 1957, I stayed off and on in digs in St John's

Wood, spending my days going up and down Charing Cross Road, dropping into all the different agents trying to get a job. Even that was fun because everyone seemed to be doing it. Sometimes we'd all meet in The Arts Theatre coffee bar and eventually end up in The Shaftesbury pub. We were all in the same boat, all waiting for the big break we were sure was just round the corner.

The digs in St John's Wood was another mixed bag, in more ways than one. Now that my old flame Ann had married her beau I was a free agent. Maybe there is a sniff around a young man who is free because on regular occasions a young French girl used to slip into my bed. She was never invited – I didn't know her name – but whichever way you look at it, it certainly was a result.

Brighton drew me back sometimes, probably because I was short of money. There the mysterious Helen would take me on board.

Rysie, my godmother, and my mum were very supportive. I was a professional actor now and all actors 'rest'. In reality, most actors just cry in their beer and wait for the phone to ring. The only 'rest' is that glorious time before you start a job. Somebody said, it might have been me, that the best part of working is being offered a job. After that it's all downhill. Not always true, but usually.

In the fifties, however, everything was new; cynicism had not been invented.

Summer season, 1958, The Alexandra Theatre, Ilfracombe
Fresh from my St John's Wood French connection and Brighton's mysterious Helen, what did Ilfracombe have to offer?

THURSDAY, JUNE 26th – For one week only

Norris Stayton and Edmund S. Phelps present the UNICORN PLAYERS in the famous comedy LOVE IN A MIST by Kenneth Horne.

Characters as they appear:

Mrs Evans – Duck farmer's wife .... JUNE GARLAND
Nigel – Bridegroom .... LEON WELLS

Pat – Bride .... CAROL BOYER
Mr Evans –Duckfarmer .... WALLY THOMAS
Howard – Late comer .... JOHN BLANEY
Rose – The girl with him .... JOY M. AINSLIE

The comedy produced by WALLY THOMAS

The entire action of the play takes place one week end, in the parlour at Mr and Mrs Evan's remote bungalow on Exmoor.

Act 1. Late evening in September.
 INTERVAL
ACT 2. The following evening.
 INTERVAL
ACT 3.
 Scene 1   The next morning
 Scene 2   That evening

General Manager: W.A. Thomas

Stage Director: Richard Davies
Stage Manager; Joy M. Ainsley
Assistant Stage Managers: Caroline Leigh and Raymond Brooks
Set Designed and Painted by Jill Davies

NEXT WEEK – A Sensational Play
BY A HAND UNKNOWN
By C. Neilson Gatty and Z. Bramley Moore

We thank the following for their courtesy for loaning us equipment and furniture: Ilfracombe Co-operative Society (High Street), 'S & M' Electrical Co. Ornaments by Roland Squire. Extra Furnishings by Healey's, Fore St Nylon stockings by Kayser Bondor.

I feel I ought to apologise for putting all this down, but the reason for doing so was to show you what it was like in those days. All seaside resorts during the summer months had variety theatres *and* repertory theatres, the latter showing a different play every week. Can you imagine that now? And you might have noticed that a new play started every Thursday. Why? Most people stayed on holiday for a week, so with a play starting on a Thursday, you could capture them twice. You have to get bums on seats.

You might notice some names on that programme whom I have mentioned before: Richard Davies, my Welsh singing partner and his wife, Jill, who also sang a bit but came from Birmingham. Two other names are of particular interest, especially for someone who carries a handkerchief: Carol Boyer and Joy M. Ainsley.

Carol was beautiful, tall, elegant, her parents were both professional ballroom dancers, she'd studied acting in Paris, and was sophisticated and dedicated in spades. She told me she had slept with Peter O'Toole when she was at The Bristol Old Vic. But most women said that they'd slept with him somewhere or other. I warmed to her greatly.

Joy was totally different: a stage manager – so a few more rungs up the ladder from me. She was engaged to a rather successful business man, though whether she was happy with this arrangement I never found out. She didn't seem to take her engagement very seriously. I think the phrase is, 'She played the field'. And I was included in her game.

On Sundays, our day off, we'd all lounge around in the sun reading the papers and drinking coffee. I salivate thinking about it now. Everyone bought the broadsheets and, from what I could tell, only played at reading them. Certainly I did.

The one dark cloud on the horizon was my National Service. For people who don't remember, National Service was a compulsory two year stint in the army, airforce or navy for all young men of eighteen or over. The Government had announced that they were stopping it but I was one of the last group who would to have to do it. It seemed very unfair to me – I had started my career, and two years square bashing or painting the grass green seemed to be a complete waste of time.

Nevertheless, I had my call up papers and I would have to have my medical in Exeter. It was rumoured that the best way to fail the medical was to tell them that you were a serial bed wetter. As I didn't know what tests they'd put you through to confirm this medical deficiency – I imagined something to do with pipes or sticking a telescope up your arse – I decided on another route. I stayed up three consecutive nights before my trip to Exeter. Carol stayed up with me, feeding me coffee interspersed with handkerchief activity. It was lovely and I was well and truly knackered. In this condition I turned up for the medical with the rest of the poor saps. It was horrible. I heard exchanges like:

'You've qualified for the R.A.F.'

'But I'm married with two kids. How much will I get a week?'

'Two pounds ten shillings.'

The young man's head dropped, just like his salary. Two pounds ten a week with a wife and two kids!

I *had* to fail. Forget bed wetting, I was going for the Full English – depression, broken by having no father, deprivation, cruelty, a general mess. I was going to convince them that I was such a quivering wreck, they would believe I was incapable even of tying my shoe laces. I managed to put sufficient doubt in their minds that I was referred to a specialist in Harley Street at a later date.

Triumphant, I returned to Ilfracombe. Carol treated me like a hero. Peter O'Toole, eat your heart out. I could play Hamlet, Jimmy Porter, Romeo – I could play anything. I'd given the performance of my life in Exeter that day.

The sun shone. Dickie, the leek, and I practised our song on our guitars, little knowing the 'great future' we had ahead of us as the British answer to the Everly Brothers; Carol and I caroused; plays tumbled out weekly. I collected props in the mornings and rehearsed in the afternoons: the summer was long and glorious.

There was the occasional cock up in the props department. Our task, Caroline Leigh's and mine, the ASM's, was to convince shop owners to lend us some of their goods for a week in exchange for free tickets for the first night of the play in which their stuff was appearing.

For one show we had persuaded a jeweller to lend us some silver cups and trophies. With two free tickets in his hand, he seemed happy.

The silverware was placed in a glass fronted cabinet, upstage by the main door. The stage had a severe rake, which means that it wasn't flat, to keep this cabinet steady we tied it back to the scenery.

My part, although not monstrous, was tricky. I had to come on laughing. Not being RADA trained, keeping silent off stage and then appearing on stage laughing as if I'd been doing so for ages was a problem. I think it was Caroline, who'd been to some obscure acting school that specialised in laughing, who gave me the answer.

'You keep pumping your stomach as if you're out of breath, and as you come through the door just laugh. It really works.'

In the dressing room it *really* worked, even when Joy popped in to see what was the matter and suddenly felt in the 'handkerchief' mood.

Feeling 'pumped up', I obliged – but not to her satisfaction.

'It's like cleaning your teeth with you, isn't it?'

It was not a relationship that was destined to last.

On the first night, pumping up, getting out of breath, I burst onto the stage, laughing crazily, and slammed the door, whereupon the cabinet fell over and disgorged its silverware which rolled down the stage virtually into the laps of the jeweller and his wife.

Another time, we borrowed a grand piano. On the Wednesday night change over we had to get it up onto the stage. The legs wouldn't come off. So some bright spark decided we should turn it over and slide it onto the stage. Even though there was a sheet under it to protect the veneer, there was a considerable amount of scratch damage – deep scratch damage. It must have been insured because there were no repercussions.

The plays rolled on. I was always hungry and a girl in the cooked chicken shop took pity on me. Remorselessly – to the extent that chicken legs were handed to me every day. No one can eat that amount of chicken so I used to shove them into a cupboard in my room. I didn't want to let the girl down. But I was busy and I forgot about the legs until the end of the season when I had to clear out my belongings. Among my dirty socks were the chicken legs, or what was left of them, and a teeming mass of greasy, fat maggots.

On the 27th of September, the season ended and it was back to London and Brighton and to doing rounds of the agents – and to Carol.

She lived in a flat in Holland Park with another lady. It was very smart. I stayed with her a few times, when her flat mate was out. But things had changed.

We weren't in sunny Ilfracombe away from home; it was dark, drizzly London. Unemployment for me, while she was back among her friends. Understandably, she wanted to see them and spend less time with me. It was the fag end of a relationship, but it had been a very happy one. And we were young. I met her again years later in Bristol, where she and husband were living, when I was touring in 1982. Anyway, back then she was off to Paris to study mime and, out of the blue, the great producers of the season in Ilfracombe, Norris Stayton and Edmund S. Phelps of Unicorn Players fame, wanted me to work at The Market Hall, Redhill, for six weeks over Christmas. Yippie!

December 12th 2006

Alarm early again – 4.45. Defecate, shower, wash hair: what's left of it. It's dark and bloody cold. Incontinent cats; cut grapefruits in half; toast and pot of tea. Take tray and yesterday's papers upstairs. Sadie is now sleeping in the spare room because she likes the radio on all night; I wake up to an alarm radio, so that wouldn't work. I also go to bed at nine o'clock, so it would be dodgy all round.

'Sadie!'

'What time is it?' she moans.

'Five twenty.'

'Ohhh!'

Leave the house at six o'clock. One Valentine scene. A drinking scene. Doom and gloom.

'Everyone's criticising this marriage. I just want a companion,' Brown Owl says to no one in particular.

I suppose I'm getting used to being invisible. Sue Butterworth, the line producer, follows me out of the studio.

'Thank you, Ray.'

'Okay.'

'Are you all right? Do you want to talk?'

I rumbled on about how difficult it all was.

'It doesn't show on screen. Anyway, it'll be easier when Bert comes in.'

That's dear Dave Hill. I decide to button my lip from here on in. This series is taking over my life. I don't seem capable of thinking about anything else. Tonight I saw a bit of *EE*. Me useless – looking like shit. A waste of space. Very depressing. Turn it off and go to bed, resolving never to watch it again.

Tuesday 13th

Early again. The usual routine and in car at six o'clock. Knackered.

June Brown says, 'You were good last night, you and Wendy. Very good.'

High praise indeed. Bless her! Need a bit of a boost every so often. Do a bit in the market. Bit in the launderette – Brown Owl brighter. Maybe June spoke to her as well. Mother Teresa! A pick up in The Vic. Then out into the Square. John Bardon says, 'Fuckin' hell, this should have been done before lunch. Booked a hotel in town for the night. Going to the theatre with me missus. Fucked, mate! This takes over your life.'

Where have I heard that before? Two late scenes with James. Back in the car at 7.30. Everything's aching.

Wednesday 14th

Early again. One scene at Tube station. Arrival of my daughter Megan, (Nicky), for the wedding. All messy chaos. Home by lunch. Beer. Bed. Ahhhh.

Thursday 15th

Early again. Still tired. Café – James. Fine. Vic. – James, Natalie and Wendy. Atmosphere intolerable. Phone Kate Harwood, exec. producer, for meeting at 12.30. I've had enough.

Kate wants me to stay.

'We've got story lines. When Bert comes in things change. (I've heard that somewhere before too. It's the 'party line'.) Wendy has been in – worried. I don't know how to deal with her. She wants to see the plans for the story lines. The relationship works on the screen.'

And on and on and on.

81

'There, there, there. Ah, it's all right now.'

Bollocks!

Who's schizophrenic? Me or Kate. It's a game – all the cajoling, playing on the actor's vulnerability, vanity – actor on his high horse, making a point, his sensibilities bruised: 'Listen to me, I'm important.'

'No, you're not. Get back in your box and do what you're told.'

Praise, praise, praise – that's the way it was couched; so I left half happy, half despondent. What a fool! If I'd used my getting out of National Service technique I might have pulled it off. But producers are vulnerable too. The first thing they learn is 'stickability': be nice to everybody but when the chips are down, dig the knife in deep. Yes, it's a bloody game.

Afternoon. A scene where we agree to marry. Brown Owl is supposed to say, 'Joe, will you marry me?' She cut it. Didn't want to appear submissive, I suppose. What a silly lady.

Saturday 17th

Last day before the Christmas break. Everyone arriving back at The Vic after the wedding ceremony. Phil Daniels' first day. Terrific, energetic, good stuff. Barbara says, 'Listened to LBC on the way in. Really horrible DJ. He was saying what a great actor you are.' Babs and June know the way to an old fart's heart.

The bride and groom entrance. Third take.

'You tarrahed on the first take, you laughed on the second. It won't cut.'

Here we go. Deep breath.

'What shall I do this time?' I say with a hint of sarcasm.

'Do what you like. You're always ad libbing.'

I had to walk away. There can't be an explosion now. It would be the shortest marriage in history! With hindsight I realised that that was my moment to have it all out. But I missed it. I was definitely on the ropes now.

The last shot of the episode is Phil Daniels, pissed, leaving the pub, and Kellie, his estranged daughter coming in.

'Dad!' Dum dum dum. *Finito*.

A voice, under a hat, mutters next to me, 'He isn't going to be the last shot. I've been upstairs. It's going to be me and Joe.' The whole scene was reshot after Christmas with a new director: totally rewritten, two fights added, then me and the hat. Dum dum dum. She got her way.

I think I'll find I'm off to the knacker's yard quicker than I expected, whatever producer Kate says.

The power lies under the hat.

11

Now Newcastle – 1959

This was printed in one of the Newcastle Playhouse programmes:

PROFILE

OUR AUDIENCE

Actors will tell you that every audience is different and no doubt they are right. I suppose, however, that the audience which can matter so much is the Monday Night Audience. And certainly ours is different from any other night of the week. Mostly it consists of ladies, but that does not exclude the fact that we have some gentlemen in the audience whose record attendance at Monday night shows goes back many years.

But back to the ladies. They like to make their little comments on the play as it proceeds, punctuated by the stealthy rustle of sweet wrappings as they grope in the dark for – food for thought no doubt!

I love the last sentence.

Four shows in, we had the gala opening of *The Rape Of The Belt* to mark the official take-over of The Playhouse Trust. A special programme was produced. Although I knew everybody, there wasn't a lot of time to ask about their backgrounds. The programme contained all the actors' biographies – in truncated form, of course.

John Irvine's was very interesting.

John Irvine
Commenced theatrical career with the O.U.D.S. Designed costumes for their productions of As You Like It *and* Macbeth. *Acted with the Oxford Rep. during long vacations. When the war started was at Sheffield Playhouse. Enlisted in the Intelligence Corps, became Lt. Col. in H.Q., served with M.I.5 and was awarded the Croix de Guerre by General de Gaulle. Returned to the stage in 1952 with tours and appearances in television and has since played in repertories at Preston, Tynemouth, Hastings, Sheffield and Derby.*

It tears me apart reading that now. It's humbling. The photo, accompanying the biography, shows a slim intelligent face, Brylcreemed hair, a half Windsor knot in his tie, a double breasted suit and a coloured hankie in his top pocket. This man did all that during the war and here he is down the hill in Jesmond Rep. I think I'll have a cigarette.

The last line of my biog says: *Have tried television and failed.*

Michael Cooper, the director's biog says: *During the war served in the Royal Signal Corps and the Paratroops.*

So, here's a squaddie with a parachute *directing* a member of the Intelligence Corps and MI5 with the Croix de Guerre medal.

The mind boggles, doesn't it?

Also in the programme was Brian Moorehead. He opened the batting for the other side and was a very funny man.

One review read: *It couldn't have a been a better send-off, for the antics of the two heroes of ancient Greece, the dragon-slaughtering Hercules (Brian Moorehead) and forgetful Theseus (Ray Brooks), provided superb entertainment.*

What heroes? 'The 'Dragon-Slaughtering' Brian loved wearing his short skirt, threatening frequently to leave his underpants off. Our beards were stuck on with copydex, and slipped and slithered the more we broke sweat. The diaphanous white gowns of the girls left little to the imagination. No wonder the audience flooded in, the ladies dragged by their men folk, no doubt.

The most revealing gown of all was worn by Cecily Smith, who played Hera. She and I got to know each other very well. The last line of her biog says: *Her ambition is to be in a position to spend part of every year in Italy.* But I didn't let ambitions like that get in my way. The man with no passport was out to conquer the girl with spaghetti in her hair.

I was a fully fledged actor, albeit with copydex under my fingernails; no more farting around looking for props, things were getting better.

The one thing I'd love to have done, but couldn't, would have been to go to St James' Park to watch the legendary Newcastle United.

The great centre forward, Jackie Milburn, stayed with his Newcastle team in Brighton the week prior to the FA Cup Final. It was at the beginning of the fifties and it was rumoured in the town that the fleet-footed Jackie would race against the fastest greyhound in the land behind closed doors. Jackie was quick. All we'd ever seen of him was on news reels or read about him in the papers, but we knew he was the quickest man in the world. Forget Jessie Owens this man would leave him at the starting blocks.

Then the whispers came back from those in the know that the fastest man in the world *had* beaten the greyhound. We kids were stunned. Heaven knows what the opposition thought, because there's no doubt they'd have heard about this in their hideaway. Alastair Campbell up there in the 'baby waiting room', must have spotted this trick before he unleashed it on the British public many years later: spin, fabricate, spin. How strange that, Tony Blair, as a young man, also supported Newcastle United.

The board at the Jesmond Playhouse was trying hard to make a success of the theatre. The programme notes pleaded that they needed three thousand people to come through the doors a week to make it a viable local facility.

The company worked hard, a different play every week, a new set to be painted. And there we were, waiting for these three thousand members of the audience to arrive – and not to rustle sweet papers, you understand, but to guarantee they would come back next week. A big problem. Unlike *EE* and other big soaps, who have a captive audience, we had to get people out of their front rooms and to walk down to the theatre and buy tickets. That's the difference. There's no difference between the personnel: all actors are much of a muchness, though not one of the *EE* cast had been in MI5, and the soap's audience don't even have to get out of their front room.

Our Jesmond audience could have Cecily Smith, in *The Rape Of*

The Belt, swanning about in a state of undress every performance. Their front rooms could never offer a near naked beauty, so they'd rush out of their houses and set their minds to higher things and soak up a bit of culture. Higher things and culture!? Bouncing, bra-less boobs to knock your eye out (you might need the other one to catch the finale). Well, it beats a Shakespeare sonnet for entertainment. It was a bit like the Windmill Theatre, except that Cecily had ants in her pants, and the Newcastle lads loved it.

But, in truth, what did we offer these potential 'culture vultures' as the season went on? *Reluctant Heroes, The Kidders, Detour After Dark*. The programme announced:

> *What is Entertainment?* Is it something to give you a good laugh or conversely a good cry? Does it make your flesh creep and your temples throb? Is it ladies in tights and gentlemen with red noses?
>
> Perhaps Bevan was right when he said the other day, 'I leave my brains in the cloakroom when I go to the theatre.'

I think Mr Bevan was right. I think the management was right. They don't want you to think after a hard day with the kids or in the office. Give 'em 'ladies in tights and gentlemen with red noses'. Or throw soaps at them five nights a week. But they'd have to wait fifty years for that – but it was coming.

All we could do then was to keep up the great tradition. So why not *Jack And The Beanstalk*? There's lots of tights and red noses in that. I played Simple Simon, with my guitar and my three chords.

> The repertory actors do well in what is for them an unusual venture. They enter the world of fairies and beanstalks, of catchy little songs and tricky dances with zest and vigour. The whole approach is bright and breezy, even to the extent of a rock and roll scene in which young actor Ray Brooks – putting Simple Simon behind him for a moment – provides a song as the dance team goes into an ultra modern routine. Most of the laughs are provided by Pat Becket, the most unfairy-like beanstalk fairy the kiddies are ever likely to see. She is undoubtedly the star.

Following close behind in the laughter parade are Bernard Severn and Alan Paton. Beth Harris is a vivacious Jack and Elspeth Bryce a delectable Alice.

The rest of the cast never misses a trick and the colourful settings and costumes add to the enjoyment of this worthy Christmas venture.

Indeed one small girl summed it up as she left the theatre. 'Wasn't it funny?' she said.

Yes, it was fun, it had all been fun but now, as the panto ended, my rep. days ended, I packed my bags and left the Jesmond Playhouse for London – The big boys' rep.

12

No More Little Boys' Rep.

I was musing the other morning – as you do at 5.00 a.m., before launching yourself onto the North Circular to see what Fate has in store for the Fowlers after a wedding – that I didn't remember having baths or showers in the fifties. In fact, the last bath I do remember was when my mother and I (she was pregnant with Paul and I was about fourteen) went to a neighbour's house to have a bath, not having a tub of our own.

My mother went in first, then me – same water, it was very expensive in those days, especially if you were allowing mangy neighbours a dip. Before that, it was always the public baths. 'More hot water, please.' But after that nothing.

'Paws and pussy,' actresses used to say, so I suppose it must have been the equivalent with the lads. Maybe we all stank, so nobody noticed. 'Cleanliness is next to Godliness' they used to say. But I assume all those dirty people in the old days still went to heaven. It's a mystery.

London. 1960 was an extraordinary year. I got my first television job. But there was much more. Mateus rosé, scotch and curry appear in my life. I eventually move in, with Michael Kilgarriff, to Gloucester Crescent, Camden Town: two beds in a basement room the size of three snooker tables, a two bar gasfire, Killy and his surgical stockings, and a kitchenette.

From Brighton, following a failed abortion, a separation, hearing a Tommy Bruce record of 'Ain't Misbehavin'' in a steamy café, a pregnancy, and a fire, Sadie moves into Gloucester Crescent with Killy and me on the 27th of December. The best part? Sadie's ever expanding tummy and sharing our staple diet of Plumrose Ham and Pork on toast with as a special treat, an egg on top. Bliss!

The details of that chaotic year would take more pages to tell than I have in this book, so bye-bye 1960.

We settled into the cramped room with Killy. We were very poor. We kept an empty half pint bottle of milk on the mantelpiece for our loose change. This fed the gas meter and paid for the occasional trip to the cinema.

Killy was at the London Palladium, playing the Giant in *Jack and the Beanstalk*. Chloe Gibson, the director of my first television job, *The Secret Kingdom*, was going to be very helpful. She offered me a part in *Tuppence in the Gods*, a show about old time music hall. Dandy Nichols was in that, best known for her role in *Till Death Us Do Part*. Now she was the business.

I don't know whether June Brown ever knew Dandy but they are out of the same mould: that breed of actress who've always worked hard at their craft. Timing, application, enthusiasm, phenomenal concentration, spiced up with a wicked sense of bitchy humour. Maggie Smith is in the same bag. They're adorable.

Then Sadie lost our baby. My reaction was one of sadness mixed with relief, if I'm to be honest. It's forty six years ago. We were so young, living in one room – what chance would we have had? I don't know. Maybe I was less attentive than I should have been, but Sadie seemed to be thinking the same. It's different for a woman, though, isn't it? If you carry a baby inside you for all those months and then it dies, it must really hurt. Men are not trained for parenthood; with women it's an instinct and the loss must hit them hard.

Sadie came home and she rested. I remember thinking that this could be the end of us. The shock must have put a strain on our relationship. But we talked and walked and went to the pictures, and gradually things got back to normal.

Sadie got stronger, I looked for work, Killy finished his 'Fee, Fi, Fo, Fum, I smell the blood of an Englishman' routine at The Palladium and then announced that he thought that we ought to move. Maybe because he had made a few bob from his job, he wanted to live in more salubrious surroundings. Anything would be more salubrious in those days than Gloucester Crescent, Camden Town.

9, Dunster Gardens, Kilburn became our new abode: two bedrooms (handy), a tiny living room and a kitchen. Four pounds, ten shilling a week, plus key money.

Our landlord, a Mr Cohen, lived with his family in Golders Green. I don't know what the law was then about buying a second property to rent, but I do know he said that if anybody came enquiring about him not to say that he lived elsewhere, just that he was away. Crafty stuff. That's the way that you got rich.

Chloe Gibson, the director, came up trumps again with *Girl on the Roof*, about a pop singer who has to talk down a fanatical fan on the roof, threatening to commit suicide if she doesn't meet her hero. The sort of thing that Nigel Harman must face daily, whether he's in *The Caretaker* or *Guys and Dolls* or in Tesco Express.

The rehearsals were interesting. Chloe stopped the scene on the roof by saying, 'I can't hear you, Ray. Speak up.'

'But I'm trying to be real.'

'There's no point in being real if no one can hear you.'

If Chloe were still with us, what would she have made of *EE*? I can be standing next to some of them and I have to lip read.

'There's no point in being real if they can't hear you.' That should be first on the list in the rule book for every director coming on the show. But no. 'Do it, clear it, get on with the next scene' – that's the mantra.

I've also got a theory about soaps. One way of anticipating an imminent exit is to watch the actor's eyes. You'll see flickers of panic, the growing fear about the fact that they're going to be out of work soon. That safe haven of the soap world is being snatched away from them. Do it. It works.

Girl on the Roof was going to be transmitted live from the BBC's Manchester Studios. 'Live' was normal in those days. The floor manager, during a live transmission, had what was called a 'cut key', which meant that if an actor 'dried' the floor manager would press the 'cut key' and that would 'cut' the sound being transmitted from the studio; then he would give a prompt. So us actors planned that, if we were even uncertain, it would be a clever ploy just to keep silent but to mouth away like some beached fish, then the floor manager would press the key and give us an indication of where we ought to be going, dialogue wise.

Except that this concept contained a minute flaw. Background noise. During a 'live' drama at Granada TV about a tube crash, before the first commercial break, three survivors, one injured, had to make their way through the underground tunnels. The injured one had dialogue but seemed to have passed out with the stress of it all, so the other two busked their way through it. The commercial break, thankfully, arrived whereupon it was discovered that the poor man was dead.

Chloe Gibson came up trumps again – long forgotten play set on a canal barge. Kevin Stoney was in it. The last time I saw him was in *I, Claudius*, a smashing actor. Pauline Boty was also in the cast, not really a full time actress but a very successful pop artist. She died of cancer, tragically young, in 1966.

Then I got an interview for the film *Play it Cool*, starring Billy Fury and directed by Michael Winner. In 1962 Michael was a slim, confident, rich young man. It was rumoured that his parents owned most of Marble Arch. His films included *Some Like it Cool* and *The Cool Mikado*. Cool. But laid back Michael certainly wasn't.

Billy Fury was busy on his endless tours of one night stands, so I was pulled in to read his part when they screen tested the final two girls for the rôle of Billy's leading lady. It was rumoured that Michael was keen on one of them; the powers that be selected the other. Michael wasn't happy.

I was playing one of Billy's group, *The Tornados*. Jeremy Bulloch and Michael Anderson Jr were the other two. I was the bass player but the instrument wasn't electric; it was almost as big as me. I had to lug this thing everywhere: onto planes, running for taxis – it was a nightmare. Peter Barkworth, Denise Price, Lionel Blair, guest stars Bobby Vee – who was a younger version of Buddy Holly – and Helen Shapiro were also in it. The word was that thirteen-year-old Helen 'Walking Back To Happiness' Shapiro, who was on it for three days, was earning £1,500 a day! I was on £40 a week. Barkworth used to brag he was on £60, but when the thirteen-year-old turned up the bragging stopped.

I like Michael Winner but in those days he was very arrogant. I watched him reduce the leading lady, the one he didn't want, to tears before a close-up. In the studio he used a megaphone to bark out orders. We used to put lighted candles under his director's chair and on the last day, everyone had megaphones and shouted at him. It worked. He knew. Maybe we should have done it earlier. Over the years he's matured and mellowed. He hasn't made a film for years but writes a newspaper column critisising restaurateurs in posh newspapers. Some years ago, I went to see him in his vast house in Holland Park. He was going to film Alan Ayckbourn's *A Small Family Business*. He looked at me across the desk and said, 'Well, we've both survived, Ray.' I didn't get the job. But we both survived.

A word or two about Billy Fury. He came from Liverpool and was under contract to Larry Parnes, who had a stable of pop singers. Vivid surnames like Johnny Gentle, Marty Wilde, Georgie Fame, Cuddly Dudley were Larry's trademark. Larry was parodied on a track in Peter Seller's album, 'Balham, Gateway To The South.'

Billy's contract with Parnes tied him up for a paltry £60 a week. There was also a free flat in Marble Arch, probably one owned by Michael Winner's parents, a car and a personal manager/driver, Hal Carter. Girls were in and out of Billy's dressing room all day. When I said something about this to Hal he replied, 'He loves it. I tell you something, if Billy lost a leg, he wouldn't limp.'

Billy did forty weeks a year of one night stands; he had twenty Top Ten hits and when he got ill and retired to a small place in Sussex, he sued Larry Parnes for his 'mechanical rights'. In other words, he had never received any royalties from his records. Parnes and he settled for £15,000. It must have been like suing McDonald's, you can't win: so get out while you can. Billy died in 1983.

But Billy did me a favour because when I took his place for the screen test, unknown to me, another picture was being made but the lead who had been cast had just dropped out. They needed another likely lad, quick. They were shown the screen test and I was chosen. Wow! Back to back films! Strangely enough, the lad who'd pulled out was Terry Palmer, whom I'd worked with in Newcastle Rep. two years previously.

I had to lose weight to play this young, leather jacketed, motorcycling rebel. Easy when you're young. Two stone, two weeks – gone.

So svelte me and Sadie go down to Bristol. The film was *Some People* directed by Clive Donner and starring Kenneth More. It was about how young tearaways could be brought back into the fold by taking part in the Duke of Edinburgh's Award Scheme. There was a love interest between Anneke Wills and me, a lot of racing around on motorbikes, smashing things up and playing guitars, and generally making a lot of noise – a touch of *Rebel Without a Cause*. But along comes Kenneth More on his white charger and we all live happily ever after.

In my gang were David Andrews and David Hemmings. My dad was played by Harry H. Corbett and my mum by Fanny Carby. Corbett was an amazing actor. I'd seen him often on television but never known it was him until the credits came up. He was that versatile.

I only had one big scene with him. It was to be in a pub, a father and son heart to heart.

The first time I met him was in the taxi going to the pub to shoot our scene.

'Do you want to run the words?' he asked.'

We did.

'Right now I'll play your part and you play mine.'

I knew that he'd worked at Stratford East with the great Joan Littlewood so here was a real actor. We did it. He was better than me; I was a very poor second. I don't think he did it to intimidate me. It was just his way of working.

During rehearsals and the various takes of the scene, he cried on the same word every time. He'd absorbed his Stanislavski and grafted on an astonishing technique.

I met him years later in The Pickwick Club. He was sitting at the bar drinking. I was a bit more successful then and he certainly was. He had been doing *Steptoe and Son* and it was a terrific hit. But I could tell that it was getting to him. He knew that he was better actor, but now he was being pigeon-holed, stuck. He did do a stage play in the West End between series, but the critics slated him – 'All those Harold Steptoe gestures we've seen before...' etc. He never got taken seriously again.

David Hemmings was a bit younger than me and, in his way as astonishing as Corbett.

When 'the gang' was being taught how to ride motorbikes on a disused airfield by a police instructor, David Andrews and I fell off all the time, but show Hemmings where the gears were and how to change them and he was away. Instinctive.

When he was thirteen he played the lead in Benjamin Britten's *Turn of The Screw*. As he was a minor, he shared the the performances with another thirteen-year-old, Michael Crawford. Connections, connections. It's like a jigsaw. Britten thought David could be an opera singer and offered to pay for him to study in Italy. His parents, however, decided against it. There were bigger fish to fry.

He could play the piano, do conjuring tricks, could score 100s at darts, swim like a fish, roller skate ... but he always sounded as if he'd got a permanent cold, a constant nasal blockage. Blowing didn't seem to help. I got a touch of solace from this. He may have been clever in every way but his proboscis was bunged up with concrete. Mine was as clear as a bell even if I was rubbish.

We kept in touch over the next few years. He, his wife Jenny, Sadie and I went for a weekend in Tenby. David drove, naturally (he had a sports car). He seemed so mature and accomplished; I liked him a lot but he still made me sick.

The last time I spoke to him was in the summer of 1965. I had an interview for a Walt Disney film starring Peter McEnery.

I was a bit early, it was a lovely day, so I went to a pub across the road from where the interviews were being held, in St James's. Who should come in but the conjuring piano player, Hemmings. I told him I was just going over the road for an interview and he said he'd just been.

'They're all there: John Hurt, the usual faces. It's a waste of time.' So I decided not to go and we had another drink.

'What've you been doing?' he asked. I told him that I'd done a film called *The Knack*. 'It's been entered for the Cannes Film Festival and Sadie and me are flying out tomorrow.' I told him it was a small film, shot over six weeks, mostly in Shepherd's Bush. 'How about you?'

'Oh, I've got this part of a fashion photographer. I think they offered it to Terence Stamp, but anyway, it's going to be directed by an Italian, Antonioni.'

Neither of us had heard of him. 'It's called *Blow Up*.'

There we are, on a sunny day in a pub in St James's, two young actors: one going to the Cannes Festival where his film is going to win The Palme d'Or, the other going to make *Blow Up*. Arguably, two of the seminal films of the sixties and we didn't have a clue. Halcyon days.

Back to 1962 when David and I first met. With *Some People* finished, the premier was going to be at The Plaza cinema in Piccadilly, attended by the Duke of Edinburgh with a reception after at Claridges Hotel. The evening before the opening, the cast were taken to The Plaza, where we sat in the Royal Circle of the vast empty cinema for a private viewing.

When the lights went down, the curtains parted and the opening titles began, it was overwhelming. The music, the colour, we all looked fantastic. It was the first, and nearly the last, time I was so blown away. This great screen was where we must have been born to be – shining up there forever. No wonder they're called film actors, film *stars*. We shone out, big and beautiful forever.

I read an article in *Film and Music* about Nicholas Cage, the American film star. It details his marriages and his impressive list of films, and has a full length picture of Mr Cage. He would have found it hard to get into *Emmerdale Farm*. If most of his films had gone straight to DVD, he would have been nothing. He *needs* to be on the BIG screen. The twitch of an eyebrow, the wry smile, the 21st take, the lighting and the editing. Yes, that'll pull you through, Mr Cage. On the following page two relevant articles caught my eye.

How to destroy the ICA with drills

The gist of this was that a company, the German group Einstruzende Neubauten's Concerto for Voice and Machinery, were to give a performance of their work at the ICA in London's Mall. The article blew the gaff. A cement mixer would be on the stage, together with a piano, electric drills and jackhammers. The plot was about smashing the piano, drilling a hole in the stage and tunnelling through to Buckingham Palace.

This couldn't be entertainment, I thought. What was going on? I don't mind experimental theatre – *The 39 Steps* imaginatively done with four actors, for example – but what kind of people spend good money to see a group of 'actors' drilling holes?

Buried Secrets of The British Cinema

At the Royal Mail Archive, under the enormous Mount Pleasant postal complex, there is a treasure trove of long forgotten films from the GPO film unit: *The Night Mail*, in which the rhythms of W.H. Auden's words and R.Q. McNaughton's editing propel letters and parcels along the contours of the country; *At The Coal Face*, in which Alberto Cavalcanti's camera follows a filthy squad of miners beneath the surface of the earth to the music of a Benjamin Britten score. John Grierson, the guru of documentary, said the U.K. was '... the only centre in Europe where the artist is pursuing not just entertainment but purpose.' Can you imagine those pin sharp images? The only drilling in those days was to rip the coal face a thousand feet underground.

Entertainment, purpose. There's not been much purpose in most of the things I've done, apart from earning a living – the people who produced them wanted to make a profit too. Do you think there's much 'purpose' in *EastEnders*? There's not much 'purpose' in the scripts and I'm not sure entertainment is top of the list either.

Recently a journalist from *The Observer* phoned me about *Cathy Come Home*.

'How did it change your life?' he asked.

He meant had it affected me politically? I was honest.

'All actors are whores. They work for money to keep a roof over their heads.'

He didn't like that. But there was a purpose about *Cathy*. Ken Loach and Tony Garnett were, and in Ken's case still are, out of the John Grierson mould. It was never about money but it was certainly about purpose. That's why it lives on.

Immortal. Well, the image is. Not the actors. Not poor Carol White.

When I was doing *HMS Defiant* in Spain, we had to travel out to the galleon ship, moored about two miles off the coast of Benidorm, to film. It was not the Benidorm of today, that sophisticated seaside hideaway (!). It was a one horse town or, to be more accurate, a one hotel town with no air-conditioning.

The small boat that took us out to the galleon ship bobbed around like a cork in an emptying bath. One day the sea was really rough and the galleon was jumping up and down on the horizon alarmingly, with the two stars of the film, Dirk Bogarde and Alec Guinness, on board our little vessel.

All I thought during that terrifying, bouncing journey was that the boat couldn't sink, not with Mr Bogarde and Mr Guinness on board. Both of them are now dead, not in a boating accident. Stars or not, the grim reaper scythed them down as he will all of us.

An old lady, who lives near us, fell down in the street the other day. My friend, David Collison, picked her up. She'd smashed her nose. Did she ever think this would happen to her? A dignified woman, falling, hurting herself, feeling helpless? Thirty years ago she must have thought she'd never get old like other people, she'd keep her marbles, keep her balance, just wrinkle up a bit but the old brainbox would still be ticking over, co-ordination as fluent as clockwork.

And here's me – an actor from the fifties, the sixties, the seventies, eighties, nineties, the 2000s – up to my neck in *EE*, plagued by cysts, forgetting my lines, hair falling out, trouser waistband getting tighter; I've never been so unhappy in my life. But I'm not dead.

13

Back To The Plot

Kenny More took the cast out for lunch after the premier of *Some People*. I don't know how it cropped up in the conversation, but it turned out that Angela Douglas had just moved into a flat in Baker Street. Question marks flicked over everybody's faces. How could this be? A young actress, poor like us, suddenly going smart.

I have a photograph in my room of the introductions at the premier. I'm shaking hands with the Duke. On my left is David Hemmings, on my right is Kenny More and next to him his wife, whom we heard was part of the Hartleys jam family. It turned out later that Kenny had left his wife and moved in with Angela. Angela's not in my picture.

They eventually got married and when Kenny became ill she nursed him. Kenny died and Angela's married again.

Within months the BBC called and offered me a series for thirteen weeks, that would take over the Saturday slot while *Dixon of Dock Green* had it's summer break. Bill Owen, Sid James and I would be taxi drivers sharing a flat. I found out later that Val James, Sid's wife, had suggested me for the part. They needed a young 'handsome' character to pull in the spotty, pubescent viewers. There seemed to be a lot of acne around in those days. It turned out she'd seen *Some People*. Thanks, Billy Fury, for doing all your one night stands which allowed me to take your place in the screen test and thanks, Mr Winner, for giving me the job.

The first series of *Taxi* was written by Ted Willis, an old compatriot of Bill Owen's from the Unity Theatre days. My mother loved Bill. He made a speech at the bus company's staff retirement presentation in which he slated the bosses, announcing to a packed hall, that he was disgusted that these men and women, who had worked for this company for twenty or thirty years, were getting nothing more than a gold watch. He was never asked back again. Showing his true colours, he wrote a musical called *The Match Girls* about women who worked in a match factory, how the sulphur affected their health and their struggle to get compensation. When he was working on *Last Of The Summer Wine*, in the first week of the National Lottery, the company had a whip round, a quid each, to do a few lines. The following week, Bill refused to join in. He'd heard that Lottery funding was going to places like The Coliseum in London.

'The poor buggers are trying to win a few bob and the money goes to those well-heeled twits!' he was reported to have exclaimed. The language was probably a bit fruitier, but that was Bill.

The last time I saw him was at the Television Centre. I was doing a sketch on *The Paul Daniels Show*. During a break, I went to the BBC bar for a drink. The place was empty so I went out onto the terrace.

'Hello, mate.'

It was Bill, dressed as Compo. He was doing studio inserts for *Last of The Summer Wine*. After a couple of drinks, it was time to go.

'I'm dead lucky,' he said. 'This is my pension.'

Where have I heard that before!

At the time of his death he was still doing it. He was over eighty. They erected a statue to him in the Yorkshire village they used for location shots. He was a well loved man.

The second series of *Taxi* was to be written by Jack Rosenthal and Harry Driver. Harry was a fascinating man. His previous life had been as a trainee manager for Woolworth's and in the evening he did a comedy act in the Working Men's clubs. Then a terrible illness paralysed him. He had only the use of his neck muscles and the little finger of his right hand. What he did have were his brain and his imagination. He decided to write. Flat on his back, a typewriter positioned on his chest and a knitting needle clamped in his mouth, he hit the keys with the head of the knitting needle and, amazingly, wrote scripts. There were no electric typewriters in those days; those keys had to be banged hard. Imagine how exhausting it must have been. Talk about dedication. Granada signed him on as a scriptwriter for *Coronation Street* and he teamed up with Jack Rosenthal.

For the *Taxi* read-throughs in London, he used to be driven down from Manchester, flat out in the back of the car, by his secretary, to sit in his wheelchair listening to us Londoners mashing up his script.

Then, after we finished the second series of *Taxi*, suprisingly, I got an offer of a couple of weeks on *Coronation Street*. I grabbed it, not that the money was as good as the BBC – only £60 an episode, but two a week meant £120, so I was happy. It was a bit of a journey to the Manchester studios but we didn't have to start rehearsals until twelve o'clock on the Monday, and they paid subsistence. We finished recording the two shows on Friday at 6 o'clock and that meant I could go straight back to London, have the weekend at home and start again Monday morning. Very civilised. I finished my two weeks, then they called me back at Christmas for a few more episodes.

Manchester – what a smashing place! Full of lively people who played hard and worked hard. *Coronation Street* was extraordinary. It had massive audience figures, and the people in it were almost as famous and sought after as The Beatles. It was big. For instance, Violet Carson, who played the spiteful Ena Sharples, when hearing that the railway line between Manchester and Lytham St Annes was going to be axed by Dr Beeching, wrote to him to complain. She threatened that if he didn't do something about it, she would go above his head and get him the sack. She might even resign from *The Street*. Now that *was* a threat.

Bear in mind, that Ena was a frumpy old bag, who always wore a hairnet, gossiped and played the church organ. But Violet Carson could sing like an angel, had played piano on Wilfred Pickles' weekly show, which had been compulsive listening in the dark days after the war, and she had a lot of clout. Beeching changed his mind. Ena had her railway line back.

Soaps are a drug, aren't they? They have been around for ages. I think the earliest one on television was called *The Grove Family*, when there were only two channels, done in black and white and definitely 'live', because recording on tape hadn't yet been invented. It was watched by fewer people than go to church on Sundays. In fact, when George Orwell's 1984, was done live starring Peter Cushing, it was repeated the following week, the cast had to go in and do it all over again.

Then there's *The Archers*, all the month's episodes recorded in one week in Birmingham, gloriously sent up in *The Bowman's*, Galton and Simpson's vehicle for Tony Hancock. The list goes on forever. I was in *Coronation Street* for a few months in 1964. There were two episodes a week. Once you started recording you couldn't stop; if you did you had to go right back to the beginning because the tape was too expensive to edit.

Corrie started in 1961, originally with just twelve episodes, but it caught fire. It's hard to imagine now but the cast was recruited from experienced actors who had spent most of their professional lives touring the U.K. in North country farces. Some were almost at the end of their careers while the younger members had just begun scratching around in rep.

Arthur Leslie played Jack Walker, manager of of The Rover's Return. I was told the other day that Tony Broughton, Arthur's son (I assume that Leslie was his stage name) had a visit in London from his dad in 1960. Arthur was going to disband his small touring company because it was becoming too expensive to run. The impression Tony had was that he was getting fed up with things, work was drying up and he was becoming too old. Tony, also an actor, was keeping body and soul together by working in The Cricketers pub while June his wife was selling programmes. It must have been a rather depressing meeting. Arthur said he had to get back up North because he had an interview at Granada Television the next day. This is the sort of story that keeps actors going: out of the blue something wonderful happens. Just as it did for Arthur Leslie.

When I did *Coronation Street* in '64, I stayed with the most famous theatrical landlady in the country – Alma Mckay.

She'd come bustling out of her parlour, in her usual uniform, the well worn pinny, to greet a new guest.

'I'm just giving Mother her tea.' Mother could be seen chewing toothlessly on a piece of jam sponge in the background.

'Now, I'm putting you in number six. One of my best rooms. Ralph always said...'

'Ralph?'

'Ralph Richardson, love. One of my favourites. He always said, "I love that room, Alma, I want to take that room back to London with me it's so comfy".'

There were two lounges, one for her variety people and the other for her theatricals. She had rules and they were not to be broken.

She also had her ear to the ground about gossip. Anything that happened in Manchester she knew about it. When I went back on one occasion she said, 'I hear the last time you were up here you stayed at The Grand. Not posh enough for you here, are we?'

Bite you and then make you a cup of tea – that was Alma for you. It had all been noted.

I saw Freddie Jones in The Grand one night. I didn't know him at the time. He was in the lounge, surrounded by young actors listening to every word he said. He is one of the great actors; unrecognised by the multitude, but by his peers he is adored. They were like kids at the feet of Father Christmas. And he was loving it.

Freddie is currently in Emmerdale Farm and I'm sure millions know him now.

At Alma's I got to know one of the 'variety' crowd, Mike King of the King Brothers singing trio. We kept in touch over the next few years. His wife was actress Carol White.

Brown suitcase. 16th November, 1956
I have found two replies from theatrical agents to my letters asking for work in the 'theatrical profession'.

The first is from Wardona Productions Ltd, Evelyn House, 62, Oxford St.

Dear Sir,

We are in receipt of yours of the 15th inst. and, whilst we appreciate your desire and are pleased to hear that you were impressed by the medium of Television, we have no idea from your letter as to what your abilities are or what you think your value to our organisation would be. If you could give us some enlightenment on this perhaps we can discuss the matter further.
    Yours faithfully
    Oliver Ward (managing director)

Read that letter carefully. It's rubbish, 'enlightenment' – 'appreciate your desire'! It's painful. A seventeen-year-old boy, hoping to get a break receives this stuff. It's enough to send an innocent soul into a lunatic asylum.

The other also dated November the 16th 1956, and is from Daphne Scorer Ltd, 43, St Martin's Lane.

Dear Mr Brooks [There's a nice start. Not 'Dear Sir']

Thank you for your letter and your photo which I am keeping for the files. If you would care toxlet [she'd obviously made a typing error] us know which day you are likely to be up in town, we will fit you in for an appointment.

That letter was encouraging. Within a month Daphne Vasper had got me my first job at Nottingham Playhouse.

After my last few weeks on *Coronation Street* in November 1964, I got my big film break – *The Knack*. It had been a play by Ann Jellicoe, staged at the Royal Court Theatre with Rita Tushingham, who'd had a big success with her first film, *A Taste of Honey*.

Rita was a Liverpudlian, she had big eyes and was pretty but not the classic Julie Christie type, all legs and flowing locks. Rita had an elfin look. But she was bankable, and Woodfall Films, backed by United Artists, the big American group, loved her.

I think my first audition was with Michael Crawford, who had already been cast. My character was called Tolen, a serial womaniser. Michael played Colin, a school teacher, who couldn't get started.

The scene we read was Tolen explaining to Colin how he should go about getting a woman.

I must have felt cocky because, instead of calling him Colin I called him 'Colen' to rhyme with Tolen. It was a big risk and certainly something I wouldn't do now. In fact if I heard anybody doing something similar, I'd think he was a prat. Well this prat got the part.

It was six weeks' work and filming in deep winter. I was supposed to ride a Harley Davidson motorbike. American coppers ride them; they're huge. Good for Tolen, I suppose, this sexy, big machine. They took me down to a showroom to see one. In one scene I had to push it with a punctured tyre. I couldn't push it with both of them inflated! So they got a 250 cc bike and tarted it up. I must have told them I was *au fait* with bikes. After all, I'd ridden one when I was doing *Some People*. But I don't suppose I told them that I kept falling off. Little things like that tend to slip your mind when auditioning.

Richard Lester, the director, was a crazy American. He'd been in advertising, had directed The Goons in the *Running, Jumping and Standing Still* film. Then The Beatles, who loved The Goons, in *A Hard Day's Night* and was going on after *The Knack* to direct them again in *Help*. He was a big cheese – squeaky, quick and clever.

I think he saw Michael Crawford as an extension of himself: all elbows and slightly cracked.

Our main location was a house in Shepherds Bush. It was used for exteriors and interiors. One morning, a Friday, there was a long four page scene – just Michael and me. It followed a scene in which Michael fell into the Ruislip Lido. That Friday we were shooting him drying himself and getting dressed. I'm doing most of the chat, while Michael puts on bits of clothes, always having to step over my outstretched legs to get to the next item of his attire, always managing to avoid stepping into the bowl of water in which he'd washed his feet.

Every time he came to putting his socks on, then having to step over my legs, he stepped into the the bowl of water. This was wrong!

'Sorry, Dick,' he simpers.

'Don't worry, Michael, we'll go again.'

Again and again, we did it – or rather *I* had to do it, going through the dialogue again and again.

'Sorry, Dick.'

On and on. 'Take twenty three,' the clapper boy shouted.

Then there is a shout that Oscar Lewinstein, the producer, has arrived outside. They wiped the chalk off the clapper board and changed it to 'take three'. We finished the scene at take six.

Lunchtime. Donal and I go to the local pub. Michael, first time ever, makes an appearance. Two Guinnesses later the group is walking back to the house. I pull Michael aside.

'You did that on purpose, Michael. You do that again, I'll fucking kill you.' The sly little face crumples up and looks as if it's about to cry.

That night Dick Lester is at London Airport in the departure lounge, flying to Paris when an announcement comes over the tannoy.

'Mr Richard Lester, telephone.'

'Dick, it's Michael. Ray said he's going to kill me.'

Monday morning, Dick called me over.

'Michael says you're going to kill him.'

'Well, he was mucking about.'

'Michael is a real actor. He lives his part. You just go home and get on with your life. He takes his job seriously, a real actor.'

What could I say? What's a real actor? Someone, who seemed to me, to be extremely selfish. Me, me, me – that's not acting. Teamwork is the name of the game. That's what I thought but, in all fairness, he's done astonishingly well. Dick employed him again: *How I Won The War*, which starred Michael and John Lennon; he went to Hollywood, he starred in *Phantom Of The Opera*. What did I do when *The Knack* was over? A small part in *Dixon of Dock Green*. So, what do I know?

But I think Michael always felt he needed to impress me, because every time he did a show in the West End, he would ask me come to come and see him. And I did, sometimes. I felt he was a sad person, a person who needed approval. As a result he got hurt but didn't realise that he hurt other people. He was a perfectionist and, deep down, despite my carping, I like him.

The Knack was intended as a small budget picture, to go out on the filmhouse circuit as second feature to a re-run of *Tom Jones*. But, out of the blue, there was a gap for a picture at The Cannes Film Festival. Being out of work, as was Rita Tushingham, Sadie and I were invited to the South of France.

It was amazing. A Rolls Royce arrived in Dunster Gardens in Kilburn and whisked us to Heathrow. When we landed in Nice, we were met by an American from United Artists, wearing teak sunglasses. There were flowers for Sadie and Rita. Then we were driven to the Carlton Hotel in Cannes, reputed to be the second best hotel in Europe. What was the first, I can't imagine!

We had a suite with a balcony, overlooking the Carlton's private beach, with a complimentary bottle of Johnny Walker Black Label Whisky and more flowers for Sadie. We'd come from a £4 a week flat in Kilburn and now we were in Cannes, in the second best hotel in Europe. We thought we were in heaven. Maybe we were.

'Just sign for everything you want,' Teak goggles had said, so we did. Champagne and strawberries everywhere. Wonderful! Fill your boots.

Jacqueline Bisset and Charlotte Rampling had been among a dozen or so wet-suited non-speaking beauties decorating the Ruislip Lido in *The Knack*. Jane Birkin was one of the multitude of virginally dressed young girls winding up the stairs to my room in Shepherds Bush. Jane Birkin can also be seen in *Blow Up* rolling around virtually nude in front of David Hemming's camera. They were all keen as mustard to get on. Rampling turned up in Cannes. She hadn't been invited, of course but when did that stop a Coleman's girl?

'Daddy and Mummy have got some friends who live here. So I thought I'd pop over.'

And pop she did – in a bikini. If any photographer made an appearance, she popped for England. I think if it had been La Bisset, the popping might have been more interesting.

The Knack was shown at The Festival Theatre and when it ended, the audience, as one, turned towards Rita and me and applauded us crazily. We couldn't believe this little film, shot in six weeks in Shepherds Bush, could inspire such enthusiasm.

The press swarmed around for the next couple of days. In the foyer of the hotel, there were lots of stands displaying films not in the competition, their producers all trying to get a distribution deal. Michael Klinger, unknown to me at the time, but displaying on his stand some semi-pornographic film designed for sleazy 'art houses' in the back streets of Europe, approached me. 'Ray,' he said grabbing my arm, 'when you get back to London, we've got the perfect part for you. A maniac.'

The last night in the hotel, Sadie and I ate in the Carlton restaurant ('Sign for everything you want.'). Sadie had had a few drinks by the time the sweet trolley came round – a beautiful sight on many levels. The waiter stopped at our table and gestured towards his chocolatey, creamy, strawberry, sugary, tumbling vehicle. Sadie squinted at the trolley.

'Have you got any bread and butter pudding?' she smirked.

'Mais oui!'

From the lowest level of the trolley, the waiter produced what turned out to be the best bread and butter pudding in the world.

I seem to have done more television and films during the sixties than at any other time. It was an amazing decade. We were young and carefree. We knew everyone and understood everything. It was a time of great optimism. But, in reality, we understood nothing and little did we know that it would all turn to dust.

14

Back to the 'Funny Farm' (and other stuff)

Tuesday 10th of January 2006
Back to work early (up at 4.30 a.m.). Seven scenes in the Fowlers with my new mate, Bert, played by Dave Hill. This is the character who's going to liven up the show for me, give me something different to do, give me a chance to do scenes with someone other than Brown Owl and Betty.

Dave Hill's got balls. So have June, John Bardon, Barbara and a few others, but, as A.A. Gill said, 'Soaps turn good actors into bad actors.' I would prefer to put it another way: 'Soaps turn good actors into zombies.' It's the scripts, the plot lines, the churning out of clichés week after week, year after year, never being stretched and ending up flat as a pancake.

Wednesday 11th
Nicky Henson's first day. Another actor I seem to have known off and on for ages. Nicky's had cancer and is in remission but he's a workaholic. He phoned me when he was offered the job because he was concerned about the schedule, the hours, etc. I told him it was very hard at times. The producer had told him it would not be too arduous and he had decided that if his calls were early he would stay in a hotel near to the studios.

In the first scene, Nicky's character had to drive his Land Rover round the square and park it outside the Vic. The vehicle had no power steering and he had to do it again and again. He was lively to start with but soon began to wilt.

'I know what you mean now,' he said, Nicky is a theatre man. Television, particularly this kind, if you're not 100% fit, is arduous.

111

He was married to Una Stubbs, who had been in all the early Cliff Richard films, like *Summer Holiday* together with Richard O'Sullivan. There are connections everywhere.

Richard moved into our area a few years ago. Things hadn't been very good for him and he was suffering from loss of confidence. We drank together, talked, and agreed about the 'confidence' thing. It applied to both of us.

Sadie and I were invited down to Tessa's house – Tessa is the mother of Richard's son, twenty-one-year-old James – for Richard's sixtieth birthday party. Tessa was married to someone else by that time but was still very fond of Richard, hence she had organised the 'do'.

Mike King was there, though I didn't recognise him at first. When he was married to Carol White, Sadie and I used to go round to their cobweb festooned, basement flat in Hammersmith for the popular dish of the time: spaghetti bolognese, followed by Black Forest gateau and cream. Ugh! But we were young. They had two sons, Sean and Stevie.

Carol had worked for Ken Loach in *Up The Junction*. Now he wanted her for *Cathy Come Home* and he wanted Sean and Stevie to play her children. She was nervous about their being involved because of the upsetting scenes – bailiffs hammering down doors, the fires on the caravan site – and the general bleakness and despondency of it all. So would I, who knew Sean and Stevie, play her husband Reg and be a part time *au pair*? As I've said before, we're all whores to a man – the smell of a bit of the folding stuff and we're in.

In 1968 I was out of work but, inspired by the American singer-songwriter James Taylor, I thought, with my three chords, I'd try and write some songs.

I strummed away and warbled into a Phillips reel to reel. All self indulgent subjects, like lost love. One song was about two-year-old Emma, Sadie and me: 'Children's toys trip her as she walks, she's bored with the way all her friends talk, she stands in the kitchen, her tummy sticking out...' Others were about The West Pier in Brighton and a few rockers. The only person I knew in the music business was Mike King. He still had a few contacts, even though The Kings Brothers act had stopped.

He played them to Ray Cameron, who had produced the big hit

'Grandad' with Clive Dunn. (Incidentally, he used to write sketches with the glorious Barry Cryer, for the amazing and sadly missed Kenny Everett.)

Cameron liked them and contacted Doug Flett and Guy Fletcher, who, through their production company, Egg Productions, got a deal for an album with Polydor. These were very exciting times.

When they'd recorded the backing tracks, I went in to 'lay down' the vocals. (I'd got all the jargon!) When I heard the tracks, with violins, honking saxophones, pianos and electric guitars, I couldn't distinguish one song from another! Finally, it was all done and dusted. Then the round of interviews began.

I thought, in my naive way, that I was up and running. I got £2,000 advance, a massive sum of money. A single 'Lend Me Some Of Your Time', was released in America and got into the top 100. But soon everything went quiet and nobody played the record. I'd hardly started before I was finished. It was 1969. Then, amazingly, my recording career forgotten, in 2007 I got a letter from Manchester.

Mr Robert Cochrane had found the album in a junk shop, loved it and written about it on a web-site for a New York Retro Magazine. He also sent me a CD copy of the album. Next, a guy at RPM Records wanted to know if I still had the masters of the recordings. They wanted me to phone them. I did.

Polydor Records don't exist anymore and their catalogue had been bought by Universal, he told me. As it was an independent production, he was going to try and get in touch with Guy Fletcher, an important person at the Performing Rights Society. I await the outcome. I'll let you know if anything happens before the end of this book.

1969 saw a complete switch round for me. Apart from the odd bit of television work it was mostly back to the theatre. But I did a film, *The Last Grenade*, and that changed everything for us. I'd appeared in *Doctor Who and The Daleks* with Peter Cushing and Bernard Cribbins a couple of years before. Gordon Fleming had directed it. His wife, Fiona, had been a dancer on *Cool For Cats*, a sexy, pop based television series of the sixties. Gordon phoned offering me his new film – £300 a week, for twelve weeks, playing a part I wouldn't have got under normal circumstances: an army officer, a bit top drawer, not my normal type of rôle.

Hong Kong, Spain, Shepperton Studios – not bad. Hong Kong entailed a sixteen hour flight. The props and electricians on the film had demanded First Class seats, so off we went to Stansted Airport, where we boarded a plane that had been so long on the ground they would have had time to take out the Economy Class seats and stick in the First Class ones that are, or were, only five inches longer.

We took off, with difficulty. It was an old plane. A stewardess asked me what I would like to drink.

'A vodka and tonic, please.'

'Do you always have tonic with your vodka?'

'Yes. Why?'

'Because we've only got one bottle on board.' That summed up the flight.

I went up to watch in the pilot's cabin.

'There's a bit of a headwind. We might have to land in South Vietnam for fuel.' The Vietnam war was raging at the time. We didn't have to refuel, thank God!

We landed in Hong Kong in the middle of the night and I went straight to the Peninsular Hotel and crashed out on the bed.

Wake up – the sun is shining – wander into the bathroom in a daze. It's mirrors wall to wall. The image that looks back at me is of a hundred-year-old man – even older than I look now. Scary.

Hong Kong was magical to me, a man who had never in his life been 'abroad': masses of small people, rickshaws, building work everywhere with bamboo scaffolding, and no cars. In fact, I heard that there were only two Rolls Royces in Hong Kong, both owned by the Rum Rum Shaw brothers, the filmakers, who, it was said, regularly went to Switzerland for 'monkey gland' injections to tickle up their libidos.

To walk up Nathan Road, the main street, was weird. I was the tallest man in the world! But to turn off into one of the side streets was a different matter.

There were fresh food shops selling chickens, snakes, frogs and meat that didn't seem to have come from any animal I'd ever seen, all hanging on hooks. I had the feeling that, if they wanted to, these tiny people could gang up on me, drag me into the shop and within minutes I'd be hanging up on one of those blood-stained hooks.

114

I had four days' filming over two weeks. Wonderful! One of my scenes involved meeting Stanley Baker, coming off an aeroplane. Stanley was a star and not very communicative; for him people like me didn't exist. Before a take he'd stand there with his eyes closed. The minute they said, 'Turn over,' he barked, 'Drops.' A makeup man would rush over, administer the eye drops and retire. Stanley's eyes would remain closed. On 'Action' they would fly open, shining clear blue and he wouldn't blink during the whole take. It was fascinating.

Later in the studio, at Shepperton, we had to walk side by side, the camera on a track profiling us as we moved. During rehearsals I glanced across at Stanley on our walk. I remember thinking, he isn't taller than me; in fact, he seems a bit smaller. That was a surprise. But when it came to the take, he *was* taller. By this time, he had let me talk to him, so I said what I'd noticed during rehearsal and how on the take ... etc.

He said, 'You c**t. I always want to be taller than twit actors like you.' Then he demonstrated – no lifts or anything, he simply walked on tip toe. Clever.

We went out occasionally – not Stanley, of course, he had other fish to fry – but the lads, Gordon and I. Nightclubs were extraordinary. There were licensing laws in those days, even in the mad world of Hong Kong. But when the shutters came down, that didn't stop them: we had our beer and wine in teapots. The local police didn't do anything; there were always a few of them 'having a cup of tea', just to be sociable.

On my birthday they took me to cabaret club called Les Girls. 'Les Wanne-Be-Girls' is what it should have been called. They were a bunch of men, mostly Australians, working there, miming to Shirley Bassey records, to get the money to have the operation. After the show, Gordon, because it was my birthday, invited a group of them to join us for drinks. Sitting next to me was Zizi, who was German. I was drinking vodka and tonic. Every time my glass was nearly empty, this fluttering hand topped it up. She/he was the most feminine person I'd ever met.

Watching the dance floor, Zizi said, 'See Frank over there?' Frank was this big red-headed 'girl' dancing with a very drunk American. 'That gentleman's going to get a big shock in the morning.'

When I flew off to Hong Kong, Emma, who was three at the time, was watching me on TV doing *Jackanory*. Sadie told me that Emma said, 'Where's Daddy?' Then she went behind the television trying to find me.

Emma and Sadie came out to Spain when we were filming there. On the flight out, one of the engines packed up and they had to return to Heathrow. It was the start of Sadie's terror of flying. The return journey was horrendous. The day before the flight home, we were filming on some remote country road. The scene involved Richard Attenborough and his wife, Honor Blackman, being driven in a Rolls Royce, with me following behind with a couple of my 'men' in a support wagon. The Rolls hits a landmine and turns over and over in the valley. I jump out, Honor, I think, is killed, fire is raging, I pick up the unconscious Attenborough, and carry him away to safety. Easier said than done. Dickie was heavy, even in those days, and, acting like a good 'un, he played unconscious to a tee – he was a dead weight. The valley, by the way, is strewn with little rocks. Carrying this big lump of what we now know as film history, I couldn't see where my feet are going. Inevitably, I tread on one of these rocks and go over on my ankle, with the still 'unconscious' Dickie on top of me.

The next day, waiting to go to the airport, Sadie is shaking like a leaf, downing a bottle of sherry, while I, ankle throbbing out of control, am carrying Emma, who is as good as gold.

We get to the airport. Flight delayed. Sadie is a gibbering wreck. I call the airport nurse. She gives Sadie pills which don't seem to have any effect. Suddenly, at my elbow appears Arthur Askey and his wife, Arthur was a very famous comedian. He introduces himself.

'We're not travelling First Class. They always let families on first. Can we come with you as grandad and grandma?'

What with my wobbling wife, my elephant man ankle, the tiny Liverpool comedian and his wife disguised as grandparents, and happy little Emma, oblivious to all the chaos, we must have looked like Fred Karno's army.

Sadie spent the flight with her head in her hands, moaning softly. When the stewardess asked if we wanted anything, Emma said, 'Mulk.' Sadie said 'Brandy.'

116

When we arrived at Heathrow, both the inebriated Sadie and Mrs Askey stood at the carousel waiting for our suitcases.

Arthur said to me, 'We could wait here forever. Neither of them know what's going on.'

They didn't.

When we eventually made our way out of the airport no taxi would take us. Maybe it was the fact of Sadie's weaving around, or maybe they'd rather have had a fare to Birmingham. After at least three have turned us down, Sadie, getting more angry – as a brandy and sherry indulged person is inclined to – seizes an umbrella and hits the next taxi driver over the head with it. The balloon goes up and a policeman is called.

The taxi driver complains about 'this mad woman' who attacked him. I explain about the difficulties we're having getting a taxi to take us home, my wife being exhausted and how our daughter, who was learning fast and consequently bawling her head off, needed to get to bed and, generally speaking, how I was fast losing faith in human nature. The policeman, obviously moved by my case – or it might have been the threatening 'mad woman' with the umbrella – he told the taxi driver to get off the airport and forced the next one in the rank to take us.

When we got home, Sadie fell down a small flight of stairs onto the landing. I left her there all night. It had been a long day.

With the money from *The Last Grenade*, we managed to buy a house. Neither of us, nor our families, had owned one, so it was a big step. The deposit was £350 and the house cost £7,350. We took out an endowment policy with repayments of £60 a month – the equivalent of £15 a week, whereas our rent had been £4.10. It was a daunting task.

Now, we're in the house, having spent a further £600 installing central heating and having it painted and decorated; consequently I'm broke. Great start! If something doesn't happen soon we'll have to sell it. Fortunately, I started to get a few voice overs – just £30 here and there, but it all helped.

The VO agent of all VO agents was Wendy Noel, who worked for the theatrical agent Bryan Drew. She was the Bill Shankley of agents, fiercely loyal to her clients, would defend you with her life.

John Baddely told me that, as a young actor with a young family, he had gone to see if she would represent him. She had agreed and then said, 'How much do you need a week, John?' No agent in the history of the world has ever asked an actor that question. John was flummoxed – two young kids, Penny, his wife, and a mortgage…

'About seventy pounds a week,' he said.

'Fine,' she said.

And it was. She was hot.

Wendy took me on, not on the same deal as John, but I had high hopes. Sadie was pregnant again, so my responsibilities were growing.

Then I was offered a musical: *Lie Down, I Think I Love You*. It was about a bunch of students who take over the BBC. With a mad plot by a young writer, Ceredig Davies, it was in the *Hair* mould – the idealist young, shouting about their 'rights'. Four weeks of rehearsals and no rehearsal money because the union, Equity, had this ridiculous structure, that if you earned £100 a week you gave the rehearsal period free. £99 a week, and you'd be on £20 a week for rehearsals. So, I got no money for four weeks.

Lie Down had an interesting cast: Vanessa Miles, Sarah Miles' sister, an intense vodka swilling pal; Colin Bell; Lynn Dalby, constantly talking about the affair she was having with a senior National Theatre actor; leggy Antonia Ellis; Ray Davis, dancer, smashing teeth; Ioan Meredith, a serious actor, presumably thinking that *Lie Down* had a political message; the juvenile lead, Malcolm Reynolds, flowing hair and near perfect bone structure, who I can't really remember but then I'm sure he doesn't remember me; Jo Maxwell Muller, who did VOs and had lived with Tom Baker; and Tim Curry. Tim went on to have cult success in *The Rocky Horror Show*. I remember once coming across Tim munching an apple.

'I always like a big Cox,' he announced. There was no doubt which way he swung. He was the only one in the cast who could really sing – and it was a musical. The rest of the company was made up of ex-Royal Ballet dancers.

The director was John Gorrie. I had worked for him before on a television play called *The Raging Moon*.

I had my doubts about the whole project. I trusted John Gorrie but the rest of the production team were very worrying. There was

Daniel Rees (for Fairlodge Productions), the brother of Angharad Rees. He was a university pal of Ceredig Davies who had written the music. And there was Stratton-Smith of Stratton-Smith Productions Ltd, the owner of Chrysalis Records. A mixed bunch.

I had taken the precaution of having it written into the contract that if John Gorrie left the production I could leave as well.

During the rehearsal period, there was a few days' filming in order to provide back projections during the show.

The day after the first preview at The Strand Theatre, Sadie, getting rounder by the minute, and I were having lunch in Luigi's prior to my having to go back to the theatre for 'notes'.

We'd hardly started eating when one of the ASMs came running in. 'There's a meeting in your dressing room. Will you come back now?'

Everyone was there: dancers, actors, Gorrie, the writer, the producers.

Gorrie announced, 'I'm leaving the production by mutual consent.' There were gasps. 'And Geoffrey Cauley (the choreographer) will be taking over the direction.'

My turn.

'If John's leaving, I'm leaving too. It's in my contract.'

Gorrie looked me in the eyes. 'You can't, Ray, you're in the filming.'

'I'm still going.'

At this Stratton-Smith piped up. (I sensed relief. The show really was bad.)

'Well, we'll have to close the show.'

That set the cat among the pigeons. The highly sensitive, constantly smoking dancers, started crying. They hated being out of work. There were tear-dripping faces all round. Even actors used to blubbing only at night climbed out of their coffins and turned on the waterworks. I withdrew my notice. John Gorrie left. The next five previews were cancelled and Geoffrey Cauley stepped into the breach.

Most of the script was thrown out, only the bare bones were left.

'When you come on, Tim, what would you like to say?'

What would you like to say?!!! Mr Cauley was doing Mike Leigh before the bearded genius had even drawn breath. Of course, this style of directing opened the flood gates. Mr Cauley didn't know about actors. He was only familiar with high kicking, muscled, tear-

119

stained dancers. Actors love saying lines, boosting their parts, polishing their egos. It was chaos. It was so confusing that I kept the second act in my back pocket when we finally showed our wares to the paying public. It reminds me of a show, many years later, that played in the theatre next door to ours, The Aldwych. It was called *The Fields of Ambrosia*. Sadie and I saw it. The reviews were so bad they were reduced to giving the punters their money back if they stayed for the second half.

The reviews for *Lie Down* were just as bad, except for that written by the esteemed critic Michael Billington, who seemed to see some merit in the mess being splattered all over the The Strand Theatre stage.

Lie Down, I Think I Love You closed after thirteen performances.

John Gorrie must have felt guilty for what he'd got me into because he offered me a television play within a month. It was a crazy play with Leonard Rossiter and the lovely Cheryl Kennedy, whom we will meet later. They did a lot of crazy, one off plays in those days. Now we seem to do crazy soaps that go on forever. So crazy, in fact, that we seem to forget, with their 'chewing gum for the eyes' repetition, how really stupid they are. That's progress for you.

Leonard Rossiter had made his name with *The Rise and Fall of Reginald Perrin* and *Rising Damp*. Starring with him in *Rising Damp* was Frances de la Tour. Towards the end of the decade, I worked with her in Greenwich in a play called *Singles*. She told me that she and Rossiter hadn't got on. Never spoke. Could hardly bear to be in the same rehearsal room. Many years later he was appearing in *Loot* at The Ambassadors and she steeled herself to go. During the performance there seemed to be a hiatus on the stage. The company manager walked on looking very serious. 'Ladies and gentlemen,' he announced, 'I'm afraid we will have to cancel tonight's performance. Mr Rossiter has been taken ill.'

La Tour looked at me. 'He should have said he'd died. That would have been more accurate. Do you think it was because I was there? I'm not sure.'

The seventies carried on – lots of telly plays, the VO work increasing. I thought my West End theatre career was over but it didn't worry me. I was earning, paying the mortgage, and we had a miracle a new baby Mr William. A miracle because Sadie had to have a D and A, and when she returned to the hospital two weeks later for a check, they found that she was six weeks pregnant. A D and A is tantamount to an abortion, so the Chelsea Women's Hospital was astonished. 'Impossible!' But it seemed not. Then Sadie came into contact, by mistake, with someone who had German measles. Naturally, we were very nervous and worried about the outcome. But when he arrived he was, to our intense relief, healthy and fit. Now we had two perfect children.

But then, the lure of the greasepaint raised its perfumed head again. It was *Snap* by Charles Laurence, whose previous success had been *My Fat Friend*. The director was William Gaskill, a Royal Court man, and a bit left wing. He had never done a 'boulevard comedy' before. But it starred the great Maggie Smith, a marquee name if ever there was one – and she still is. Her biography in the programme read: 'Favourite music: applause and Bach.' She loved applause, entrance rounds and exit rounds. Bill Gaskill even said to her during rehearsals, 'Cut out some of the laughs, Maggie' – because she could make anything funny.

Three or four things really stick out about *Snap*. This was my first real play in the West End, with a big star and all the trappings. We were at The Vaudeville Theatre in The Strand, which is a good address, and with an audience who couldn't wait to see Maggie.

As my background had been television, the odd film and repertory theatre, I expected that acting with top-notch people would be of the highest quality. On television, for example, when you're talking to someone, that person would look at you. But not in the jolly old West End. The first couple of words that they say to you, but the rest of the speech is directed at the audience, straight out, with the final line, or word, flicked back in your direction. I found this very disconcerting.

On the morning of the opening night, I came into the theatre with my first night presents for the cast. Maggie's dressing room door was open. It shouldn't have been. I looked round and saw she was asleep on the couch. Her eyes opened. 'What are you doing here?' I asked.

'Nerves, darling. Can't sleep at home. How can you get a bit of shut-eye sleeping next to man who smells like an Italian waiter.' She was married at the time.

I had one funny line in the whole play. Bill Gaskill told me to stand centre stage and say it straight out to the audience.

'They've got to see both your eyes. It can't fail.'

It did, night after night.

'Why doesn't it work, Maggie?'

'I don't know, darling. You say it beautifully.'

'You're not doing anything, are you?'

I couldn't see her as she was behind me when I delivered it.

'No, darling, of course not!'

Still nothing.

I forced myself, one night to cast an eye towards Miss Smith. She was outlining the pattern of the wallpaper on the back wall of the set with her index finger! If Bob Hope had delivered that line he wouldn't have got a laugh, not with Maggie's finger doing a dance routine.

I still believe, in my naivety, that she couldn't help it – that it was instinctive and she didn't know that she was doing it. It was my only potential laugh in the whole play and she had hundreds; of course she wouldn't do it deliberately. Most people disagree. But I think that with her genius she's unique, '. . . because without her where would little boys be?', to quote Maurice Chevalier.

Opening nights in the West End are fraught affairs. The critics are out front, it's a full house and the actors begin to have underpants-threatening panic about whether they should stand *here* when they're saying this line or if they should be over *there* and, for fuck's sake, what *is* the line anyway?' Moreover, on this particular opening night, Barrie Ingham, the leading man, who had been flying to New York every weekend during rehearsals, trying to buy the rights of a Hans Christian Andersen musical he wanted to present in the West End starring Tommy Steele, was jet lagged.

Second act. The whole cast is on stage, the set is blinding white, the lights are blazing, full house, it's as hot as hell and we're on the last lap. It's the exposition of the whole plot – who gave who 'clap'. Here we all are, chipping in the odd line, piecing this jigsaw together. It's Barrie Ingham's important line. Nothing. Panic! Should we stop and start all over again? Maggie to the rescue. She skips Barrie's line. We limp on for a couple of pages. His line was the key to the whole play's chaos, but he's sitting there like a beached halibut. At a suitable moment the great Maggie stops, stares at the half asleep Barrie, and delivers his line herself with such aplomb that the audience roars its approval. Did they know or didn't they? It didn't matter. All I knew was that Maggie could do anything. That's genius.

Barrie seemed to be half asleep most of the time. He fell deeply asleep during a scene with me once. Maybe I was being particularly boring. Inspired by the magic finger and its owner's bewildering concentration, I tried to emulate this goddess and, I have to admit, failed miserably.

Snap had a change of cast after six months. Geoffrey Palmer came in for Barrie, who probably went straight home to bed. I left and Maggie went off to play Lady Mac on Mars or somewhere.

The twinkle in Sadie's eye has materialised into Tom. And that makes three. 'You've got your own gang now,' someone said. And they were right. Two seemed easy, but three – well, that's a whole new ball game. I do admire Sadie. She works so hard keeping these little bundles in the air while I'm out hunting, or dealing in the world of 'self-aggrandisment' as someone else said.

Friday 20th Jan. 2006

In Early. Now, by this time, I am totally convinced that some of the cast have been snaffled up by alien pods that first saw the light of day in *The Invasion of the Body Snatchers*. Wendy Richard *is* Pauline Fowler. It's not her fault, she's been taken over.

John Bardon says to me, 'Yesterday when you and Dave on the kitchen set are having a chat, Wendy looked in and went straight to June and said, "Bloody actors!" It's all a mystery.' What's going on? There has been a rumour that Wendy's leaving. But there are rumours wall to wall here; say the wrong thing and the jungle drums are bashed. But if she did go ... well, well, well.

The Brighton girls are coming up to see the world of *EE*. Jane, Kate, Mary and Sadie arrive in high spirits. Kate is the fan of fans. She's wetting herself but, being a nurse, has the secret of keeping the dampness at bay. We go into the studio. Emma Barton and Barbara

123

are doing a 'dramatic' scene. We stand as still as we can and, in Kate's case, as long as her bladder can. Barbara spots us.

'Do you a want a picture taken?'

She takes us over to The Vic set, puts her sweet little arms around the girls and beams as if it was Lord Snowdon behind Kate's phone camera.

'One for Lloyds!'

Barbara's a real pro. I click again, or whatever these cameras do.

'Bye, darlings.' And she's off leaving a trail of perfume and jollity.

I drag the girls to lunch in the bar. Then back to the Square. They're doing a shot outside Walford Station. There's a fair bunch of extras swanning around, so I try to get the girls in shot.

'Should have asked me yesterday, Ray, I might have been able to square it. Put them in now, we'll have a strike on our hands.'

They had to settle for jolly Joe Swash, bouncing around, having his picture taken with them. He's a very generous, kind kid. 'Ain't you Mr Benn?' was the first thing he said to me. That's not why I like him, I swear, but it does make me feel accepted, even if I do have to hang on to that little man in the bowler hat!

Finally, we head off home in the car. I couldn't help thinking about Brown Owl's possibly leaving. After twenty-one years! What a wrench. But why? I don't suppose she'll ever tell me. I'll just have to listen to the gossip.

I also had a call from Maxine at Voice Shop. I was wanted to do a VO for a charity.

There's no point in asking upstairs if I can do it. I've asked before. They don't like letting their precious *EastEnders* out of their sight. More to the point they don't like you cashing in while you're under contract – even though in this particular case there was no cash. For contract read handcuffs.

VOs in the late sixties, seventies and eighties had been terrific. Lead by our General, Wendy Noel, her little soldiers seemed to conquer all. On one occasion I got a job on a Saturday morning. Not usual. Sadie wasn't too happy, she'd have to do the weekend shopping with the kids in tow but the old man had to keep the loot coming in. 'Grab it while it's out,' somebody had said. It was good advice.

124

It was a studio that was foreign to me. The producer was a fat, self-satisfied American of about forty. He handed me the script. It was forty-five pages of, close type in lower case. The subject was how to cure sheep of gum rot. Forty five pages! *And* I was going to have to record it to picture. My recording booth was claustrophobic – and it was 'No smoking'. I have to match the words to the pictures, hitting the exact shots. The little TV monitor on my desk glinted threateningly. I'm not particularly good at sight reading, especially under poor circumstances. I wasn't feeling happy. The American was becoming very huffy at every mistake I made. And I was making plenty.

'Let's go back on that.'

I don't like fat Americans, apart from Sidney Greenstreet. Don't *they* ever make mistakes?

I'd taken an hour longer than the time allotted. I was shattered. The engineer was in a bad mood, the fat American looked as if he was going to explode. It was going to cost him more money for the extra studio time.

I handed him back the sweaty and mangled script.

'Thank you,' I said through gritted teeth.

He looked at me as if he wanted to strangle me. 'You did quite well,' he said. 'We usually use Marvin [*sic*] Jarvis but he wasn't available.'

I bounced down Broadwick Street to Piccadilly tube station. Marvin Jarvis! The smooth, elegant, charming Martin Jarvis! I'll dine out on that, I thought.

I bumped into Martin once in the early eighties.

'What're you doing, love?' (Actors always ask you 'What're you doing, love?') I told him I was going up to Norwich, to do an adaptation for Anglia Television of the P.D. James novel *Death Of An Expert Witness* and that I was playing Dr Kerrison, the pathologist, who turns out to be the murderer. It was a six parter and I was looking forward to it.

'Why're you doing that? You could earn more money down here. And everybody's turned it down.'

'Marvin' had probably turned it down. Muggins was lumbered now. The last actor in London to be offered the part. Bloody fool!

A few years later, I saw in the TV Times that Martin was in the latest P.D. James Dalgliesh adaptation, playing a monk. As luck would have it, I bumped into him.

'You told me everyone turned down these Norwich junkets. You could earn more money down here. Now you're doing it.'

'Yes.' He smiled knowingly. 'But I got a world deal.'

You can't win.

Fulham must have been playing away on the 'sheep gum rot' Saturday, because Fulham has been my passion since the sixties. When I was working in the theatre, if the Saturday matinee started at five o'clock, I always managed to see the first half of the match, then drive like a demon to get to the theatre on time. I must have been nuts, but I loved it.

Will and Tom, encouraged by me, started going at about five years old, are still going joined by grandson Joe ... generations of ulcers and tears. And it goes on and on.

In 1975 I appeared in *Absent Friends* by Alan Ayckbourn. *Absent Friends* would be his tenth production in the West End. Eric Thompson was to direct. Eric had already directed five of Alan's plays in the West End. Produced by Michael Codron, a producer of staggering credentials, this was a 'stellar situation'.

I'm looking at the programme now. Richard Briers, (his sister, Jane, had been in *Snap*), a master of comedy; Peter Bowles, light on his feet, a Black Belt in Judo, a worrier but *very* good; Cheryl Kennedy – I'd worked with her before – pretty as a picture, married to Tom Courtenay, hardly any lines, a bit of a grunt here and there, but a real stunner; Pat Heywood, a great cake maker, mother to all of us, but, more than that, a superb actress. We loved her. Then there was Phyllida Law, edible, married to Eric, mother of Emma and Sophie. Philly is a jewel, highly intelligent, the funniest woman in the world.

The first rehearsal was at the Globe Theatre, Shaftesbury Avenue. On the first day, everyone dresses up a bit. Richard was as smart as paint, hanky in his top pocket, etc.

Eric Thompson showed us a model of the set. Tiny doors, tiny arches, sofas, windows and tables. If producers got hold of tiny actors, there'd be no need for expensive sets, or expensive West End theatres. They could just tour plays on the Circle Line. They already pay tiny wages, so it makes sense.

126

'Right,' Eric says. 'We won't have a read through. Let's get on with blocking it.'

There is normally a read through of the script before you start blocking the moves.

'Okay, Dickie,' Eric continued, 'we'll see you about Thursday.'

Richard's character didn't come on until page forty. His face dropped; all dressed up and nowhere to go – not even a read through, another coffee and biscuit and a little chat. 'All right, then.' He sloped off.

That was typical of Richard, I discovered. He *wants* to work, he *loves* working, loves the theatre, loves people. As Philly said to me during the run, 'Dickie's astonishing. If there's only a dozen people in on a Wednesday matinee, he works as hard as he does on a Saturday night.'

The first date on the tour before the West End was Brighton. Home. I'm going to stay with my mum and Ernie. Cheryl drives me to Brighton. She's staying at Millicent Martin's flat, just off Sussex Gardens on the sea front.

Brighton, full of ghosts and memories. Millicent Martin was married to a fifties singer, crooners they were called in those days. His name was Ronnie Carroll. Ronnie was on the radio, and made the odd telly appearance but never seemed to crack it. As a kid, in those dark fifties, I saw him at The Grand Theatre in North Road in Brighton, which now is a multi-storey car park, in a variety show called *Disc Doubles*. The Doubles were little known singers who looked and sounded like American record stars who had hit records. Hard to believe, isn't it? You never saw the great American singers in the flesh, only photos, so get somebody on a stage, under lights, yards away from the audience, singing the famous songs and audiences clamoured. Ronnie Carroll was Nat King Cole – blacked up.

I was almost a season ticket holder at The Grand, every week, up in the gods, leaning over, lapping up everything that was thrown at me. I saw *Soldiers in Skirts*. Can you imagine it? They might have been in the war – it was only a few years since it had finished – but this lot could hardly have been at the front line.

That show is a blur but *Gypsy Rose Lee* I think I went to every night of the week!

She was a stripper, who danced. The Windmill Theatre in London had strippers but the law said that they couldn't move. Wobbling wasn't allowed. But Rose did. The only difference was that she was a fan dancer. Not the sort of fans that you see in museums, those little fluttering things; Rose's were almost as big as she was. She came on the stage carrying two of these elephantine fans. She didn't take her clothes off – they were off already, we assumed. She proceeded to dance. As one of the 'fans' wafted off her stunning body, in our imagination she was the most ravishing female creature God had ever created. We craned over the balcony, tongues hanging out, handkerchiefs at the ready, as the other 'fan' instantly took the place of the previous one, and the wobble, the glimpse, was magically snatched away from us – until the next time, the next night. Then on Saturday night she was gone elsewhere to tease other handkerchief toting, testerone bubbling teenagers. She had a bit of the Olivier magic. And substance. Two key requirements. Top dollar.

Absent Friends was going to play at The Theatre Royal in New Road. Opposite was The Pavilion Theatre which was attached to The Dome; it had been the stables where the Prince of Wales had kept his horses. A lot of the competitions in the Brighton and Hove Musical Festival were held in The Pavilion Theatre. I had competed there. Standing outside the stage door, waiting for my turn, I remember seeing a gent riding past on his bike and thinking that I wished I was him and not me.

When we moved from Kilburn – Sadie expecting, me out of work – the first week we were there, I saw a coffin being carried out of the house next door. I thought then, I wish that was me. It wasn't a death wish, it was that I was so frightened; it was the early days of responsibility, so I was scared about the future. Can you understand that? Maybe you think I'm mad. But, in my twenties, with baby Emma, the rent to pay, no money, no prospects, it was scary. I'm sure we all feel desperate at times.

But now, working, a play coming into the West End, a week in Brighton, the ghosts come steaming in.

My mum used to take me regularly to The Dome, opposite The Theatre Royal; it's vast concert hall with a stage. We saw the concert pianist Jose Iturbi, who did all the the piano playing for Cornell Wilde, as Chopin, in *A Song to Remember*, a film which my mum and I saw 37 times, taking sandwiches and a blanket to cover our knees to keep us warm. We saw Tito Gobbi, and Eileen Joyce, the Australian concert pianist – all I remember of her was that every time she went off stage she came back in a different dress.

I appeared there for the Brighton and Hove Operatic Society, playing Michael in *Peter Pan*. No wires, just jumping about a lot.

Next to The Theatre Royal used to be another theatre, The Dolphin. The amateurs used that regularly. It was there I appeared in the *Happiest Days of Your Life*. You may remember the film, black and white, with Alastair Sim, Margaret Rutherford and Joyce Grenfell. It's about schools during the war – a boys' school and girls' school having to share, and the confusion that caused. In the play there was only a token schoolboy and a schoolgirl. I was that schoolboy – in fact, there were two of us sharing the part. That was the occasion when I worked my bulls-eye magic.

Spending time in Brighton and being paid for it, allowed me to wander around during the day.

I remember taking Emma and Lisa Imi, when they were about thirteen, to Brighton to see a Gary Numan concert. I couldn't let them go on their own, so I drove them down from London and waited for them in a dodgy Indian restaurant in Preston Street.

I was the only one in the place. They stuck me in the window, a spider to catch a fly. I had a half of lager, chicken curry, tons of rice and the usual accompaniments. Halfway through this enforced two hour meal, the door opened and a delivery guy came in carrying a large plastic bag bursting with chicken legs oozing blood. I felt sick. I looked at the legs in the bag and the leg on my plate covered in slosh. I saw his van outside in the street. I'm sure it said Burke and Hare Suppliers on the side. I pushed the plate away and ordered another lager, figuring it would be my last drink before I was rushed off to The Royal Sussex County Hospital.

Just down at the bottom of Preston Street is a casino. My late friend, Mike Dolling, ex-dried food salesman, ex-advertising salesman for a small London newspaper, ex-organiser of pub 'entertainments', strippers, etc., employed Michael Barrymore in the early days ('He did his act standing on his head. Nuts!'), ex-gun toting copper and C.I.D., introduced me to gambling, late night and early morning drinking and hanging around with what Mike used to call 'the low life'. Phil Mitchell of *EastEnders* is a dead ringer for Mr Dolling. Rolypoly specimens, always ready to mix it – probably the first ones in – arguments galore but very, very loyal.

Steve McFadden, plays the character of Phil. I don't know what he gets up to when fishing off the Cornish coast, but Mike was Phil in real life. He certainly didn't suffer fools gladly.

I first met Mike at Griffin Park, Brentford's ground, when I saw him having a row with a bloke who was berating Keith, his wife Janet's younger brother, for scratching off a reserved sign on a seat. He went ballistic.

I should have realised then that Mr Michael was a 'noise box' and trouble followed him wherever he went. But he turned out to be a Fulham supporter, and from then on we went to games together, home and away – at the start with that little 'scratcher' Keith, until he grew up and started sniffing around girls, then we were joined by son Will and finally son Tom. Great days and hugely memorable. If there was a crowd around a bar at a football match, Mike could always get to the front. I seriously thought at the time of writing a 'How to Fiddle Your Way Into Anywhere Guide' based on Mike. He was a master.

His moods ranged from bragging for Britain to deep despair. Mike and I started to go to Brighton. We'd got our flat in 1981, and it was a good bolt hole from which to wander around having a few beers and gambling. I didn't have a clue about casinos; I'd never been in one in my life. Mike soon changed that.

In the beginning, it was all very simple and innocent. Lose a tenner in Sergeant York's, straight over to The Queen's Head, a couple of beers and work out a new system for the roulette table. And that's how it went on – lose a bit, win a bit less – but it was just a giggle.

How or when it changed I can't remember, not suddenly just gradually. Yes, gradually, it started getting serious. Mike used to note down every number that hit on every spin of the wheel. He had hundreds of these roulette cards. He became convinced there was a pattern. I said it was random, he said it wasn't.

Eventually, to prove his point, he decided to go to Brighton for a week on his own, and spend three days in the flat, not drinking, not going out, just studying his hundreds of roulette cards. After this, he would hit the tables with a system, spend two days playing the wheel and clean up. He took four hundred pounds, I gave him two, with the promise that I'd have a third of whatever he won. 'Well, I put in all the work, didn't I?'

He spent one day in the casino – no, one afternoon – and blew the lot. After that, as with some wounded animal, things got worse. The whole focus of his trips became the casino. They loved us in there, we had free drinks and meals. He was losing badly. They wanted to keep us coming. And we did. I suppose, in my stupid way, I hoped to wean him off. I thought that eventually he'd have to see sense.

Well, he did – but in a most unexpected fashion. Mike had got a bee in his bonnet about one of the controllers in Sergeant York's Casino. Mike thought that this guy didn't like him. Mike used to get pissed – the free drinks didn't help – and consequently got very loud. One night, Mike decided to tell this guy 'his fortune'. Mike roared down to the gaming floor to confront him. But he had had forgotten to put the belt on his trousers, so, with all his waving his arms about, his trousers fell down. The controller called the police. Mike had another large rum and coke. The police arrived.

'I'm a copper,' says Mike.

'Are you going to come quietly, sir?'

They took him outside; I followed, and so did one of the off-duty croupiers, who liked Mike.

'Let's go for a drink,' the croupier says. I could have killed him. Mike's up for the idea. I couldn't leave him alone in this state, so I followed along.

The pub we went to was in Preston Street, the street of dodgy curry houses. Mike suddenly got more tired than emotional. I ordered a taxi, for although we only had to go a couple of streets there was no way Mike could walk.

Preston Street is a steep road that leads down to the seafront. Trying to manoeuvre Mike to the taxi was difficult. His trousers kept falling down and his shoes came off. As I tried to get him into the taxi, he lost his balance and fell down the hill onto me. Mike was a fair old porker. It hurt. The stupid croupier had to pull him off. We got back to the flat and he snored his way through the night.

The upshot of all this was that Mike was banned from all the casinos in Brighton. There were three of them. The controller to whom Mike had told 'his life story', happened to know people, so he spread the word and Mike was out.

It was a blessing in one way. Mike stopped losing money, but the trips to Brighton seemed to have lost their focal point, so they were knocked on the head. I miss those early days – silly, sunny and cheerful – but all good things come to end.

The last time I saw Emma in Brighton, she was working for the Social Services of Fulham and Hammersmith. She had to visit a client in a hospital near Shoreham. I arranged to meet her in The Greyhound pub. It's now called The Fish Bowl and serves highballs, shots, cocktails and sushi on sticks!

It was a sunny day and when I came in, she was sitting with her back to the window – her lovely red hair (henna), little round glasses, dressed in a smart dark suit and with a tummy bump inside which two month Joe was swimming. It's an image I'll never forget. Our beautiful daughter. We had a drink and I walked her up to the station. She held my arm. I was so proud. And now she's gone.

Monday 6th February
Early. Re-shooting wedding celebrations in The Vic. Whole, dum, dum, dum moment changed and most of the rest of it. Two fights, naturally. Phil Daniels hits a taxi driver who goes all over the wedding spread. Yolande and Pat have a fight – Pat's been sleeping with Patrick, Yolande's husband. All good stuff.

The hat says to me, 'Welcome to Walford.' I reply.

'You know something. There's nowhere in the world I'd rather be.' Two shot then the dums and credits. Sometime during the day my daughter Megan (Nicky), in the show for a couple of weeks, tells me that Gerry Cowper is leaving.

Gerry Cowper is part of 'the celebrations', so I have a chance to talk to her. She'd signed a renewal of her contract last September for another year.

'Kate Harwood said there was no way of developing my character.'

What shit! Rosie Miller (Gerry) had arrived in The Square with three children, the biggest dog in history, and husband Keith (David

132

Spinx) who was the laziest bugger who ever lived. She worked her fingers to the bone supporting them, then Dawn (the stunning Kara) turns up, another miscreant, so there's another mouth to feed. What's the great producer in the sky talking about?

Someone said, when I mentioned Gerry's departure, 'Yes, I told her she needed to make her character more funny, lighten up a bit.'

Be more funny? Lighten up a bit? Come on. Gerry's a real actress, plays the part truthfully. Like Kate Harwood said about Jessie Wallace 'she plays through the line', except Gerry isn't all flashing teeth and trying to pull 'fellas'.

Gerry's just managed to get her mum and dad a house near to where she and her two children live. She's going through an acrimonious divorce and last month her father died. Now *EE* has given her the boot! Because, reading between the lines, she wasn't funny, not light enough!

A couple of months ago, during a rehearsal of a scene where Jim and Dot come round to the Fowlers for dinner, which I cook, I ask Dot if she wants a drink.

'No, I don't drink. Only for medicinal purposes.'

Brown Owl collapses on the couch with shock. It's a rehearsal.

'You must do that. That's very funny.' I say.

'No, I'm not allowed to.' Now what does that say? She's a widow worried about her son; another son has died of AIDs; her daughter, thousands of miles away in America, was raped by dirty Den. Wendy, plays the truth. She doesn't give us Lucille Ball. Gerry plays the truth, but Gerry's not a mainstay of the series. Wendy is.

Dot and Jim play pensioners. She has a part time job in the launderette, he is the occasional potman in the Vic. Pensioners. They'd be strapped for cash, wouldn't you think? Therefore life would be hard – oppressive, really.

But John and June play the parts accurately if quirkily, a touch camp. They've been around enough, and struggled at times in their careers. They've been doing *EE* for a long time and have adopted a 'house style'; they treasure their 'camp' moments and play to the hilt the drama. Adam Woodyatt – in it from the beginning, over twenty-one years, very young when he started – did everything that was written for him. His 'house style' evolved over the years: he goes along with the marriages, his meanness, and plays it for all it's worth. He never plays for sympathy. It makes his character interesting, rounded and a touch ridiculous. But he doesn't mind.

Gerry, forty-four when she started, wanted to make a fist of it, but 'funny', 'quirky', 'camp', were difficult adjectives to find in her part of the down-trodden Rosie.

If they'd given her story lines where she'd had the opportunity to change direction for a few episodes, she'd have grabbed it with both hands. But no. 'There's no way of developing your character.' What's the matter with these scriptwriters? Kate's job was to kick them into shape.

That's the dark side of being in a soap. I felt, after a few weeks that, the actors were constantly auditioning. Writers with upcoming scripts would watch the show. If they saw something 'a little bit different' in the performance of one of the actors, they would fall on it like a ton of bricks. Anything to give a bit more flavour, however briefly.

I'm sure Dave Hill won't mind me telling you this but he was having a bit of trouble with his eyes. A sniff of this got 'upstairs'. Immediately, they jumped up and down – something else to use. They had the courtesy to suggest a meeting with Dave and his agent but they said 'no'. I'm not sure if that was the reason, but it wasn't long before Dave was written out.

I had worked with Gerry Cowper years ago: she was just a kid, in a show called *Two People* for London Weekend Television, running off with my young son, Stephen Garlick. If only we'd both known where we were going to end up.

The last time I worked at LWT in the late eighties was in the sit com *Running Wild*.

They suggested Sharon Duce to play my wife. It seemed we were bankable, the sort of Richard Burton and Elizabeth Taylor of the Third Division. Then they changed their minds and said maybe it was too close to *Big Deal*. I suggested Janet Key, Gawn Grainger's wife. Janet got the job. Having worked with her I felt would make life easier; it would be a bit of short hand that would help the turn round of one week's rehearsal per episode.

The rehearsal routine of sit coms seemed to be a 10.30 start, a 12.30 finish, then straight to the pub, a few pints, then home – five days a week. Most days, instead of going home, I went into town and did VOs. The episodes were only thirty minutes each – less than twenty-five with commercial breaks – but the scripts were usually over seventy pages in length and as there was only, with the odd exception, four of us, we shared quite a bunch of dialogue. It was more difficult than I thought.

The two other mainstays of the cast were Michelle Collins and Peter Amory. He was in *Emmerdale Farm* for years, mostly in a wheelchair if I remember correctly. When I was up in Leeds for three weeks doing *The World of Eddie Weary*, the wonderful Celia Imrie as my sidekick, he phoned me a few times for a drink.

Emmerdale Farm is filmed there. He'd got a house outside Leeds, and had settled in nicely. Denis Waterman was in Leeds at the same time, doing *Stay Lucky*, and also asked me out for drinks. But I had a strict routine: two pints, then straight back to the hotel to learn the next day's lines. There was a flicker, even back then, that learning was becoming a pain.

Sunday was the *Running Wild* recording day. I tried to write a sit com once. The head of comedy at the Network Centre, the organisation that says 'yes' or 'no' to proposals, told me after reading my effort, 'Sorry. What we're really looking for are three studio sets, four or five actors and three gags a page. Sorry.'

Sorry? I'm sure he was – and so was I.

Running Wild was three sets, no fourth wall, facing the audience, four cameras pointing at the actors, like a firing squad. The difference was that we *didn't* have anything like three gags per page. At a push, one and a grin every *four or five* pages. It was more Ibsen than Ray Cooney.

The custom before recording in front of an audience is to have a 'warm up' man. I'd heard that the great Tommy Trinder, ex-chairman of my beloved Fulham FC, host of the original *Sunday Night at The London Palladium*, ended up doing warm ups.

Our man wasn't a Tommy, but he was a smart, quick comic, with a bag full of gags, more certainly than three a page, and all tinged with a liberal coat of seaside blue. We should have done the show first and *then* he should have come on. He was a lot funnier than the rubbish we were peddling.

Following his 'act', tradition has it that he introduces the 'stars of our show'!

I always came on last, being *the* 'star', to say a few words.

I told a joke by W.C. Fields, but the audience now in a state of high excitement engendered by Mr Blue, hadn't a clue who W.C. Fields was and probably couldn't care less. The Fields' punch line was, 'On the whole I'd rather be in Philadelphia.' It went down like a cup of cold sick.

A graveyard silence followed. Foolishly, I bet the rest of the cast, that I would continue during the next six weeks to do the Fields' gag and eventually get a laugh. What a fool I was!

I'm not saying that Mr Blue followed by Mr Fields sent *Running Wild* down the toilet but something did.

For instance, at the first recording we did, most of us were confused as to how we should pitch our performances. Should we play to the audience or to the cameras? It seemed an uncomfortable mix. No one got more confused than the bloke with whom I was doing the first scene.

Constantly, he was told, not very kindly I thought, to draw the level, loudness and pulling faces, back – to be more subtle. They 'pulled him so far back' I thought I might have to take a crash course in lip reading.

When the cameras started rolling on the first Sunday, they kept stopping the scene. The floor manager would creep over and whisper into this poor actor's ear. We'd start again from the beginning, and they'd stop it again. The floor manager would repeat his walk and whisper. Off we'd go again. Then we'd stop. The poor actor was getting more and more confused. Every time we started again, his performance level got broader and louder. By the time we actually did it for real, my lip reading skills were wholly redundant. Cotton wool in the ears would have been more appropriate. He was King Kong with lip gloss and a funny walk.

Instinctively, some of us picked up the baton and joined the gurning club. It became horrible.

Rummaging around last night through my stock of old VHS tapes, I tried to find that episode of *Running Wild*. I must have recorded it. It was so terrible. There were three mystery tapes, unlabelled, so

I had to play them through to find out what they contained. *Randall and Hopkirk (Deceased)* starring Mike Pratt and Kenneth Cope, episode called 'The Man With No Name' – that was me.

Another tape had chat shows – *Pebble Mill,* Sharon Duce the presenter and I playing poker (naff!) and Bobby G. launching into the *Big Deal* song. He wanders around the table, hair all buffed up, miming his heart out. Sharon and I are smiling at him. The whole programme looks like something out of the fifties.

There was *The Wogan Show* – me berating him for taking over the Flora ads from me and my starving family. Funny how photos and old tapes bring memories back.

The morning after *The Wogan Show,* I was in John Wood's studio. At 9.30 I went in to voice a commercial. Billy was the engineer.

'Wogan was just in doing a Flora ad. I said, 'Thanks Terry' – he'd done six takes. Then I said, 'But Ray would have done it quicker.' Good old Billy.

Then there was BBC's *Breakfast Show* with Frank Bough. In the bottom right hand corner of the screen was a clock. It read 7.05.

'I've just got out of bed,' I say. 'Must say good morning to Sadie, Will, Emma and Tom – and apologise to Duncan, Emma's boyfriend, for the row last night.'

Then I find it. And it is *the* episode. And it's exactly as I remember it. The credits have that 'here comes a comedy, bouncy, jolly music over the pieces of jigsaw flicking across the screen with our faces on them. Oh, it's terrible. And here's the scene in the office! Whoosh! We take no prisoners! As high as kites, but nowhere to go. Everyone's at it, looking out to the audience, winking, double takes every second. I'm waving my arms around like a tic-tac man on drugs, Janet's eyebrows seem to have a life of their own, Michelle Collins looks like a Barbie doll on roller skates while Peter Amory, on the other hand, says his lines as if he means them, which makes him seem like he's a day visitor in a mad house. It looks exhausting. It's exhausting to watch it.

In the LWT bar after that first recording, we're all throwing down drinks to wash our mouths out and trying to erase the memory of that recording from our fried up minds, when over slides our producer, Marcus Plantin.

He puts his hands on my shoulders. His eyes, behind his horn rimmed specs, one arm of which had sellotape holding it together, seemed to be brimming with tears. He held me in this position for what seemed like half an hour; I was like a rabbit in the headlights of his watery eyes. Eventually he spoke, and the sincerity sent a shiver down my spine.

'Ray,' he said, 'you're a star. Every time we cut to you it's money in the bank.'

I remember that in detail because it was the biggest load of rubbish I'd ever heard in my life. Even a pathetic, quivering, shell-shocked actor knows what's true and what isn't. Did he take me for a fool? Producers were spinners, the sugar coated kind, long before politicians realised that that was the way to run a country and drag us into wars.

The morning after the first episode was aired, we got to rehearsal as usual. The day before, a cross channel ferry, The Spirit of Free Enterprise, had sunk. They'd left the dock doors open, and many people had lost their lives.

This morning, the day after, somebody said (I'll save embarrassment by not naming the person), 'I bet our audience ratings went down after that boat sank. In fact, we both sank.' A stunning remark.

The first series limped on; we certainly weren't setting the world on fire.

Nevertheless, it was decided to make another series. One thing was worrying me. For a start it had been a nightmare experience, but if we carried on doing it the same way, thinking that if you shouted, grinned and generally bounced around like maniacs, that was the way to get laughs, we were snookered. But the money had gone up. So...

I spoke to Marcus. 'Do we have to have an audience? Can't we do it like a play?'

I had a theory that the studio audience could be a liability. Marcus, who thought I was a star, agreed that we could do the show without one.

Would you say that Judi Dench was a star? I don't think there's any doubt on that score. She was doing As Time Goes By, a sitcom. with Geoffrey Palmer, and she hated working in front of an audience in a studio. She asked if they could do the show without the audience.

They wouldn't let her. I was working for LWT and Geoffrey and Judi were working for the BBC. There's a lesson there somewhere.

I didn't really help. Doing *Running Wild* without an audience, the script was exposed. The screaming crowd had covered up the text and the waving arms, double takes and flying eye brows had obliterated the dialogue entirely. Now it was there for everybody to hear. If cynics call television chewing gum for the eyes then *Running Wild*, without an audience, was like red hot needles being pushed into your brain. It was very painful.

I'd had the phone call offering me *Running Wild* when I was in Manchester doing a chat show with Sharon about the 'state of television today'. The last episode of *Big Deal* was going out that night and I didn't have any work in the offing. *Running Wild* was a huge contrast to *Big Deal*.

I thought that a drama series, like *Big Deal*, was the way to make some sort of impact. In the early days, if you did a *Play for Today*, a one off, and everybody saw it, it was a good showcase for actors. Now it was a series. *Big Deal* was just what I'd been searching for.

I was sitting in the stand at Fulham, when a blonde bird on the terraces in front of me turned round and shouted 'Robbie Box!' We hadn't started filming. I didn't know who else was in it. The blonde bird turned out to be Sharon Duce. I didn't know her from Adam – but I got to.

I heard rumours that I was third choice for the part. But that's the way things go. David Jason wasn't first choice for *Only Fools and Horses*, for example.

Brian Lighthill was the director for the first episode. He looked like a nephew Ken Loach might have had. He was very intense, took it all very seriously. Rumour had it that he had directed *The Archers*, so maybe that was the reason.

We rehearsed in The Baden Powell Scouts' Headquarters on the Brompton Road.

He gathered us all together and started asking each of us about our character's background and history. We'd only just got the first script and he seemed to be working from the Joan Littlewood handbook; he was certainly jumping the gun. Ken Waller, playing Ferret, was a wily old bugger. When his turn came, he played along and created the most bizarre history of 'his family'. War records, pre-war liaisons, unemployment, working down the pits, an Irish tinker, a great, great, grandmother who lost a leg in the First World War – he went on and on. Brian Lighthill took it all in, nodding – this is what real directors do.

After about two weeks Duce and I were bussed out to a greyhound track just off the M4. It was nice to be *working* after all this navel gazing nonsense. We did a couple of scenes and it was fun. Sharon and I got on, the dogs ran round the track, it felt good.

After that, we stopped again and had to endure more Lighthill psycho-babble. It seemed a strange situation. We were ready to go. Why didn't we carry on filming after we'd filmed at the race track? Later, the truth came out. It was rumoured there was going to be a strike at the BBC.

The producer, Terry Williams, had decided that we had to get some of *Big Deal* in the 'can'. If we didn't, and there was this threatened strike, they might scrub the series altogether. In other words, the BBC having spent money on a night's filming was much more likely to let us get on with it. There was no strike, so off we went.

We shot every episode in sequence – no rush and panic – and we had eleven days for each one: two days rehearsal in the Acton Hilton, where everything from *The Morecambe and Wise Show* to obscure plays that have never seen the light of day were rehearsed, then nine days on the road filming from dawn to dusk. We loved it.

It was hard work. I worked every day, leaving the house at seven in the morning. I seemed to be in every scene, to one point, after a couple of beers I have to admit, I fell asleep at the traffic lights at Gunnersbury Lane. Woken up by the tooting of the the car behind me, I limped home. Next day at work, I told somebody what had happened. The following morning there was a car and driver waiting outside the house. I never had to drive to work again.

The job was a joy. Sadie found it difficult though, because I had so many lines to learn every night that she felt I was never part of the family. It reminded her of the time I was in *Snap*.

She had said then that I seemed to 'shut off' at about four o'clock every day. I tried to explain that I supposed I was beginning to think about what I had to do. The drive into town was horrendous, finding a parking space nightmarish; then into The Vaudeville Theatre and do the play for two hours. It was inevitable I would start to think about it the nearer it got to the time I'd have to leave.

'But you've been doing it for weeks. What's to think about?'

'Well, you've still got to get it right – remember the lines. The audience is different every night and you've got to do your best because it's *their night* out and ... well, it's the job.'

'I still don't understand.'

One Friday, Sadie was going to a theatre in town. The play she was going to see started at 8.15; *Snap* started half an hour earlier. I suggested she come backstage with me before my first entrance, to get the atmosphere and see how I felt having to go on 'every night', with, owing to Maggie Smith, full house, roaring away. And once I got on, I stayed on. Scary.

She stood with me behind the door where I had to make my entrance. I whispered to her my cue to go on, telling her that it was coming nearer and nearer. Then, bang! I was on – onto that overbright, white carpeted stage.

I met her after for dinner. 'Well?'

'I can't see your problem.'

So *Big Deal* was a hiccup at home as well. I started trying to learn my lines at lunchtime, on location, during tea breaks. The strange thing was, that the nature of the series seemed to be 'enjoy yourself'. Not as far as the bosses were concerned, of course, but the cast had a rip-roaring time and, I suppose, we made up our own rules. We played about with the dialogue. Sharon and I used to rehearse our scenes, trying to get the best out of them, altering words, applying paint where there wasn't any. Occasionally it was the wrong colour but, to hell with it, it seemed to work.

Here's an example of teamwork. Jeremy Irons joked, in an interview, that his performance as Robert Dudley, Earl of Leicester, alongside Helen Mirren as Queen Elizabeth had been helped when he put his hand on Mirren's thigh during the first read through of the script. She didn't slap him. You see, even the high and mighty believe in tactile communication to enhance their artistic endeavours.

Someone once said to me that *Big Deal* was 'second division stuff'. I remember saying that I was second division, when talking to that

141

reporter in Nottingham about Gemma Jones. She certainly is First Division.

If some people thought that about *Big Deal*, I didn't really care because I knew it wasn't Chekhov or Stoppard but we made it the best we could. I'll give you an example. Scripts started coming in late ... a bit like *EastEnders* ... a lot like *EastEnders*.

We'd finish filming, then we'd come into our two day rehearsal period. This particular time, the new script for the next episode arrived at the same time as we did. So we did a read-through without ever having seen the words before.

When we'd finished, I looked at the director, who hadn't seen it before either. We both looked horrified. It was awful. The producer, Mr Williams, was away on holiday, the writer had sent the script in from France or Spain, wherever he lived, and he wasn't at the rehearsal. Gawn Grainger, one of the writers, *was* there.

All the locations were booked. The guest actors for that episode – Warren Clarke was one of them – were sitting there after the read-through looking a bit confused. They hadn't seen the script before either. Jeremy Summers, the director, and I asked Gawn to rewrite the whole thing entirely – change the plot, do anything to make it workable. As this script stood, it would be like pushing treacle upstairs.

He did rewrite it, over those two rehearsal days, working like a demon, and pulled the whole thing, and us, out of the fire.

We shot it, it was edited, then Mr Williams came back from holiday and saw it. He hit the roof. This wasn't the script he'd commissioned.

Jeremy Summers and I were hauled up to see Jonathan Powell, head of series and serials. After opening statements from both sides, our defence went into action: late script, rubbish (I think Jeremy and I said this together), our writer sunning himself on some continental sandy beach, having pocketed £6,000, meanwhile we in Acton have to sort out the mess that Monsieur Scribbler has submitted. And who turns it into a sparkling number? Only Gawn Grainger, who will get a mere £4,000. Jonathan Powell's eyes narrow; there's a wigging looming. Then it burst, but we won our case and Jeremy and I went straight to The Bush pub to celebrate. This happened over twenty years ago. If we'd done that today we'd have been marched out into the car park and shot.

Everything changes, not always for the best, but at least we enjoyed the good times. A VO actor, one of the younger variety, in all seriousness asked me, 'What was it like to work in black and white films?' He wasn't a good VO, and an even worse actor, so I didn't kick him in the balls.

Pam St. Clement and I were sitting next to each other in the make-up factory at *EastEnders*, a smattering of the younger ones dotted around. In the general moaning that was going on, a voice said something about a breakdown in recording the previous day. I piped up with, 'There might have been a hair in the gate.'

This was ignored by the youngsters, who hadn't heard the phrase, but Pam's ears pricked up. A 'hair in the gate' meant that a sliver of the film running through the camera had split away from the edge of the film and flicked across the image on the pictures being taken.

'What do you know about that?' the earring queen said.

'Well,' I started to say, 'when I was in...'

'I was in the business before you were were.'

Then I started throwing around a few dates and years and she stopped me.

'No, you're right. I was still at school then.'

The funny little games you play. Everyone tries to be in the box seat, except if you're a pipsqueak – first television job and you're getting hundreds of fan letters – listening to old wrinklies waxing on about the 'old black and white' days. It must be anathema.

I was a comparative 'pipsqueak' when I was doing *Big Deal*, except that Sadie and I had three kids and I was forty-five. Forget my age, I was still a bit 'pippy'. A late developer.

I had been lucky. I'd met Wendy Noel who had introduced me to voice overs. Without them, Sadie, the kids and I could well have been struggling.

There were only thirty or so of us doing voice overs in the early seventies and if you could do things within the allotted time and hit the pack shots you were in. It was suggested by my then accountant, always a sharp eye to make a bit more, that I should form a limited company.

I was hoping to call it Excelsior Limited or Mighty Fulham Finance, but they were all taken, so I got Subtle Productions Limited. And subtle it was – £30 here and there, hardly Bill Gates' Microsoft Corps.

Then I had to a have a self-administered pension fund. In those days who had heard of that sort of stuff? The accountant said it was a good idea, so meekly I agreed. The advantage seemed to be that I could put most of my earnings in the fund, tax free, minimising my personal tax. Interest rates were high so the fund built nicely. It was not mine to spend, of course, 'but it'll be there when you retire'. But danger lurked. This world gave me a wedge which allowed us to feel comfortable. Not that we'd *ever* be in danger, but it gave enough flexibility to take the odd risk. *Big Deal* was a risk. In money terms, it was shallow water; without the water wings of VOs and the so called cushion of the fund, the game could have been up.

The BBC always took an option on a second series, in case the first was successful. For the first series they paid me £1,600 per episode, which is £100 more than I get per episode on *EastEnders,* but there are four *potential* episodes a week plus the 80% for the Sunday omnibus. So (potentially) more episodes, more money. But with *EastEnders,* you can have an affair with somebody, or kill somebody, either of which might give you a couple of weeks' mileage, or you can order a pint in the Vic, then disappear for five weeks. It's a mystery.

For the second series, the money was to be £1,900 per episode. We did ten episodes per series and from wink to blink it took about twenty-four weeks to complete. Although there was about half a year left to earn a bit more money, the opportunities for doing so were limited. With VOs I'd been out of the spin, so I'd get a few but nothing like as many as before. Financially things were not critical, but it chipped away at the savings.

EastEnders started in 1985, when *Big Deal* was in its second year. When I think how we were on *Big Deal* – enthusiastic, excited, really enjoying ourselves – I assume, no I could almost could guarantee, that they, in *EE,* were in the same state when they started. Now, twenty-one years later, they all seem tired, spark gone, and 'enthusiasm' certainly isn't in their lexicon. I realise that if we'd been doing *Big Deal* for twenty-one years, we'd have gone down the same route. So if I criticise them, it's because I turned up, excited in a 'new start' kind of way and expected everyone to be the same.

But back to *Big Deal* for a moment. By then the danger of the pension fund had reared its ugly head. Foolishly ('Don't worry, Ray, you can put it back any old time.') I had borrowed over time from the pension fund around £180,000 in order to supplement my income from *Big Deal* and keep my family on an even keel.

During the three years of *Big Deal*, the voice overs had dried up. It was difficult to recapture the same momentum. Paying back the pension fund loan was put off and put off, until things eventually came to a head about ten or twelve years later.

I was summoned into Jeffrey's, my new accountant's, office to face the Inland Revenue. Nigel Sloam, the actuary of the pension fund, was also in attendance. I was going to face the firing squad. My only allies were Jeffrey and Nigel. Side by side were the stern faced Inland Revenue men, the law behind them. I could almost see the prison gates opening to welcome a new inmate.

'Mr Brooks,' the older one said, 'with compound interest, the amount of money you owe the Inland Revenue is £860,000.'

I've never been so shocked in my life. The office was only on the second floor, so there was no point in throwing myself out of the window. In a flash, I calculated that we'd have to sell the house, the car, whatever we might have in the bank and spend the rest of our lives in a cardboard box.

My allies, however, were as cool as cucumbers. Why wouldn't they be? It wasn't their money.

'Surely, we can come to some arrangement,' said Nigel, lighting a cigar.

The older Inland Revenue man turned his attention to the cigar smoking actuary.

'When I was going through your papers referring to Mr Brooks' accounts, I found a letter your client had sent you. I quote: 'Do you think if we change the name of the company that we can pull the wool over the tax man's eyes?'

Nigel laughed. 'That's Mr Brooks' humour. Do you think I'd have left it in the file if I thought, for one minute, that he'd meant it?'

I *had* meant it but I echoed Nigel's laughter. Nigel warmed to his theme.

'Now Mr Brooks had no intention of cheating the revenue. The advice he's had in the past has been very shoddy. Mr Brooks is a

145

busy family man with three children. He's naive in the ways of finance. If he's culpable of anything, it must be that he had no knowledge of the financial ramifications of this loan.'

He puffed his cigar. I felt in my water that these men were beginning to realise they were in the presence of a master.

'Now, surely, we can come to some sort of arrangement?'

He wrote something on a piece of paper and handed it to them.

'If you'll excuse us for a moment. We ought to phone head office.'

They left the room. Nigel was all smiles.

'It'll be all right now, Ray. They'll settle for £70,000.'

'Seventy thousand? I haven't got seventy thousand!'

'Not you. The pension fund will pay it.'

The tax men returned. 'Yes, that's acceptable.'

Nigel had pulled a rabbit out of the hat!

They shook Nigel's and Jeffrey's hands and then turned to me. The older one smiled; he had pointed teeth.

'I always enjoyed your performance in *Big Deal.* I understand you do some writing. Maybe you can put us in one of your books.'

You *are* in one. Count.

The younger one shook my hand. 'My children and I love your Mr Benn.'

Why doesn't *he* pay the money then? He's always slipping in. Even bloody tax men talk about him.

Needless to say I went round the corner and straight into a pub. I phoned Sadie and told her the full story. If she could have squeezed down the line, she'd have been tucked into a large white wine. But we did all that when I got home. What a day!

15

Thursday 9th March, 2006

Bit later today, thank God. I leave home at 7.00 a.m. Five scenes in the Beales' house. A kids' party – four of them including Kevin, a five-year-old. Difficult to control, running around when he shouldn't, leaping off the set during takes, trying to find his mum, the usual five-year-old shenanigans. There's me and Brown Owl, Babs, Laurie and Adam. Babs and Brown Owl don't have children, and they were getting beady. You have to understand that Brown Owl's bead is very different from Babs'.

Adam has to offer Kevin a cup-cake. Brown Owl leaps up as if to save little Kevin from certain death.

'Not that one! It's got a blue smartie on the top. They've got chemicals in them!'

She snatches it away and gives it to a prop man. Blank faces all round. Kevin looks as if he's going to cry. She shoves a green one in his face. One day, when Kevin's an old man, he will bless a photo of Pauline, holding Betty, in Albert Square, and mutter to himself, 'She saved my life.'

Eventually all the genuflecting was over and I went back to my dressing-room to get on with the fan mail. I find it a bit tedious, but then I'm lazy. Two new scripts arrive! I do know what Steve Mac does when he gets scripts. He sings, pathetically trying to imitate Abba, 'Money, money, money.' I don't bother even to read them.

Back last year I was on the phone to Elstree almost every day asking where the scripts were. Understandable then. But now it's a matter of time. Each script is between eighty-five and ninety pages long. And most of the time they have printed the scenes in sequence with the characters' names. This is very handy. It's much easier to 'fillet' the script, that is take out your scenes and sling the rest. But you can't just 'sling' them. In all the corridors near dressing-rooms or the sets are small steel pillarboxes, locked and marked 'Confidential'. Used scripts have to be posted in these, away from prying eyes.

In my 'filleted' scenes, Dot is suddenly in a wheelchair! Why? Doing the episodes, all shot higgledy piggledy, she might be in a wheelchair in one scene and sprinting round the Square for charity in the next. I've always said that I might have a scene in the Minute Mart buying a plaster for a cut on my knee, but were I to ask the director how I'd got the cut he'd be quite likely to say that he doesn't know! I certainly have done scenes with people when I've had to ask who they are in the scheme of things. It can be embarrassing.

I scramble around on the floor to try and piece together all the scenes I've slung away from the two scripts. Here is a scene with Bert going into the Vic with a woman. Mo sees him. She's angry. Dot is at the window of her house. She bangs on the glass to attract Mo. Mo goes in to see Dot. She's furious because she's been jilted by Bert. She spills the beans to Dot.

'They've both been in prison.'

How does she know that?

'Bert had a short stretch. Joe had a longer one.'

Dot's eyes widen.

Here's another one, Dot's now in the wheelchair and for some reason I'm pushing her.

'I know about you being in prison. I won't tell Pauline yet, she's worried about Ben. But I will. It's my duty.'

The episode goes out in April; my year's contract is up in June. There must be a connection. But I asked Kate Harwood a month ago if I could leave and she said, 'No, we want you to stay. Everyone loves you.'

Not everyone, obviously. She said they've got story lines. But *this* story line is terminal. Dot doesn't like me. Mo doesn't like me and Brown Owl is going to go flaming mad. Wendy didn't want us to get married – I think words have been said. They want to get rid of me. That's my prediction.

Clockwise from left: 1. Before me; my mum on Brighton beach. 2. John Lewis Brooks, Rysie, my godmother and my mum. 3. Polyphoto me. 4. My mum at nineteen, a cigarette kiosk on the Palace Pier.

Left: A schoolboy.

Below: Pulling rope, second from left, on the *Hispaniola* to *Treasure Island* in 1956.

Above: Learning the guitar and singing.
Below: *The Knack* with Jane Birkin.

Above: With Sid James in *Taxi*.

Left: Cannes Film Festival 1966, with Rita Tushingham.

Right: *Cathy Come Home* 1967.
Below: The John Barry Seven and me.

Above: Carrying the great Richard Attenborough.

Below: Gemma Jones, *A Nightingale Sang*.

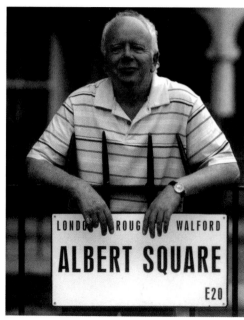

Above Left: *Big Deal* with Sharon Duce.

Above Right: First day *EastEnders*.

Below: Will, Tom and Anna Brooks with Maisie. Sadie and me poking through the holes of the cut-out, Joe, Will's girlfriend Anna, Nel, Jane and Rob.

Clockwise from right: 1. For Father's Day.
2. My Sadie. 3. The Helford River. Little
darlings in the rain.

16

More Reflections

I'm writing as if those characters are real people. 'They don't like me.' (!) But that they should want to get rid of me: that hurts. I feel as if I haven't really been given a chance. There's been a lot of duplicity. Whispering. It hurts because actors are weak vessels – they want to be wanted.

Except *Big Deal*, I really loved them all; it was a very happy time. Almost from day one we came together, relied on each other. Yes, it was a joy. The icing on the cake was that the public liked us. I must say that after recording the first show of the first series, I ended up in a pub, with Scotty Jarvis, my mate, and Sadie. I was exhausted. I had *nine* more to do; I couldn't see how I was going to do them. How many scams, bets, general gambling could you do!! Nine?!! I was shattered. But we went on. Apart from falling asleep at traffic lights, I got through it. And the buzz around was wonderful. So there was the second series of ten.

The second ten were better. Everything was better; we got more and more comfortable with what we were doing. There was only one dissenting voice. One actor took Terry Williams out to lunch to talk about 'developing his character'. It didn't happen. I didn't blame him – every actor wants to do more. But this was a company piece, like an Alan Ayckbourn play. Everyone was as important as everyone else.

Talking about Ayckbourn, I remember Anna Massey telling me about being offered an Ayckbourn play. Her first job, after leaving drama school, had been in the West End playing the female lead in *The Reluctant Debutante*. I did that in Reading with insulating tape over a hole in my sock. I suspect the production Anna was in was a classier number. But the point about Anna's career was that she was brought up in the 'structured' West End play/comedy times. There was a distinction between the lead players and the smaller parts. So when Anna read the Ayckbourn script and saw there was little or no difference between the size of the parts, she didn't understand. She thought she'd be playing the lead, but where *was* the lead? There didn't seem to be one. She turned it down. But Richard Briars, an old friend of Anna's, with whom I did *Absent Friends*, has done about six Ayckbourn plays.

During the run of *Absent Friends*, Richard was doing two sit coms back to back over fourteen weeks, recording them on Sundays. One of these was *The Good Life*. Richard told me that the BBC was having trouble casting the characters of Barbara, Richard's wife in the series, and Margo, the posh neighbour next door. Richard spoke to Eric Thompson about the problem. He suggested Richard and the BBC producer of the show should go and see Ayckbourn's *The Norman Conquests* which Eric had directed.

'There's a couple of girls in that might be all right.'

The main name in *The Norman Conquests* was Tom Courtney. The cast also included Michael Gambon, Felicity Kendal and Penelope Keith. Eric was right – Felicity and Penny were perfect for Barbara and Margo.

I first worked with Penny in *Emergency Ward 10*, a big show for ATV. By the time Penny and I got to it, it had dribbled down to showing on Sunday afternoons. My character was a footballer, who had scored three goals in the first half of a match, then collapsed at half time and been rushed to Ward 10. The football inserts were shot at Watford's ground, using Watford players. I scored my three goals against Pat Jennings, the then Watford goalkeeper.

Who is my physiotherapist? None other than the great Penny Keith, big and strong. She never really played leads until *The Good Life*; she was usually cast in 'ordinary' parts because she would make them more interesting. I don't know whether she will remember, but I saved both our lives during filming.

One location we used was Queen Mary's Hospital in Roehampton. They had a physiotherapy unit, part of which was a large swimming pool. In the scene Penny was supposed to be dragging me through the water to try and get some movement into my limbs. While we were in the pool rehearsing, the crew were setting up the camera equipment, etc. I became aware that there were 'brutes' – big lamps – being positioned round the edge of the pool, with cables snaking back to the generator. I dragged Penny out of that pool in a flash. (Inappropriate word, I know.) The director poured scorn on my concerns but I insisted.

'Anyone could trip over a cable, in drops a lamp and we'd be fried to a crisp.'

He agreed, muttering, 'Fucking wimp actors!' as he shuffled away to get the scene re-lit.

I never worked for him again. I reasoned that if he'd got his way and a lamp had dropped I'd never have worked for anybody again. And nor would Penny.

Eric Thompson was a clever man. He gave me a 'note' once, advice I suppose you could call it. Just before *Absent Friends* opened, we were both in the gents' toilet. During this silent pee he said, 'Be brave, Ray.' That's all he said. It was the most brilliant note I've ever had. It's similar to one I heard when Eva Marie Saint was interviewed. She'd always been a very serious actress: The Actor's Studio in New York, the sort of place Al Mulock was going to open in London, and films like Elia Kazan's *On The Waterfront* with Marlon Brando and Hitchcock's *North By North West* with Cary Grant. She said that the only note Hitchcock gave her during the entire picture was, 'Keep looking into Cary's eyes.'

Eric and Phyllida Law had two children, Emma and Sophie. Emma Thompson married Kenneth Brannagh. They were a glittering couple. They did big shows together and separately, Ken directing and acting. A joke circulating at the time ran: Emma comes into the house.

'Where are you, Ken?'

'I'm in the kitchen.'

'Can I be in it?'

Phyllida and I were both in *Absent Friends*. One of the first night reviews read, 'Ray Brooks and Phyllida Law should both be arrested for mugging.' I know. 'Be brave', but not that brave. It was a smashing company. Nicholas Bromley was the company manger – smart as paint, little moustache and always smiling. The IRA bombs were going off in London at that time. Sometimes you could hear the bangs in the distance when we were on stage. Nick Bromley had told the cast that if he had notification from the police that there could be a bomb in the vicinity...' So as not to panic the audience, I'll stand in the wings and wave a white handkerchief and then you must leave the stage in an orderly manner.' Fortunately, Nick, in his dinner suit, was never called upon to wave his white silk handkerchief.

After the show, Peter Bowles, Richard and I would go round the corner from The Garrick to The Marquis of Granby for a couple pints of Guinness. When we left the pub, aware of the IRA's habit of leaving bombs under cars, we would all go round to each other's cars, and get down on our hands and knees searching for strange packages.

One night I was driving home after an evening when many bombs had gone off. At The Mortlake Brewery there was a police cordon. They stopped me. I'd had a couple of pints of Guinness, which was a popular Dublin drink. If they smelt it on my breath, I could end up in clink. I wound the driver's window down half way, so that my mouth was parallel to the glass, hoping that they wouldn't be able to smell the Guinness. A big copper ambled over to my car, I was shaking, vowing never to let another drop of alcohol pass my lips.

'Where have you been this evening, sir?'

I started saying something, my words bouncing back at me off the driver's window.

'Oh, it's you, Mr Brooks. Sorry, off you go.'

It was our local bobby. I hadn't recognised him in the sweat and panic of my situation. Aren't policemen wonderful? Especially if you know them.

When *Absent Friends* closed after nine months. I went round to all the dressing-rooms after the last night to say goodbye to everyone. It's a sad time. Finally, I came to Peter Bowles' dressing-room. The door was open. He was squatting on the floor in his underpants doing yoga exercises.

'We will keep in touch, won't we, Ray?'

Dear old Peter, such a sentimental guy.

We did keep in touch. Peter and his wife Sue, Sadie and I used to go out to the theatre regularly and have a meal afterwards. It was a nice habit.

Peter loves theatrical stories, particularly stories against himself. He told me of one night, I think before he was married, when he was having a late night drink in Gerry's Club, a basement establishment in Shaftesbury Avenue. A drunken actor whom he didn't like very much, a well known lush, spotted Peter and made a beeline for him and put his arm round Peter's shoulder.

'We are friends, aren't we Peter?'

'Yes,' Peter said tersely.

'We really are, aren't we?'

'Yes.' Peter was steaming.

'You're not just saying that, are you?'

'No.'

'You mean it?'

'Yes.'

Peter, who does yoga and judo, was about to sling this limpet across the room.

'Do you mind if I tell you something?'

Now Peter's intrigued.

The lush's voice went soft as he whispered into Peter's ear, 'Do you know why you'll never be famous?' Peter went tense. 'Because ... because nobody likes you.' Peter didn't tell me what happened afterwards. Maybe he went home and cried, but he didn't say anything. That story typifies Peter. But the lush was wrong on all counts. He went on to star in *To The Manor Born* with Penny Keith, my physiotherapist, and has never looked back.

17

Monday 20th March

Early in. Big week. Confession time. After recording the scripts that I got on the 9th, all has become clear – or clearer.

Seems like I've been in every day for weeks. Cyst is playing up. This weekend at home has worn me out. I'm exhausted. In the Vic all day, not many words. Tried to sleep in a break but couldn't. I feel as if I'm falling to pieces. All in all, it's been a down day.

Tuesday 21st March

Cyst diminishing. Slept well, feel much better. Ain't nature wonderful: one day I feel fucked and here I am feeling as a bright as a new penny. But today is a mountain to climb. I've got to readjust my thinking about this job. Do I need it? More importantly, if I got out, it would more than likely be back to the old routine. What would it be like?

But it has been an amazing day! Extraordinary the way I got through it. Five confession scenes in the Fowler's ... yards of dialogue ... the Jackanory kind and more. Then five scenes in the Branning's!

Barbara said, 'Everybody's saying they don't know how you did it.'

Thanks Babs, but you have to take everything with a pinch of salt in the Boreham Wood World of Disney. Deep down, however, I knew that I'd climbed a mountain. It may be much easier to learn a bunch of dialogue than nipping in and out with the odd line. But, whatever, well done Ray! Home for a well earned kip.

Thursday 23rd March

Leave 7.00 a.m., weather shitty, sleet and rain. Out on the lot. Stop, go, stop. Ready to start scene. No. Quick change of clothes for another scene. On truck, unloading ten-foot lengths of timber, handing them to Bert. Us builders! What a joke. Two feebler actors you couldn't find. Lots of dialogue, me plot driving, Dave just 'Oh, ayeing.' Bloody Northerner! Snow now! We stop. Now start. Fucking difficult, planks off truck, Dave taking them, chatting, making sure that you say 'that line' towards camera. 'It's important.' More snow. That's one thing they can't cope with; snow gets on the camera lens. Now it starts spitting icy rain.

'Action.'

Bugger us getting soaked. Get through at last in six takes. None of them accurate. Another break. Then me, Dave and John. Again making a mess of it. It's so cold and unpleasant. I'm beginning to think that I can't walk *and* talk at the same time. Finally, it's lunchtime. Due to do a scene after, now it's dropped, reinstated, dropped again. Big break ... snooze.

Final scene, night, breaking into the Brannings'. The designer proudly told me that they had painted the window frame yesterday, 'Ready for its close up.' Pleased as punch.

I have to climb through it. Rehearse for cameras. Back to starting position for a take. No, can't – there's paint all over my jacket. Bloody chaos.

'It should have dried.'

'Costume, got anything to clean the paint off?'

Costume try; everything smudges. Eventually have to get through the window, almost backwards, like a crab in reverse, to try and keep what looks like large dollops of seagull shit on my back, away from the camera.

'Check it!'

'That'll do.'

Home. Knackered.

Friday 24th March

Leave home 6.00 a.m., eye very sore ... falling to bits. No fags in car. Second time – *that* part's getting better. Big day, lots to do. Morning, one scene no dialogue and one with bunches of it. Lunch then *eight* more scenes. Trying to forget about my sore eye and emerging cold, I seem to sail through them. Big achievement for me. Home. Knackered again, aching, sneezing. Bed 9.00 p.m. Bliss.

Next week, a strange thing happened, I went on ITV's *This Morning* show. Fern Britton is smashing; Philip Schofield doesn't like not being in control; me, with the nerves, trying to get in references to The Greyhound pub (I'd promised Mel and Jason), plugging Brighton and Hove Albion, apologising to Sadie about a row we'd had that morning, talking about my *EE* diary (repercussions to come later) and offering to take over the show. Young Philip gets decidedly beady.

Fern says goodbye, old Philip just checks his finger nails.

Car back to the studio, straight to the bar. Just settling in with a sandwich and pint when over to my table comes an *EE* person, not quite sure who. I start rattling on, probably still suffering withdrawal symptoms from the *This Morning* débacle, about trying to get out of the show, my contract being up in June, and how 'she'll most likely bury me in the allotment.' The *EE* lady says, 'They won't do that. They'll want you to stay, I'm sure.' And that was it. Three scenes, no dialogue and home.

I'd had an idea for a series for Felicity Kendal and me when I was doing *Big Deal*: a married couple, now divorced; she has become a successful business woman; I've slipped badly down the ladder, doing Dickens tours of London; but we still both long for what we had. Gentle, romantic, with lots of twists.

She liked the idea, so I thought it would be good to show her an episode of *Big Deal* directed by someone who could be interesting for our project. As the particular episode I had in mind had not been shown yet, I phoned Terry Williams our producer to ask him to lend me a copy.

'What do you want it for?'

I told him about Felicity and our idea for a series.

'Does that mean you wouldn't do a third series of *Big Deal*?'

I could hear the panic in his voice. Within a day or so they were on the phone to the agent. I didn't try to put the squeeze on him, I really fancied the series idea with Felicity. Now, it would have to wait till later.

The third series was still great fun although the stories started getting a bit repetitive, so we stuttered on, but there were one or two great episodes. One moment that sticks in my mind typifies the pleasure we all got out of it. We were rehearsing the last episode in the Acton Hilton. It was a very sunny day and I was standing over by the window. There, on the other side of the room, the whole cast were rehearsing a scene in a pub, all discussing how they were going to get me out of prison: Sharon Duce, Lisa Geoghan, Pam Cundell, Jimmy Ottaway, Steve Tate, Andy Mulligan, Deirdre Costello, Frank Mills, Alex Tetteh-Lartey, Roger Walker and Ken Waller. That moment of all those lovely people is a crystal clear picture in my head.

As the years have passed, I've kept a look out for all of them. Ken Waller went into *Bread,* Lisa Geoghan into *The Bill.* Frank Mills was for a while, in *Coronation Street.* Roger Walker went into the BBC's ill fated, short lived and much derided series, *Eldorado.* Andy Mulligan, Ken Waller told me, has more or less retired and just does 'extra' work. Steve Tate, who'd done *Cats* and other musicals, I've seen spasmodically. He used to live over in Brentford, but what he's doing now I have no idea. Deirdre Costello was in *The Full Monty.* Pam Cundell, the sweetheart, is directing amateur productions. She turned up in *EastEnders* for a few weeks and was a breath of fresh air; she never changes. Lovely Jimmy Ottaway died, as did Ken Waller – such a dear man, a trouper; he used to take his false teeth out when playing Ferret. I do miss them all so much.

Tony Caunter played Diamond – the big business man with a drunken wife, Marion Bailey – who hanged himself at the end of the first series. I know he was disappointed to leave. He came to the end of series party, and I could see that it was difficult for him to join in. Here we were, all celebrating the commissioning of the second series, but he wasn't going to be in it. He disappeared for a while, then turned up in *EastEnders* playing Pam St Clement's husband.

He was in it for a while and I was pleased for him. I remember the plot line when he left. Pam told me he was very unhappy about going. He and his wife now live abroad, Pam says. She keeps in touch and they are getting on fine.

Memory is a fickle friend and, like all friends, sometimes not there when you want them. I would never have been able to write this memoir without my magic cardboard suitcase. In it are all the programmes from my rep. days, letters, elocution exam results and notices in local papers. Without the DVDs and video cassettes with their cast lists that roll up at the end, there's no doubt I'd have been snookered. Even the most important sequences in my life seemed to be edited – just flickering images and snippets of conversation.

18

Sweet Emma

Emma's illness and the surrounding pain sits like a weight in my heart. Maybe it was that pain that edited the sequence of events, the visits to the Marsden hospital, my poor daughter lying there so ill that I seemed to be anaesthetised, as in a dream. If the reality had hit me I would probably have been screaming at the injustice of it all.

When she learned she had breast cancer and had to have a mastectomy, she went home to be with little Joe and Nel, her partner, in Acton. She had regular visits to the Marsden for radio therapy and for chemotherapy every three weeks.

Once, as she rode her bike across the park, with Joe in his seat on the back, her wig on because of the chemotherapy, Joe's seat slipped and he fell off. Emma screamed and she fell off. People ran over to help but when they saw that Emma's wig had also fallen off, they ran away. People don't like bald women.

After the Marsden gave Emma the all clear, she decided they ought to get out of London. Her job as a social worker at Fulham and Hammersmith was too stressful to go back to, so they moved to to Carvoeiro, in Portugal. Nel's parents worked there, dealing with holiday lets, and Emma and Nel could help them out.

In 2001 we went out to see them and because Sadie hates flying, we went by train. It was a lovely trip, especially the overnight sleeper from Irun to Lisbon. We had dinner in the dining car. Because we didn't know what they were talking about, nor could read the menu, which consisted of chicken, boiled potatoes and cabbage. It wasn't very good but we were so hungry it seemed like the best dinner we'd ever had. The carafe of wine was from the table of Bacchus and we kept the jug.

Lisbon was as sunny as the posters. They were late picking us up, so the coffee we had was the icing on the cake.

Laura and Manuel, Nel's mum and dad, had organised an apartment with a balcony overlooking the sea. Emma and Nel had stocked the fridge with bacon, eggs, sausages, tomatoes and milk.

They toasted our arrival, they took us out for dinner, we took them out for dinner, we went on a boat ride into caves along the coast, sat on the beach and drank wine, we had leisurely breakfasts on our balcony and in the village, we explored the area, sat up late in the piazza listening to the bands and watching the performers, we caught the sun and slept like logs. Every morning was sunny and the world seemed wonderful. Emma was full of beans.

This is where the confusion starts. I had to ask Sadie when they came back. Sadie does crosswords daily and they say that's good for stimulating the brain. She told me it was March 2002.

Emma had been riding a moped with Joe around Carvoiero. She said she'd hurt her back lifting it onto its stand. She needed to come back to see her doctor.

We picked them up at Heathrow. She was shuffling along, obviously in great pain. She could hardly get up the stairs in our house.

Next morning I was at work. Sadie had to call an ambulance and Emma was taken into Kingston hospital. She was then transferred to the Marsden. We went to see her. She was in bed. She said, 'I've got it in my bones now.' She looked heavenwards and said, 'What the fuck have I done to deserve this?'

She had more treatment, she came home to us, she had more treatment, they moved into a flat, we had rows, we made up, she had alternative treatment, she had a pure water system installed, she went on a special coffee diet. Nel was fantastic with her. Joe was very young, and didn't really understand the gravity of her condition. We talked and I suppose we avoided the subject. What could we say? One of the sisters at the Marsden had said that she knew people with Emma's condition who had lived for twenty years. Twenty years! She was thirty six and had a young son.

We had Christmas at their flat. Nel did his turkey in flour, Joe jumped about and played games, we all opened our presents, drank copious amounts of wine and Emma sat on the couch with a blanket round her legs.

There were ups and downs with her health in the next couple of months. The treatment continued; the chemo. really knocked it out of her. There were always the same people there on her three weekly trips to the Marsden and they got to know each other well. Emma noticed that one lady had a bandage round her wrist. She told Emma that during her last chemo. visit, during the treatment, which takes three hours, the needle had fallen out of her wrist and the fluid had leaked onto her skin. She was severely burnt. And that was the stuff that was going through their bodies.

We'd sometimes go into Kew Gardens and ride around on the tourist bus. She said that if Joe jumped onto her bed in the mornings it used to hurt her.

An email on March 13th, 2003, at 13.16:

We're all well today ... and Joe is having another day off ... dreadful parents we are ... just couldn't get up really.

His spots are falling off all over the place and I can't help picking them up. (Don't tell anyone.)

Today I am really hoping to go to Madame Tussaud's. I have such an urge to go. Joe would really be interested in the Kings and Queens bit.

It's Education innit????

We love you and now we're going to get dressed. Lazy slobs we are. Just finished breakfast. Love Em xxx.

Within a few weeks she was back in the Marsden. They had put her in a private room. We'd go in daily. Sometimes she was sleeping, sometimes half awake. We'd hold her hand and talk or be quiet.

These days all seem to roll into one, as they must have done for her. It was all like a dream, up the two flights of stairs to her room, always passing the intensive care ward on the first floor, with its armchairs outside.

As the weeks passed, she seemed to be asleep most of the time. Sadie would hold her hand and I had to keep going out for coffee and a cigarette.

One day we took Hannah, one of Emma's oldest friends, to find that overnight they'd moved her to intensive care. This ward had an atmosphere of deep foreboding. There seemed to be more doctors and nurses than there were patients. There were monitors around each bed; the lighting was subdued. They ushered us into a waiting room while they got her ready. It was a smoking room – this was a stressful place.

When we saw her, this tiny girl, there seemed to be wires everywhere. They had introduced a line into her groin to feed her drugs intravenously because she couldn't take injections.

Hannah started crying. She hadn't expected to see her looking so ill. Sadie took her out to sit in one of those armchairs. That's what they were there for.

Emma's eyes were closed. I thought she was asleep. I took her hand.

'Dad?'

'Yes.'

'I think I've gone blind. I had to ask the nurse whether she'd opened the curtains this morning. Will I get better?'

'Yes.'

'Pray for me.'

On the morning of June 3rd she had a fit – or that's what they called it. Will and Nel went in. The nurses calmed her down. Will and Nel left.

That night I was watching television – Sadie had gone to bed – when my mobile rang. It was Nel.

'Ray, Emma died half an hour ago. Will you come in with me?'

I woke Sadie and told her; we'd go in together tomorrow.

There wasn't much traffic on the road, just the odd car going in the opposite direction. Nel and I didn't say much during the journey. I found myself, as in the old days, wishing I was someone else.

She hadn't changed. I don't know what I had expected, her body was straight, not curled up as it had been. The one disconcerting part was that the undulating bed, to stop her getting bed sores, was still switched on. But the pain had stopped.

I kissed her forehead and stroked her hair. It didn't seem possible, to have to say goodbye to my daughter, leave her forever, never to row again, lose a friend whose nappies you'd changed, whom you'd walked to school, whom you'd taught to ride a bike, who made you laugh, made you tear your hair out, made you proud. Maybe that's

164

what keeps them alive to you, the craziness ... this indefinable quality of not knowing what they're going to do next, but knowing that it will end in laughter.

I left Nel to say goodbye. I went to a waiting room nearby; it was a smoking room. There are smoking rooms everywhere. It's a tough place.

When I got home, Sadie, Caroline Hamilton and Sandy Collison were there with a bottle of brandy. We talked and talked. Caroline had brought some of her husband's beautiful linen handkerchiefs – Patrick had died ten years before – to mop up our tears. Emma had loved Patrick.

Next day, Sadie and I had to get the death certificate – it all has to be official although it's very personal. While at the Marsden, we went to the Chapel of Rest to see Emma. It's in the basement of the hospital. We went down the stairs, the corridors festooned with heating pipes and water pipes, or whatever, snaking along the walls. Next door to the Chapel of Rest was the rest room for the cleaners. It's hard to remember, but there seemed to be plinky-plonky music playing. Not what you'd call appropriate, although I'm sure Emma wouldn't have minded.

The door of the chapel was very serious and suitably solemn. Inside there was a low table with a box of tissues and a couple of chairs. An ornate but sombre curtain stretched across the room. When the door was closed, the curtain drew back. It was an incongruous sight, but it was part of what people expect, I suppose – everything sad, almost theatrically holy in the presence of death. The music next door was wrong and, in a way, so was this.

I left Sadie on her own for a few minutes.

'There seemed to be tears around her eyes. So I wiped them,' she said.

We went to the local council offices and got copies of the certificate, sat in a pub, talked and drifted. Then went home and the world spun around us. People phoned and wrote letters of condolence but it was all still like a dream and my tears didn't come as easily as Emma's seemed to have done.

A week or so before, Will had been at the hospital. When I got there he was sitting on the steps outside. I went in. She was very,

very ill. I came out and sat next to Will. I started crying and he put his arm round me to console me. Tommy arrived and went in. He came out and sat with us, he started crying; she didn't have long to live. We consoled each other. If only she'd been there to console us and tell us that everything would be all right.

I told Tom the other day that I was writing this section about Emma and I told him how confusing and almost vague my memory of the time of her illness was. He reminded me that during her illness he'd seen me in Richmond and hadn't recognised him. Tom had thought I was taking the piss and played along for a bit, then realised that it wasn't a game. When he told me this, I was terribly shocked.

'You were in a daze, dad.'

It seems that people have an idea of the correct way to grieve. Like Doctor Spock told us that was a way to bring up children. Some people can feel guilty about not reacting in the right way. Other people might make us feel like that.

A couple of weeks after June 3rd, I went to Brighton. I turned up at The Cricketers and told Dec, the manager, about Emma. He knew that she'd been ill. He had lost his mother and that had hit him hard, so he was very sympathetic. Miss Tig, who bounced about the pub serving food and being happy, a mate as well, came into view. I told her. She burst into tears. Big tears, really painful, an emotional outpouring. It was overwhelming. I'm not saying that dear Tig made me feel guilty about my reactions but it's just an example of how easy it might be for someone to feel that they haven't reacted to personal tragedy in the perceived right way. Incidentally, her father died recently and that cloud will take a long time to clear. I don't think it ever will.

After Emma died, Will moved into the flat with Nel and Joe to be a support. Will can be amazingly strong. He sort of took over, which he often does, and in this case it was a wonderful thing to do.

The day of the cremation was beautifully sunny. Paul, Sandra, Sharon, Wes and the kids came from my side and Mary, Brian, Jane, Rob, David and Sharon from Sadie's. Mike Dolling, my boozing, gambling mate, seemed to have his arm round my shoulder all day. Phyllida Law, Pam Cundell, Peter Bowles and Sue, Richard Briers and Ann, Killy and Sarah, John and Betty from The Coach, David and Sandy Collison, Ian and Tessa, and dozens of Emma's ex-workmates from Fulham and Hammersmith, plus all her friends and many of Sadie's friends, filled the crematorium. Quite a few of them had to stand outside.

I really don't know what to say about it. All I know was that Emma wasn't there; everyone that knew her was. It was a very bleak occasion for Sadie and me. I don't know what was going through her mind, I don't know what was going through mine.

It's left a massive hole in my heart and in Sadie's. She often asks me why we don't talk about it. It's almost too big, too painful. Out would come the guilt, the 'Why didn't I?', 'Why didn't you?'; the 'Where were we when?', 'We should have...' stuff. Raking over the past, tearing ourselves to pieces. But maybe that's what you've got to do to get yourself back together, back to the time before everything was horrible.

I always thought that age brought maturity, that you could somehow rationalise events, take things more calmly, but I don't see any evidence of it. Only one or two people I know seem to be 'mature'. But are they? Maybe it's just outward appearances and inside they are as angry and burning as the rest of us.

As I've got older, I feel like an old man sitting on top of a mountain in the wind and rain who doesn't know how to get down to the valley to find shelter and warmth. It's lonely getting old, invisible, with opinions that nobody wants to hear, until eventually you keep your mouth shut, watch the cut on your arm that seems to take forever to heal and that pain that never goes away. But it doesn't matter – stand up, as long as your legs work, walk down that mountain and shout. Don't stew in self pity, always aim for something.

After the cremation some of the Brighton contingent ended up in our garden drinking wine. I sensed that it could turn into the nonsense that happened when my mum died. Jane and Rob took Joe down the the green to play football, Dave fell off his bike, Sandy got cross with him. Dave phoned later wondering if he could come and stay with us. 'I've been banished to the garden.' Other things happened, promises were made that were never kept – all the usual stuff at funerals.

And then it was over. Will went to Cornwall on his own for a week. He was exhausted.

'Don't you die yet, Dad. I couldn't go through all that again for a long, long time.'

When Emma, Nel and Joe were living with us, I was ironing in my room one day. She came in.

'Let me do that, Dad.'

'No, it's all right. I don't mind ironing. It's just shirts.'

'I love ironing shirts.'

'It's just the sleeves, really.'

'Oh, I don't bother with those.'

When I was going up for *EastEnders*, I was in that same room, ironing a shirt to wear and I thought about that moment three years ago. I wish she had appeared that day and I'd told her where I was going. Then she in her wisdom and knowledge might have said, 'Don't bother, Dad, it'll be crap.'

She *might* have said that, but she might not have done. Anyway, I'm in it now and I have tried to get out but I'm still here.

'Maybe you should have tried harder.'

Shhh. Oh, dear! Goodnight, baby.

19

Coming Out of Moth Balls

2001. While we were in Portugal I had agreed to be in *Two Thousand Acres of Sky*. Emma was thrilled.

It was filmed in Scotland. I hadn't flown for twenty years or more and the planes had got bigger. I settled for 'Valium' Airlines. Three of those smarties, a couple of pints at the airport and I could have flown the plane myself.

The star of the show was Michelle Collins. When I arrived I knocked on her caravan door.

'Hello?'

'Ray Brooks. Hello, Michelle.'

'Good God, I thought it was Barry Cryer.'

Thanks, Baz.

The other star was the gangly Paul Kaye, relatively unknown, apart from having played Denis Pennis, the crackpot, red-haired lunatic, who interviews celebrities in a dangerous style. I was playing his father, later to be revealed as homosexual.

Michelle was clever. She had learnt her trade the hard way – a bit of rock singing, working with me, *EE*, married to Ian Beale, dozens of affairs, trying to get him killed, then dying in prison. There's a learning curve, if there ever was one. But, above all, she is very talented.

Paul, I didn't know before, but he was a painter, had designed sets for the theatre, wrote and now was star of this show. As an actor, he seemed a bit all over the place, though somehow getting there in the end and being very impressive. Scenes with him were tricky. There's me hanging on to my lines like a leech, Paul whizzing here and there, approximating dialogue mysteriously and then landing

169

unexpectedly, as far as I was concerned, at my cue. As I said to him at the end, 'I like you a lot but I don't like acting with you. You remind me too much of when I was young.'

We were based in Stranraer, which is a port for ferries to Ireland. There were many late night drinking sessions in the hotel. One particularly heavy night the conversation got round to the subject of money. I don't like this subject. It's on a par with religion and politics, it causes upsets, so I try to avoid it.

'How much are you getting for the series?' I was asked.

As I was in only three episodes out of what I think were ten, and the assembled company were in the whole series, I felt confident that I wouldn't be treading on anybody's toes when I replied. 'Thirty thousand.'

Jaws dropped and eyebrows flew to the ceiling. The temperature in the room dropped to zero.

'How much?' The faces staring at me were frozen – or they might have been angry. Money is important to people north of Hadrian's Wall.

I repeated the figure. The smallest and angriest – I'm sure kilted and dirked at the time – said, 'Christ! We're only getting forty thousand.'

It was a difficult moment, until a lone voice said. 'Well, Ray's a star. Fair enough.'

Was it the sellotaped Marcus Plantin drifting up from a hundred years ago from LWT?

I didn't spot the person who threw me that lifeline, but if I had he would have been a friend for life, whether he knew what he was talking about or not. If I'd have been braver, I might have said that I wished I was earning forty thousand pounds for ten episodes when I was your age. But that would have been a difficult concept to grasp at that time of night and particularly if your knees were sticking out from under a kilt.

The base hotel was very pleasant. My routine on days off was very simple. It had to be, there wasn't very much going on. Walk up to Tesco to get a newspaper, see big ladies with big kids carrying big bags of shopping going into the The Star café opposite which specialised in deep fried pizzas and deep fried Mars bars. Back for breakfast, read paper, 12.00 go to pub. Walk past Tesco, see big ladies with big kids carrying big bags going over to The Star café for lunch.

The pub was small, populated by half a dozen punters who could have been there since the dawn of time. There was a lot of, 'Ohhh, Jimmy', 'Aye, dinna, Jock?', 'D'ya ken, Mary?', etc. I hid behind my paper, avoiding eye contact, drank my couple of pints and scurried out. Back to the hotel, bit of *Countdown*, then a kip. About six o'clock to the bar – a few drinks, back to room, telly, dinner, bed. 'Hi diddle de de, an actor's life for me.'

Michelle was good company, at work and socially. Paul and I were always on to her to use her influence at *EE* to get him and me in.

I did enjoy my time up in Scotland. I'd got back into 'acting'. Valium Airlines had cured my fear of flying and some money had gone into the bank. But, more than that, it made me realise, after ten years of not working, that I missed the company of actors. Not always, mind you. Some actors drive me up the wall. I'd rather be stuck in a toilet with twenty-four-hour diarrhoea than be in some companies again.

Once on a train, coming back for the weekend from Leeds during the filming of *The World Of Eddie Weary* with the glorious Celia Imrie, snoozing like a big bunny in the corner, was Anthony Daniels. He was in the show with us but more famous for having played the robot C3PO in *Star Wars*. His percentage from the films had made him extremely rich. He also came from a very privileged background. He was waxing lyrical about the joys of being an actor.

'I always had a nanny when I was a child – acting's the same really. You get a call sheet, telling you what you are going to do the next day; they drive you to the studio; they make you up; they bring you a cup of tea; you play around and then they drive you home. Perfect.'

I bet he'd always had a car. Apart from when I fell asleep at the Gunnersbury traffic lights during *Big Deal*, I've never had one.

Except when a curious thing happened on *EE*. I got a call from Carolyn Weinstein, whose job it is to look after the actors.

'You've been working very hard lately, Ray. You must be getting very tired. You can have a driver and car when you want one.'

I couldn't believe it. Yes, I was tired. Very. So no more having to stop and start down the North Circular, jousting with lorries and travelling salesmen in Cortinas. Only June, Wendy and Barbara had drivers – and now me. How nice! I was delighted.

A couple of days later, I'm up in the offices getting some more *EE* photos to send out to the punters when I bump into Kate Harwood, our mysterious producer. I tell her about Carolyn Weinstein's call.

'That's nice,' she says. Nothing about my deserving it.

I see Will, our eldest, at the weekend and tell him about the car.

'Oh, it worked then.'

'What?'

'I sent an email to Kate, saying you were looking tired and that you ought have a car. She sent one back and said, "As if by magic, he's got one".'

Mr Benn again. But why didn't Kate say anything? Anyway, it's always wise to have Mr Will in your corner.

Tuesday March 7th 2006

Early. Driven in. Thanks, Will. There is a slight drawback. Some of the drivers never stop talking – you can be exhausted before you start work. But it saves on the nerves and the horrendous homeward journey in the dark. Two tiny scenes. Brighton Thursday and Friday. The relief of it all. Keep hanging on. I felt I did well on Friday's aired episode but not a whisper of praise. I hoped. But nothing.

Tuesday 14th

After a few days in Brighton, an irrating cyst has reared up. Typical – a hint of the factory and the cyst farm goes into to full production. Early start. Bacon roll. Hard to be back but only two scenes in the Fowlers'. One with Brown Owl, who seems more cheerful today. The odd flicker of a smile. What's happened? Got through the scenes reasonably. Then I go to get some more fan pictures from the offices. Bump into Kate Harwood.

'The confessional episode is good.'

(Me telling Brown Owl about my murky past.) Only good? Surely she could have been a bit more encouraging. I don't say anything, of course.

So what happens now, I ask her?

'She kicks you out. You stay at the Brannings' for a bit.'

'So, when do I move back with Pauline?'

Pause. 'Well, not yet, er ... other things...

'Do I move back?'

'Yes, sort of.'

Now the panic sets in. Why did they get me to sign for another year? Are they having second thoughts? Do I care? I suppose I must do – it's that old devil the ego. Even though I hate doing it – this turgid plot, marking time, never laughing, just ploughing on – I still want to be wanted. I thought back to Brown Owl's cheerfulness earlier in the day. Does she know something that I don't? I'm tying myself into knots. I've tried to get out, now I want to stay! I'm going mad.

People say that actors are children, and we all know that children need encouragement. I think everybody is like that deep down. We all liked to be liked, don't we? We all want to be wanted.

As I've got older I've become more neurotic. I only wanted to be an actor in the first place because my girlfriend, Ann Thompson, having gone to RADA, kept going on about how 'wonderful' they all were. Also, because I was shy, I wanted to be 'famous' so that people would want to talk to me.

Let's go back to Miriam Margolyes – 'The trouble with you, Ray, is that you don't like yourself and you're ill educated.'

The 'ill educated' bit is correct and the 'don't like yourself' is set in stone.

Tuesday 11th April

Seven scenes looming. I read them and read them. Amongst all the chaos, the work is a sort of lifeline, something to keep me occupied. Alice, the director, is very sweet and thoughtful. When it looks, in a roundabout way, that Pauline is inviting him back to stay with her (after she has kicked me out), Joe has to say, 'I love you, you know.' Pauline is supposed to be pleased, according to the script. Nothing.

Alice says, 'It says that you smile in the script, Wendy. After all, he does say that he loves you.'

Wendy takes Alice aside. Not so far aside that I can't hear what is said. Maybe it was intentional.

'Pauline doesn't trust him. He lied to me. He's been in prison.'

Alice started to say something...

'*He lied to me.*'

Whatever she did on the take I never really noticed, but then my eyes are bad. I know she doesn't like me, for whatever reason, but she's an actress for God's sake. Just *act* it! You don't have to *mean* it.

I've had my confessional scenes, acquiescing and abasing myself to her, as all men seem to have to do to women in the 'Soap World'. So I have an idea that might be a clever way of me getting out. Let's say that she accepts me back into the house, smiling or not, but that she has a secret agenda. Not murdering me, as I'm sure that she'd like to, because 'Pauline doesn't do that sort of thing'.

She takes me back because she doesn't want to lose face, doesn't want to appear to be a woman who is abandoned by her 'husband', particularly one that she's only just married. Certainly the gossips in the Square would have a field day if she kicked me out, she'd be the recipient of every snide remark going, and that would make her life a misery. No, 'Pauline's a strong woman' but she's also very shrewd.

Whom could she tell about her dilemma, the marriage that's dying in that dark house? Who'd understand? Pauline's gay mate, Derek. Yes, he's the one. So, we see her go off to see him. He's sympathetic, agrees with everything she says and says he'll help. He suggests that he comes back and stays at the Fowlers' for a while and try subtly to suggest that I leave her.

This would make her the victim, elicit sympathy all round, tears and sherry, lots of 'aren't men awful' which is the mantra of all soaps. Bingo! A few scenes with Ian Lavender, wriggling around trying to get to the point, eventually I get the message and slink off with a tear in my eye. Maybe there'll be a bit of sympathy for me, but mostly I'll been seen as a doublecrossing bastard. That's OK. I'm not really bothered – I just want to get out now. The alternative is too dire to contemplate. Marinading in misery on screen and off for a whole year. No, no.

I'm happy with projected plot line, but how do I go about getting it implemented?

Thursday 13th

In early, head spinning with my idea. Four scenes with Dave, directed by the smashing Paul Annett. A joy. If only it was always like this. I arrange to see Kate Harwood and tell her my idea.

She thinks it is a reasonable one but she says that she doesn't want Derek back in the show. However, her main concern was that James and Natalie were leaving and plans for that are occupying the 'planners'' brain cells.

'Losing big characters like that has to be carefully organised.'

So my idea is small potatoes a non-starter.

'I've only told Wendy about them leaving. So keep it to yourself.'

Friday 14th

6.30 in. *The Sun* newspaper was everywhere.

'Sonia and Martin to Leave *EastEnders* Shock.' Headlines on the front page. Kate had said, 'I've only told Wendy...' Oh, sure! Believe people here at your peril! Still, I've a two week holiday after today and Sadie and I will be off to Jersey. Shut down the brain box and enjoy yourself.

20

Famous in Far Off Places

We go off on holiday!! We'd been to Jersey once before and we'd had a peaceful time. Sadie had been there a good few times with her sister, Mary. Mary had been there with her husband John, and when she was widowed Sadie went with her. They had accumulated many guide books of 'fascinating walks'. Sadie always took them with her.

Sadie won't fly, although by air you can get to Jersey in about forty minutes, so we go by train and ferry. It's Sunday.

I didn't realise how *EastEnders* had grabbed people outside London. The minute we hit Weymouth it all kicked off. The taxi outside the station: 'Oh, it's...!'

We hadn't booked a hotel as we'd only be there for one night before the early morning ferry.

Sadie says, 'There's a pub by the quayside, I'm sure they've got rooms.'

I go in.

'Oh, it's...!'

No rooms. 'Could you sign this?'

The mobile goes off. It's Nigel, an old mate from Brighton.

'What are you doing in Weymouth?'

'How do you know I'm here?'

'Mates of mine own that pub you've just been in.'

We find a hotel. The lady taxi driver won't take any money.

'It's been so lovely to meet you. We don't have many celebrities down here.'

'Don't be mad.'

I give her over the odds. Natch. There's the usual photograph and kiss on the cheek.

177

Book into the hotel.

'Oh, it's...!' Smiles, blushes, etc.

Go to a recommended restaurant to fix a meal for the evening.

'Yes, that's fine. Sorry, name? Stupid because I've been watching you all afternoon on television.'

Early morning ferry. Lots of 'Oh, it's...!' Even the French staff on the boat watch it. I'm seriously thinking of growing a beard over this holiday, but of course there isn't time.

Jersey is a small island, and most of the residents have cars, so there's not much room for visitors to bring theirs. Hence a weekly season ticket on the buses. And there are bikes aplenty.

I've always liked bikes. Unless I have cysts, of course. When the kids were young, we'd whizz everywhere. On Sundays, to give Sadie a break, I'd take the three kids cycling along the towpath to Putney Bridge. It was a fair old cycle ride, summer and winter.

At Putney Bridge we'd stop for a drink and a packet of crisps, rest our aching legs and build up our strength for the journey back. Once, when it was very cold, we passed a bonfire on the river bank; it was too tempting not to have a warm up before departing. Tom was only five and he had a small bike with tiny wheels. The outward journey used to exhaust him. More often than not, I would have him on my saddle, while I wheeled my bike with one hand and carried Tom's with the other all the way back. I was certainly tired out when I got home. Sadie had to take over again while I had a lie down.

I miss those days very much. The kids were young, and so were we. But did I enjoy them then? At the time it seemed like hard work, but now...? I'd grab that hard work again with both hands.

The holiday was full of smiles, kisses, signings, photos – total madness. Nevertheless, Sadie and I had a great time. It was too short and the nearer I got to the end of it and the *EastEnders* juggernaut got closer, the more frequently I began to have headaches. The fear of the scripts on the doormat waiting for me, the 'marriage' on the rocks, doom and gloom dialogue, endless scenes in the Vic and the café, muttering around, going nowhere for a whole year. God help me!

Then, two days before we were due to leave, the mobile rang.

'Ray?'

It's the *EE* office.

'You're not needed your first week back.'

Ten minutes later, 'Ray?'

Someone else from *EE*.

'You've got one week off. Yes? You can have the following two weeks as well.'

Now another fear appears. It must mean there are plans afoot for my demise. The old ego's feeling wobbly.

21

Home Sweet Home

Three weeks off. I could get used to this. The weather's good, the beer's good and I'm feeling chipper.

A week goes by – two weeks to go. I'm sleeping well; the Vic and the Fowlers are too far away to worry about.

I'm lounging around one afternoon watching *Deal or No Deal* when suddenly there's an ad break. Paul O'Grady is interviewing Wendy Richard. Wendy comes on. She's got a fair old tan, must have been on holiday like me, except I don't go brown. Smiles all round. I haven't seen her smile for ages.

'Natalie and James are leaving. I'll miss them, such good actors. But I've still got Rebecca, little Jade – such a sweet girl.'

'And there's Joe... What's happening there?'

'Of course, I've still got my beautiful Betty.'

'Yes, but Joe. What's going to happen?'

Pause. Smile dies.

'I don't know. I've just got back from holiday.'

'You'll be back together, won't you?'

'Don't know.'

'Come on, he's only done a bit of porridge.' Paul's doing a Paxman.

'Pauline doesn't like people who lie.'

The shutters come down. Then praise about cast, dressers, make-up, cameramen, directors, writers, security guards, cleaners. I didn't hear my name mentioned. Maybe I missed it. Maybe it was edited out. Maybe I don't care.

I go for my annual blood pressure test. I'm sitting in the waiting room with only one other person. As on trains, nobody talks. He didn't look like a knife carrying maniac, so eventually I spoke.

181

'What are you here for?' Not too tactful but it just slipped out.

'I've had a heart attack.'

There's me worrying about a needle!

'I'm only forty-five. My dad died of a heart attack when he was the same age. I've just come to get some more medication.'

Forty-five! We sit in silence for a while. Then this sick man speaks.

'You're an actor, aren't you?'

I wish my name would come up on the electric scoreboard; I'm looking forward to that needle now. Nothing. At last I say, 'Yes.'

'You're very good.'

'Not really.'

'It all depends on the writers, doesn't it?'

Wise words. Very wise words.

Writers. Watching *EE*. A spectacularly good episode: Steve McFadden, Jake Wood, Phil Daniels, Sophie Thompson and Charlie Jones – a company episode, the group of them holding half an hour between them. It was written by Sarah Phelps and beautifully directed by Michael Owen Norris. It was wonderful, and made me wonder why there wasn't a group of equally talented people who could create this regularly. But no. Even though Kate Harwood had assured me that she was going to instigate a writing 'school' in which inexperienced writers would be under the tutelage of a senior writer who would teach them how to write soaps. It didn't happen.

People have said that if Dickens were alive during our time, he would be writing soaps. Just imagine! If he were part of *EastEnders*, I would vote for Sarah Phelps, the best of the best, to be on his team and, if he would have him, Michael Owen Morris to direct the scripts. And I would love Steve, Jake, Phil, Sophie and Charlie to be the nucleus of the company, not forgetting, of course, June, John, Derek and Babs.

Back to work. People say, 'Where have you been?' Holiday. No sun-tan, so it's not obvious. Champagne in the dressing room for me. That's what they do when you first get here.

'When's your birthday?'

'Why?'

'There's always a bottle of champagne on your birthday. That's what happens.'

'Oh, thanks.' Terrific. Here it is; I'll take it home.

John Bardon's back from his holiday.

'Have you seen the scripts? Fuck my storyline, it's not right for my character. I'm going up to see Kate.'

Of course, nothing changed. His son, Jake Wood, from his first marriage, will turn up with his wife, Jo Joyner, and two kids, with hidden secrets about John's past. That's the nature of soaps. I doubt if there's anybody in the Square who hasn't got secrets and if they're not out yet, it won't take long for them to be exposed. It only takes a pissy Friday lunchtime. The writers flop back into their comfy office, scratch their heads and mutter in unison, 'Who shall we put the knife into now. Burp!'

The fact is that soaps are full of dysfunctional families. *EastEnders* is packed to the gunnels with them. Peggy and Pat were married to the same man; one of Pat's husbands died – 'driven to his grave, poor sod!', as someone lyrically put it; her children have pissed off, during her leisure time she has been bedding Patrick; in between that, she runs the bookies, is always in the Vic, has a great ear for gossip and the rest of the time is trying to get into the Guinness book of records for fitting the most people possible into a two-bedroomed house. At the latest count it was eight.

Peggy's got a daughter on the run – although, funnily enough, it's a different daughter from the one she started out with – hiding from the police, currently shacked up in South America. Phil, one of her sons, whose wife married someone else and recently died in Spain, has recently got out of prison where he was banged up for murder. The miraculous brief, Marcus, somehow got him out (never quite explained how) and Marcus has now absconded with the money given to him to get his sister to South America – last heard of, I think, in Brazil. It's amazing where two hundred thousand can get you – you can live the life of Riley.

Kevin admits that he's not the father of Kyle and Deano. Kevin's ex-wife turns up in the Square (Why? you might well ask. Never mind, there she is, blond and brassy) obviously a bad lot, and proceeds to have a one night stand with Kevin. Yolande is on the brink of taking her knickers off for Patrick's best friend. There's so much interconnecting it would be tedious to go through all the ramifications but they are ongoing and legion.

All these events must seem preposterous to the current generation. Even if they don't because it's on television (chewing gum for the eyes) things certainly couldn't happen with that ferocity in the real world. It's only in soaps. Or is it?

When I was a kid, in the forties, there was more confusion around than there has been in any soap. Who's your dad? Who's your mum? Who's that man upstairs in the bedroom? Why are the police knocking on the door? These were certainly the kinds of questions that cropped up. And the answers weren't very forthcoming.

I was born on 20th April 1939. Paul, my brother, August 24th 1953. I remember, Bert Beagley, his father, living with us at 4, Buckingham Place. He killed himself when Paul was six months old.

There have been rumours over the years that Bert wasn't Paul's father. Hence the suicide. Muriel had told me that John Lewis Brooks could not have been my father. He had a high squeaky voice, she said, not like yours. But I've smoked all my life, which makes my voice deeper. She wouldn't have it. She was adamant. I began to wonder if John Lewis could be Paul's father. Maybe we were full brothers' despite what Muriel said.

The uncertainty about my parentage was getting me down. Looking at the watercolour by John Lewis Brooks that Joyce Woodhouse had sent me jumbled me up again. I've always enjoyed drawing. It was the one O level certificate that I got. Emma was a great drawer too, so it must have been something that we had inherited. The two books I still have, that John Lewis Brooks gave me, have beautiful, jokey, pen and ink drawings in them.

I decided to have a DNA test done for Paul and me. He agreed, so we each had to have a mouth swab.

We both went to see Muriel, who now lived in South Wales. I thought it would be a good idea for us both to go – two heads are better than one. I messed up on the train tickets. I booked to arrive in Port Talbot, but then discovered she lived in Sandersfoot, so had to re-book to go to Tenby, which was the nearest station to her. It meant waiting in Swansea for an hour and a half to make our connection.

Swansea at 8.30 p.m. We were hungry. The only place to eat outside the station was a twenty-four hour breakfast café. We saw a bunch of drunks trying to pull a post box out of the ground! We had the worst fish and chips we've ever had in a café run by Martians, then wandered back to the station.

Swansea station is lit by 40 watt bulbs. I suppose most of the people wandering around at that time of night don't need any kind of illumination – the glow from their noses must suffice.

The Tenby train was a single carriage. We were exhausted. If it had been a pony and trap we wouldn't have cared. Saundersfoot was a 'request stop', so we didn't have to go all the way to Tenby.

Muriel was amazing, and did she talk. She went back over all the stuff she had told me when I had been to see her in Reading in 1995.

We walked and walked, as she showed us the local sights. We had to struggle to keep up with her, although she was eighty-six. Gradually more things started leaking out. Paul got more animated. He started talking about the accident he had had, being hospitalised and how he thought that he'd changed after that.

'I've seen programmes about how a bang on the head alters your personality.'

Muriel started talking about Bert.

'I'll tell you, but only if you want me to.'

This time mum *thought* she was pregnant, and told Bert that it was his. In her Reading story she had told me that mum *was* pregnant but then lost it. Either way, she *did* go to London and get pregnant by a man called Smith and, either way, poor old Bert thought it was his baby.

Herbert Beagley lived with his mother and worked in the bus company's wages department. Ernie, was mum's driver. Mum was going out with Bert. Whether she encouraged it or not I don't know, but Bert started paying mum and Ernie more overtime than they earned. Fiddling the books. He must have loved my mum. The company found out about his juggling the figures. Bert got the sack. He'd never get a job in an accounts department again. He married my mum, and lived with Rysie and me in our small flat. Rysie doesn't like him. I'm fourteen and he seems to be getting in the way. He must have been at a loose end. Paul's born and then he finds out the truth. The last time I saw him, he said, 'Don't worry, Raymond, you'll never see me again.'

185

Muriel's version is that he confronted Rysie and my mother and threw his wallet on the table.

'That's all you ever wanted from me, so take it.'

He bought a garden hose, drove into the woods in his Ford 8 car, attached the hose to the exhaust pipe, fed the hose through the driver's window and switched the engine on.

There was a report in the *Brighton and Hove Herald*. I was in the flat on my own when the police brought his clothes back. They had been ironed.

I'm not diminishing what happened, but if that was in a 'soap', some people might think it was too far-fetched and silly. Recounting that story sends shivers up my spine. Poor Bert. How desperate he must have been.

When Paul was seven, mum married Ernie and moved to Whitehawk with Paul, leaving Rysie, my godmother, on her own. She was old and ill. My mother found her with her head in the gas oven.

'Rysie was a very bitter woman. She never married and she treated your mother as her daughter. She loved you and I suppose she wanted you both for herself. A jealous woman.' That's what Muriel said.

When she told Paul that Bert wasn't his real father, Paul said, 'All those years I blamed Bert for Ernie coming into my life. I kept thinking that if he hadn't killed himself there wouldn't have been any Ernie. Ernie was so cruel to me. Now I know it wasn't Bert's fault. I didn't realise it at the time. Poor bloke.'

So, a curtain had been lifted on Paul's life.

I'd told Muriel about Joyce's letter, which she didn't think at all important; she believed her own version of events was more truthful. Finally, she dropped a real bomb shell.

'You're dad's name was Smithy, Raymond – Smithy the father. Paul's dad's father.' She was saying that my mother had got pregnant by both the father and the son! And with a fourteen year gap in between! This was madness.

'Vera went to see Rysie, after your mother had married Ernie, and she showed Vera this picture of Smithy. Who does that remind you of? Vera said, "it's Raymond." Vera told me about this.'

Vera! This thirteen-year-old who hadn't gone off to war was the ears of those who had. Muriel was never at home so Vera told her

186

the gossip. After the war, she was still Muriel's ear. Now she was living in a house, which she thought had been bought for her by her grocer lover. She was hardly whiter than white and yet she was the one passing judgement on other people. I loved Vera but I was beginning to think that she wasn't the most reliable of sources.

The day ended with us all going out for dinner. The information about Smith senior was a shock. If it was true, my mother had played the same trick twice: lied to Bert about Paul being his son and lied to John Lewis about me. I assume, she wanted to marry Bert because of his money but that went wrong when he got the sack and then found out that Paul *wasn't* his son. But in the John Lewis case, he was already married, according to Joyce's letter. Therefore, marriage wasn't on the cards, *so why did John Lewis give me his name?*

I went back to the DNA people. There had to be some way of unravelling this chaos. 'We could do a specific test on the Y chromosomes. That is for the father only,' they said.

The first test report I received back from them had said, 'An alleged father is excluded as the biological father if STR markers found on his DNA profile are not shared with the child's. However if the alleged father's profile shares common STR markers with that of the child's then he is not excluded as the true father. A statistical analysis is then carried out to calculate the probability of paternity.'

Not very clear, is it?

The report concluded: 'The results of DNA analysis for this case are INCONCLUSIVE. Based on this result we are unable to determine whether the relationship of Individual 1 (Paul Christian Beagley) and Individual 2 (Raymond Michael Brooks) is that of full or half siblings. This result occurs in approximately 10% of kinship tests...'

So no answers there.

Then the Y chromosome test came back.

Explanation of the Y Chromosome Test:
The Y chromosome is inherited with little or no change through the paternal line from father to son. DNA profiling of the Y chromosome in *male family members* can therefore be used to verify whether individuals being tested are biologically related through the paternal line. When comparing the DNA profiles from the Y chromosome,

males *who are biologically related* in this way will have *practically identical* DNA profiles, while males who are *not related* will have *distinct* DNA profiles.

Interpretation:

A comparison of the haplotypes identified for Individual 1 (Paul Christian Beagley) and Individual 2 (Raymond Michael Brooks) shows a MISMATCH AT 11 OUT OF THE 12 LOCI TESTED.

This result is consistent with the statement that Individual 1 and Individual 2 SHARE TWO DISTINCT LINEAGES, and supports the hypothesis that IT IS UNLIKELY THAT THEY SHARE A COMMON PATERNAL ANCESTOR WITHIN A REASONABLE NUMBER OF GENERATIONS.

So, Paul and I were not full brothers, and it was very unlikely that Smith father and son had anything to do with me.

I still don't know whether John Lewis *is* my father. Similarly, Paul has no way of knowing whether the mysterious Smith family had anything to do with bringing him into this world. The DNA test just compared Paul and me. The only way Paul could find out if he were be related to the mysterious Smith family would be to dig them up.

He does know that he is illegitimate, as am I, I have a hint as to who my father might be but Paul doesn't. All we can both be certain of is that we have the same mother.

My mother's life must have been a switchback ride, in those dark days before and during the war, and I don't blame her for whatever she got up to. We've only got old photographs. If only she had told us about her life. Maybe she was ashamed, but she died when I was forty. I'd been round the block a few times; I'd have understood.

After a lifetime of hiding the truth, she ended up being married to a man who hit her – she never told me about that either – and turned into a little old lady who wouldn't say 'boo' to a goose.

What upsets me more and more is the fact that Rysie really loved me, but all I've heard about her was that she was jealous and bitter. She must have had some redeeming feature. But the more I think about it, none of my family told me anything. Everyone seemed to have loved me but they must have thought that I was deaf and dumb because all their histories are blank pages.

All the scandals seemed to have come from one person: the Mata Hari of her generation, super-spy Aunt Vera. And Muriel was all ears on her visits to Brighton. The stories that had been fermenting in Vera's mind poured out in Cinemascope and Technicolor with embellishments deserving of an Oscar. That's how it seems to me sixty years later. I always loved Vera; she looked like a film star. Honey blonde hair, fire engine red lipstick, bright as a button, fag in the corner of her mouth. It seemed she could do anything. She was a mixture of Veronica Lake and Rita Hayworth. I'm sure men tumbled at her feet. When I saw her in a hospice, she was dying of cancer, yet she still had that spark. Keeping up her theatrical flair, when I asked how a young couple were getting on, she had said 'He'll stick with her. He's still treading the boards, isn't he?' Then she winked.

There's a weight in a family. Like Marley's ghost, you drag it through your life and it never goes away. And here I am, worrying about my own mortality, staring myopically back into the past trying to make sense of it. I thought when I was a kid that my uncle John, who was such a clever and wise man, could probably sum up in a sentence 'the answer to life'. I really thought then that he could, but I realised later that he was as vulnerable as the rest of us. We all get brought down to earth.

22

Monday 7th August – Brighton

Phone call from Tom: 'Wendy's leaving at Christmas, it's all over the papers. Get *The Sun.*' It's the paper for Soap splashes; the rest give a nod and a couple of lines ... maybe.

It certainly is a Big Splash. It makes Wendy almost as Olympic as Esther Williams.

She says it was the 'marriage' that made her decide to pack it in, that marrying again would be 'disloyal' to Arthur (Bill Treacher). She also says that she didn't have the chemistry with me that she had with Bill. Well, fair enough. So the rumours were true.

That same day I was in The Cricketers at lunch time and I got a call from Kate Harwood.

'Sorry I didn't let you know about Wendy leaving before. We'd known for months but decided to keep it under wraps.'

'So, I'll inherit the house?'

'No, Martin owns half of it.'

She wasn't very forthcoming. I couldn't work out why she hadn't told me before, nor even why she was calling me now. I suppose she felt it was her duty as producer – it was bound to affect me one way or the other.

It's all a bit of a mess really. Why didn't they tell Wendy that marriage was on the cards? I remember Wendy saying to me, 'Barbara wants the twenty-first anniversary show but it's going to be the marriage.'

I don't remember her sounding disappointed, so it's a bit confusing. Anyway, I think the whole decision was a miscalculation. We didn't get the cover of *The Radio Times*, which I would have thought was a 'gimmie'. There wasn't much fuss at all and, as far as I know, the viewing figures didn't go through the roof. All in all, it was a damp squib. People weren't that interested. It sunk without a trace.

I can just imagine those jolly writers scratching their heads one Friday afternoon.

One shouts, 'Eureka!

The rest gaze bleary eyed at the noise box. 'How about Pauline Fowler getting married again?'

They all cheer and run back to the bar. That's how it must have been. No thought, just a mad rush to disaster that resulted in one of the major soap stars getting the hump and jacking it in. I feel sorry for her; she must have felt let down.

The following Monday, having had a nice week in Brighton, I'm now back home when the phone rings. It's *EastEnders*. I've got another three weeks off! I calculate that in the last twelve weeks I've worked for exactly six days!

The next few weeks at home stutter along, a mixture of disappointment and elation, almost as if I anticipated this happening: the mood swings, the lack of communication, the grind of the work, and the feeling that I've been the catalyst of all this chaos – which, no doubt, I have. Maybe Steven Grief should have got the part and I could have spent the last year ironing, feeding the cats, washing up, drinking and having lazy afternoons watching *Countdown* and *Deal or No Deal* or drifting off to the land of nod.

Ian McKellen when asked about acting said, 'I've only got three performances: Gandalf, Widow Twanky and then there's me.'

A theatre producer, Peter Bridge, many years ago asked me to take over in a play at the Fortune Theatre. It was called *The Promise*, and starred Judi Dench, Ian McKellen and Ian McShane, all relatively unknown at the time – at least, to me. I declined. I told Peter Bridge I thought that Judi Dench had an irritating voice and the other two were extremely boring. It just shows you what an arrogant prat I was – probably still am. Sorry, Sir Ian.

I spend a lot of time beating myself up – 'not good enough' 'lost it' 'finished' – but I still have to go on; I've got ten months of my contract to run. On the positive side, things will have to change. Wendy's going, and James and Nat – the whole Fowler family wiped out. Will I get a new lease of life? Or will I continue to be chained to that dark house?

192

23

Answers? Or More Questions?

Now I'm back at the coal face, first time since the news.

'You've got a result there, son!' John roars.

Adam, just back from holidays to the Moon or Southend asks, 'What's happening?'

'I don't know.'

'We'd better have a chat soon.'

Barbara tells me: 'They allowed her to do *The Sun* interview and they paid her. The press office insisted on seeing the copy before going to press. They cut fifty quotes. When it came out the writers went mad. Kate was very upset. I don't know how you've been able to stand it all this time...'

It must have been a power struggle – that's all I can think. She must have said, 'You change the marriage situation or I quit.'

They must have said, 'no.'

Wendy lost and had to go. What a horrible situation. But maybe I've got the wrong end of the stick.

The first time back, there's a scene in the Vic: Pauline and I sitting together, in the back of shot. I struggle to think of something to say. When I do it is greeted with the monosyllabic grunt.

Monday 21st

Shock of shocks! Wendy smiling and joking all the way through a laundrette scene. Peter Rose directing, one of Wendy's favourite directors. I can't keep up with this.

These fluctuating moods are driving me crazy. I could accept anything as long as it was consistent. Now we've got Doris Jeckle and Deirdre Hyde.

'She's called Betty ... not that dog. Come here, baby. She needs some water.'

Got a new script, checked through it ... I've got one line! Then a call from the office: 'Rest week from 27th to 3rd. But busy for the next two.'

There's no way I could be less busy; I hardly need a 'rest week'. But do I *want* to be busy? The last few weeks have been ghastly – terrible scripts, even if I had any lines; it's almost worse listening to others saying them than having to say them myself.

I saw Michael Gambon one Sunday afternoon in a *Bergerac*, one of those drifty afternoons when 'chewing gum' for the eyes seems appropriate. During the week they had been showing Denis Potter's *The Singing Detective*, in which Gambon was sensational. How could Gambon be dreadful in *Bergerac* and great in *Detective*? Answer: it's all about scripts. Conclusion: even great actors can be crap in crap scripts. Q.E.D.

Leaving out the word 'great', I've been spouting crap for over a year, mostly in scenes with Doris J. and Deirdre H. In the words of that great director, Peter Wood, it's been like pushing treacle upstairs. Oh, for a *Singing Detective*, or even a couple of *Big Deals*. All I look forward to now is a couple of beers at the end of the day to send me into my nightmare world of stuttering sleep sweating with anticipation of the horrors of the day to come.

Then a call from the office: 'Will you come and see Kate next week?' More sweat and burgeoning cysts. What does she want? Do I care? Of course I do. The old ego needs polishing.

I told Sadie, Will and Tom about the Kate meeting, and my doubts. Text from Will: 'Hope they tell you what you want to hear. If not, balls to them.'

Next Monday I'm called in. Dave Hill has hurt himself and they want me to do his lines. Just filling in a space, you see. Was it beyond their wit to rewrite the scene, spreading the lines around? No, but it saves on paper and why should we flog ourselves to death? Anyway he's under contract. Fucking actors! They just have to turn up and say the lines; *we* have to work.

I phone the office. 'Yes, Kate'll see you after lunch.'

Much coffee, many fags, rehearsing the scene that I'm about to play out with Queen Kate. The only difference is that she knows what the scene is about – I don't.

It could have been so different. If only the company had been happy, and we'd all pulled together to try and make the best of a bad job, how much easier it would have been. How much easier if I'd spent most of my time with June, John and Barbara – a light part, with a tidge of 'gravitas'. I realise that the plots have to swing this way and that but nothing could have been worse than spending all my time in that dark, humourless Fowler house, with Betty and a fruit bowl.

24

The Meeting

There's no usual kiss on the cheek. Kate stands with her back to the window, not quite smiling. No preamble.

'We're going to have to let you go. Sorry.'

It's going to be at Christmas, the calendar Christmas, not a soap Christmas. I then went into my 'rehearsed scene'.

'Well, I have to say that fifty per cent wanted to go and fifty per cent didn't.'

I didn't know whether I was happy or not. I told her I was disappointed with the show, how the writers hadn't served the character well, and if I'd been offered it as a play I would have turned it down. Then she card-sharped me.

'I only came in a few weeks before you. I didn't know how to do things. Sorry.'

Stop saying 'sorry'. It wasn't true. She had come into the show in October, I had started the following June.

'Anyway, you'll have a good pay out.'

That was below the belt. Here is the lady who produced *Twenty Thousand Streets Under The Sky*, that classic adaptation of the Patrick Hamilton novel; a cultured lady, who had worked front of house at The National Theatre, talked enthusiastically about acting and writers, how she was going to instigate a writing school for *EastEnders*, her plans for the show, had taken me into her confidence – all in all, had seemed like a good egg. But now, excuses – not, of course, admitting any culpability, just 'take the money and run'.

'Do. I get the repeats as well?'

The repeats, you'll remember, add eighty per cent to the total. Her eyebrows shot up and there was a half laugh.

'No.' A 'Don't be stupid' look.

I kept thinking what it must have been like for Gerry Cowper, who played Rosie, to have gone through this. Poor Gerry, whom I admire. It must have been a body blow, losing a few years of security. I recall John Bardon's quote: 'It's my pension, son.' All the old stagers trundling along and Gerry, forty-six, with two kids to support and a widowed mother.

'If you want to have a shout at me, I'm here. Sorry,' were the last words that my erstwhile 'friend' said to me as I left.

As I walked back, across that full car park, I felt quite lighthearted. In truth, I couldn't care less – a year of purgatory, at least two attempts already to get out, and here was my escape. I'd failed before, been rejected plenty of times at auditions, I thought that my world was over, but I'd bounced back. Let them stew in their own juice. My background is a very rich mix and I'm happy with what I've done.

I told the boys and Sadie the way it had gone. She was very sympathetic. Text from Tom: 'Whatever the weather, it doesn't really matter. We all love you loads.'

I didn't tell any of the cast, I didn't want all that soporific sympathy: the 'Thank God it's not me getting the chop' crocodile tears; the keeping out of your way in case it's catching. I know some of them have got the elbow before but they don't want to have to join the rat race again. 'It's my pension, son' should be printed on everyone's dressing room door.

A week off and down to Brighton to lick my wounds. I drink copious amounts of beer supplied by Dec, have more beer with Tigs, Mitch and Jon and Dan, cook, watch telly, go to bed and look out of the window in the morning, plan my day, and – yes you're right – have copious amounts of beer supplied by Dec, have more beer with Tigs. Mitch and Jon and Dan. A few days of that and my wounds are healed. Sea air does wonders for you.

Then I get a phone call from Carolyn at *EE*. 'You leave on December the first, with one more day around the fifteenth.'

I ask for an early sight of the scripts.

'They're not ready yet.'

Within seconds, *EE* again: Polly, publicity.

'Do you want me to release the news? (Who gives a fuck if I'm leaving or not? It's hardly a major event in television history.) You see we're worried it might leak.'

'I'll talk to you next week.'

I won't, of course. But it is amazing. I haven't heard from the publicity department for months. But now they're all excited and I can imagine in the background the clacking of needles as they knit my soon-to-be-donned shroud.

I can't pretend that I didn't care about it. That was my problem. If Kate had just given me my cards that day and I could have got in my car and pissed off for good, I would have dealt with it.

'It'll be be like dancing on my grave,' I'd said to her. Little did I know how prophetic that remark was. Give me a shovel and let's get it over with. Instead I have six weeks of ticking off the days, knowing that whatever they give me to say it will be meaningless. I'll be serving my notice. My stupid ego's had a lot of bumps in the past but it's a bit older now and slightly more frail. This'll be a nightmare.

Quotes: 'She thinks she's a star, I'm more famous than her.'

'Don't put that in your diary, they'll never forgive me.'

'I won't be a minute, just going to get a touch of make-up.'

'With all the cracks in her face, it'll take a fucking hour.'

'I saw Shane Richie the other day, as we drove past, standing on the corner, looking scruffy, with a mobile phone glued to his ear. He was probably phoning Hollywood.'

Kind as Christmas this lot can be.

No, it won't be a nightmare – just playing out my time, an end in sight, a future to look forward to. It's been so depressing here anyway, I should be glad. And I am. I won't do what Phil Daniels had said when hearing about Gerry Cowper's exit: 'If that happened to me, I'd just fuck up the lines, so they had to get rid of me straightaway. I wouldn't want to hang around.'

I agreed with him then but now it's different ... it's *my* exit. Third time lucky, as they say.

25

Now the End is Near

It was about this time that Sophie Thompson arrived. She's too sensitive for the back street scrapping that goes on. She looked completely out of place – wide-eyed, just ripe for a kick in the teeth. I'd save her were it not that my time in *EE* is shortening by every glorious tick of the clock. But she comes from tough stock. I'm sure she'll deal with everything they throw at her.

I first met her in the seventies when I was doing *Absent Friends* with her dad and mum. She's now married with two children. When she was doing her first television job, Eric asked me if I could get a VHS recorder so he could tape the show. At that time they were as rare as hen's teeth. I found one. I don't know if he pressed the right buttons because he never reported back. Eric did a lot of voice overs and he narrated *The Magic Roundabout*, so is it any wonder?

I heard that he hadn't been well when I met him at John Wood's recording studios. I was in the reception waiting to do a job when Eric came out. He put his arms round me.

'I can't do it any more, Ray.'

He seemed very upset. John came out of the studio.

'Well done, Eric.'

'No, it was rubbish.'

'It was difficult but you did well.'

I was called in to work. That was the last time I saw him.

Monday 18th

Bump into Barbara. 'What happened with Kate?'

I stay zipped up. 'Something about story lines.'

This is going to be trickier than I thought.

201

The old 'married' couple have go out to Radlett for four lumpy heart-to-heart scenes over coffee and cakes. It was a strange day, out of the confines of Elstree.

Her concentration is fantastic, I've noticed it plenty of times before but it never ceases to amaze me. After all these years she holds onto the lines like a limpet. The scenes were long, with lots of fiddling between takes to top up the frothy coffee. Although quite well written they could have been improved but, as always, this was not encouraged. That suffocating cloth of ether on the brain.

'I watched four *Columbo*s back to back yesterday, but I couldn't finish the fourth because it was about bullfighting.'

Ether, ether.

'John wanted to watch *Midsomer Murders* – he likes the scenery. I watched it in bed.'

My 'wife' was very chatty today.

'I think I'm going to die in the block when there's a fire.'

'But I thought you said that you didn't.'

'Well, if the house is burnt down, where are we going to live?'

This confused me. I've got two months before I go. 'Where are we going to live? A Fowler fire. So here is my wife wondering where we are going to live? I think I've lost the plot here. I've been kicked from pillar to post in this show in terms of our relationship and now, 'where are we going to live?' I don't think I've lived in that accursed house more than a couple of months in the entire time I've been in this show. All very strange. A bit mad.

Then, 'When I leave here I start work two days later.'

'Doing what?'

Pause.

'Then I do something else, then I go on holiday. When I come back I do something else.'

Ether.

You can't tell me that she didn't know the date and how she would exit the show. In other words, the fire was coming up very shortly and, if she had 'jobs' to do they must have dates. Therefore, she must have known the when and how. Not that I cared too much, but I was determined to hold tight, bumpy ride or not. Finally I would escape.

Towards the end of that day, during takes of the final scene, we were both getting tired. Wendy, having most of the dialogue, began to wobble. Start again, a little wobble, start, stop. That's when she whispered to herself, 'Don't let me lose it now.' I'd never heard her voice doubt before. It surprised me but I didn't say anything.

Text from Tom. 'The cat's out of the bag. It's in *The Sun*.' The mole had struck again!

It's The End of The Whine For Joe

EastEnders star Ray Brooks has been axed from the BBC 1 soap, we can reveal. The actor, who plays Joe Macer, will meet an explosive end after nearly a year married to the whinging Pauline Fowler. He will leave in January just weeks after po-faced Pauline is killed off on Christmas Day. Last night a show insider said: 'With Pauline going, there's not much more we can do with Ray's character. Viewers will see him leave in January, it will be a dramatic exit.' The source added, 'Ray's fine with the decision.'

It marks the end of a difficult year for the sixty seven-year-old actor who endured a difficult year with the unhappy *EastEnders* legend Wendy Richard.

Wendy, 63, previously admitted that the pair didn't share the chemistry she had with her first on-screen hubby Bill Treacher. And she told *The Sun* how she quit over Pauline's second marriage ... because she felt that it betrayed her character.

Wendy explained: 'The bosses all thought that we looked good together on the screen. But when I watched it back, I just thought it looked like I was working very hard.

An EastEnders spokeswoman refused to comment last night.

How about that? *The Sun* is first with everything! And reasonably accurate.

I've quoted the article in full because of its lurid, in your face, screaming insults. Fair enough. But how could she feel 'that marriage betrayed her character'? And that she quit because of it? Is that true? It was true that she's leaving. It was true that she didn't seem to be happy being married to me but why did she let it happen in the first place if 'it was going to betray her character'? And why had she been so friendly in the beginning? It is bewildering but it doesn't matter – nobody cares. As they used to say in the old days, 'newspaper is tomorrow's fish and chip paper'.

Monday 2nd

The marriage of Ian and Jane.

The Community Centre. We all troop in out of the rain. That must indicate something. Yes, it's going to be another disaster. We're positioned on rows of chairs, with me at the far end.

I have the occasional line but nothing important, so rarely does the camera dawdle in my area. Jane's mother is in the scene, played by that force of nature Lynda Baron. Lynda had been around for a couple of weeks but I hadn't seen her. But here she is, all guns blazing.

She and June had won a couple of alternative gay awards in the West End.

'Beat Judi Dench, dear.' And they both roared.

There were a few sniffy faces around but I'd rather this than the gloom and 'what time's lunch' attitude. They reminded me of Barbara and Muriel, two pub landladies in Brighton – always as smart as tarts on holiday and sitting on stools at the bar.

'I'll have a large G and T with you, Raymond,' they'd say as they waved blazing cigarette holders and nearly singed the optics.

Lynda reminded me that we'd worked together in *Edmund Gurney and the Brighton Mesmerist* starring Richard Todd.

'He was so small, wasn't he, darling.'

Lynda is obsessed with big and small. They were putting marks on the floor for her.

'You'll have to make the "grouchos" bigger, darling. I can hardly see over my tits.'

She's just like that Joyce Grenfell song: 'Stately as a galleon she glides across the floor, Doing the military two step as in the days of yore.' Definitely more stately as a galleon in high seas and certainly from the good old 'yore' days.

The director was having trouble shooting the scene. There were row upon row of actors and extras; most of the kids in the series were present and the Community Centre isn't that big. With lamps banging fierce light down everywhere, the place was getting hot and airless, the chair-shuffling, the occasional deep roar of a tummy rumble from Derek Martin ('What time's lunch?'), June, Lynda and I looking for opportunities to nip out for a fag, Steve taking no interest in the proceedings at all, signing hundreds of *EE* photos that could have been shot by a one eyed drunk, kids wanting to go to the toilet, Babs winking prettily at me with a sympathetic smirk, the director pulling his hair out and the cameramen picking their noses, it was going to be a very long day.

The wedding chaos had been scheduled for one day but we had to come back next morning for some 'pick ups'. There was a lot of moaning about that.

The next morning the director sees me hovering around, grabbing a last minute fag.

'I don't know how you do it.'

'What?'

He puts his hand on my shoulder, then he looks around furtively. 'To be honest, I don't know how I'm going to get through this week.'

Poor sod! It's the hardest job in the world. A lot of them, who seem to get through on a wing and prayer, have one golden rule: if, on the out shot of a scene, they haven't a clue who to linger on, they plump for any character who has been in the series for at least six or seven years. As Marcus Plantin, the producer who wrote the hand book, had said, 'You're a star. Every time we cut to you it's money in the bank.'

I'm not saying they ever cut to me for the end shot, but in *EE* the mantra was, 'Linger on the money'.

Then Lynda Baron left. The few hours that I'd watched her seemed to bring everything into focus. She and Barbara are of the 'eyes, teeth and tits' brigade. John Bardon, if he'd got the third element, could have joined them. Pam Cundell and I could cuddle from here to Christmas and June is so rich in background it's inclined to make me dizzy.

They are walking and talking nostalgia. Monuments to the days when laughter and hard work were inseparable. I hope the good Lord keeps them around forever. If I was in a Court of Law, up before the beak, and asked to prove what I have written in this memoir, I would need people like them as witnesses. They are the ones who were there at the time I was. So many are long gone, too many to name here, and I mourn them.

Nostalgia can be a double-edged sword. Sadie and I are doing our Saturday morning trip to Waitrose and, as usual, we listen to *Sounds of the Sixties* on Radio 2. The DJ, Bryan Mathews, says, 'Now we have a request for a record which was the title music for a film released in 1962 called *Some People*.'

My ears prick up. I was in that, it was my first big part.

'It's sung by Valerie Mountain and The Eagles. It starred David Hemmings.'

I didn't say anything to Sadie. I suffered in silence. What about me? I screamed in my head. But no – air brushed out, unrecognisable, not worth mentioning, ego sunk.

I don't like Bryan Mathews anymore. He never plays my record; nobody ever requests it; sunk without a trace. Who needs Radio 2 anyway?

There was an extremely heartening article in *The Guardian* the other day. Have you ever heard of Mingering Mike? Just as Robert Cochrane discovered my old album in a secondhand record shop in Manchester, a gentleman called Dori Hadar found thirty albums credited to soul superstar Mingering Mike in a flea market in Washington DC.

The covers were hand painted, all released by record companies that no longer exist. Titles like 'Boogie Down at the White House' and 'On The Beach With the Sexorcist'. There were elaborate sleeve notes, and some were shrink wrapped with old price tags still attached.

When he slid the records out of their sleeves, instead of vinyl he found cardboard discs with the grooves painted on. When Mike was tracked down, it was discovered that he had stored all his records and general paraphernalia in a lock-up garage. When he fell behind with the rental payments he decided to get rid of everything.

If he hadn't nobody would ever have found out about this extraordinary man, the soul superstar who made records nobody could play. Only in America. There's a lesson there somewhere. I'm the only man to appear in *EastEnders* who wasn't really there! That's the way it feels to me.

Monday October 9th

A maximum of forty days to my exit. This is going to be difficult. It will be like treading very choppy water.

As my 'hindsight' is but a millisecond behind my 'now', maybe I should keep in mind that I should enjoy the chaos, the moods, the mistakes (if they're mine, they won't be able to sack me), the flare-ups, the wall-to-wall half truths, the uncomfortable trousers. I'm likely to be a danger on my homeward journeys on the North Circular because I'll be laughing uncontrollably.

Tuesday

Lots of scenes. Rushing around. I'm asked to make a contribution to Kate Harwood's leaving tape. I had wondered what all the the other actors had been doing all day, some with flour over their faces, some being so sincere, all directing their various antics towards some geezer with a hand held camera. I declined.

Later I thought I wasn't being fair. I know she'd had sacked me but most of the time she'd been friendly and I didn't want to be churlish. However when I looked for the geezer with the camera, he'd disappeared, probably trying to get June and John to do hand stands in the Square. Then I had a call from the office. Would I like to go to an Awards Ceremony? Dear, oh dear! Why can't they just leave me alone to grind out all this turgid toffee?

Wednesday

Out in the Square and it's pouring down. A lot of head-scratching by the production team. They don't mind rain but this is really heavy.

They decided to do the scene with me and Babs in the Minute Mart. Rain, rain and more rain. Babs has to come in from the street; umbrellas everywhere; little Babs so obscured I could just see her feet.

Me standing in the Minute Mart surrounded by stale chocolates and rock hard baguettes.

'Action!'

Umbrellas are whipped away and Barbara explodes into the shop, hits her mark, starts – and then we stop.

'Sorry, somebody was walking through the back of the shot.'

Umbrellas up and Barbara disappears.

'Action!'

Umbrellas away. Off we go. We stop. Something else has gone wrong.

Umbrellas up.

'Action!' Umbrellas away. This routine was repeated a number of times – problem here, problem there, the usual crap that happens when everybody's in a state.

'I don't know what's the matter with me,' Barbara says. 'I'm finding the words difficult. It's doing all these episodes – I get confused.'

I know what's the matter: she's tired. It must be exhausting. She's like a lot of them: worn out, wrung out. It's understandable. I've only been here for minutes, compared to their hundreds and hundreds of hours, and I'm already a candidate for the knacker's yard.

Back in my dressing room I've started packing my stuff in bags to ease the carrying on the last day. It is amazing what you accumulate over a year or so.

Richard Briers told me a story about Paul Eddington. They worked a number of times together in the West End. Richard said that on the first day in their designated theatre he was convinced Pickfords had been around.

Paul's dressing room was full of personal stuff: paintings, ornaments, family photographs, lucky mascots, a comfy armchair. I think he stopped short at curtains. The point was that it had to be Pickfords, or someone with an enormous van, because he could hardly have brought all that stuff on the tube.

It would have been awful if the show had closed after a couple of weeks. Imagine having to whip all that stuff out again. But it never happened; Paul had instinct.

I have a cardboard box of old photographs and had been attempting to complete a photograph album. I don't know about you, but the minute I catch a glimpse of old snaps I can't stop myself rummaging. I find old photos very comforting. It's a part of your life that you can't quite hold on to any more. Most of them have my mum, Rysie, me, Paul, Muriel or Vera in them, but there's a lot of people I don't recognise. I assume people in those days weren't as cavalier about taking shots as they are today. Cameras were costly, film was expensive to process. Therefore, the subjects must have been carefully selected. But still there are these mysterious people.

The phone rings. 'Ray, they want you for your scene now.'

They always say that – even if you've got only one line it's 'your' scene.

It's one of those classic soap scenes, the confrontation between two angry women. In this case it's Babs and Wendy – no love lost. Babs is angry because (a bit of tedious plot here) Pauline's closed down Martin's fruit and veg stall and basically told him that, whatever happens, he can't have it any more.

All I had to do was dive out of the Vic when the row reached a crescendo, exit when Mrs Fowler completely loses her rag and starts hurling grapefruit at me, Babs, Martin and Sonia. But, having looked at all those black and white photographs, and remembering the sounds I heard as a little boy, this scene between the two of them – face slapping, calling each other 'cows' and with accusations like 'You've ruined your children's lives...', 'Who did you have your last affair with?' (all the clichés) – was magical. I have to wait inside the Vic, just nip out for the grapefruit moment. Barbara has to wait inside as well before the kick off. She's not as chatty as normal.

It's a tricky scene: storming out, hitting a mark, putting weight on her right foot to make sure that she's in full view of the camera for the over shoulder shot, avoiding putting a shadow over Mrs Fowler's face; then, halfway through the scene, crossing over, taking up Wendy's mark, now having to put her weight on her left foot for the over shoulder shot from the opposite side.

All this leaping around, weight this way and that, and loads of dialogue, plus all the light aircraft from the nearby private airfield that messes up the sound boys' sensitive ears makes life very tricky. No wonder little Babs was pacing up and down, muttering her lines. It's late, she's tired and this is a big mountain to climb.

I've got an old photo of my Aunt Vinnie (Lavinia), a sad creature whose life, for no reason of her own, spiralled out of control. She worked in a hospital at the end of the war and fell in love with an anaesthetist. I don't even know his name.

They got married, they had a daughter and Vinnie suffered from post-natal depression. I don't think they had a name for it back then. Her husband had her put in a mental hospital. After she'd been there for a couple of years, he divorced her and moved away. My grandparents and her sisters and brothers tried to get her released but the law was that only husbands could sanction that. So she had to stay there year after year.

Eventually the law was changed, allowing her parents the right to insist on her release. By that time Vinnie had changed. She mourned the loss of her child, and nobody knew where the husband and daughter had gone. She started shoplifting, got drunk and was put in the police cells overnight; got married again to some wastrel, was miserable, and came back to her parents' house.

This poor, unhappy woman got worse and worse. Eventually she had to go back into a mental hospital. One snowy Christmas some carol singers sang outside the hospital and the patients came into the porch to listen. When it was over, they all went back in, only to discover that Vinnie was missing. The staff searched for her in the heavy snow, couldn't find her and gave up. They found her next morning, in her nightdress, tangled up in the netting of a hockey goal. She'd died of exposure.

Watching Babs pacing up and down, trying to get her lines straight, I remembered a photo I'd just seen of Vinnie. She and Babs had that same intensity, vibrancy and striking good looks. Vinnie's hair was dark and Babs is blonde, but the similarity was unmistakable. Vinnie died tragically, but Babs bats on.

The scene went well, the grapefruits flying through the air in an utterly convincing manner. Then all the actors said goodnight and disappeared. It was 10.30 p.m.

'Right, move the cameras to the Fowlers' back door. We should have time to get this bit in.' The director sounded triumphant. 'Ray?'

I hadn't been dismissed. You have to wait to be told.

'Just want to try and get your shot in outside the back door.'

It was a standby scene, one that they really never expected to get to. I scrambled through the script pages in my back pocket. Yes, here it was.

'Wendy's tired, so, if you wouldn't mind, Jamie will read in her lines.'

It's me outside having an argument with her inside. I look at my watch. Nearly 10.45.

210

'We should have time.' I kept the script out of shot and read it. I have to say Jamie was very good.

My final line was, 'All right, I'll break the door down!'

I threw my shoulder against it.

'Cut.' We wrapped at 11 o'clock.

I didn't burst through that door, in the studio, until a week later. That's *EastEnders*.

26

Door Acting and Peripheral Vision

A few days off then back, a lot of big scenes to do, screaming and shouting at Brown Owl. And finally, of course, the famous 'burst through the door'. I'm called down to the studio, only to have to wait for a Babs and Wendy scene to be completed. Babs sees me. She's not happy.

'I had all the rabbit. It was a nightmare. Stopping and starting.' She was shaking. 'I'm glad it's over.'

Now I'm on. I wasn't looking forward to it after what Babs had said. It was going to be a rocky day.

The stunt man greets me.

'Now, Ray, I've put mats down inside the door. They'll break your fall.'

'What fall?'

'When you crash through the door you fall into the kitchen. Let's try it.'

They lock the kitchen door.

'Action.'

I throw myself at the door. It doesn't budge – the set wobbles but the door stays where it is.

'That's not going to work. Let's have the door on the latch.'

'Action.'

The door flies open, I enter like a ballet dancer on ice, attempt my dying swan act and fall on the mat like a sack of wet cement. The director is scratching his chin.

'Errr...'

'Look, do I have to fall over? Can't I just bang through the door, while you put on a bit of breaking wood sound. After all, I'm supposed

213

to be a builder. Aren't builders supposed to be strong? I'm mean. Would a builder fall over? Can't I just hurt my shoulder? Just a bit more realistic.'

My real reason is that I don't want to look like a complete prat. He grunts; the house grunt is catching, but this one's a sort of thinking noise.

The stunt man jumps in. 'I think it would work!'

The director agrees. He has to – it's two against one now. So I bang through the door, a pretty good stagger (if I say so myself), holding my shoulder, in builder's fashion. Wendy's in the doorway looking shocked. I give her a builder's look, then…

'Cut. Check it.'

Now a big scene. She's giving me the wedding ring back.

'I never wanted to marry you in the first place.' Never were truer words spoken in the long history of *EE* histrionics. I look depressed (good acting that), then I start smashing the place up. Shocked Brown Owl. While I'm sweeping all the photos off the sideboard, she bashes me across the side of the head with a dinner plate.

'Here's the "stunt" dinner plate, Ray. Have a feel of it.'

It's bloody hard, like a real one.

The AD is apologetic. 'The fake one was a bit too soft. It wouldn't have looked real.'

I tap it on the side of my head. It's very hard.

'It's the best we could do.'

The stunt man is trying to be helpful. 'How's your peripheral vision, Ray?'

Ah, that. The rest of the vision, sans glasses, very blurred. In the film *The Daleks Invasion of Earth 2150*, with Peter Cushing as Dr Who, I had to throw a Bowie knife at a cyberman. I'm so blind I almost take the cameraman's head off! And in *On The Razzle*, at The Lyceum in Edinburgh, in a quick scene change in the dark, climbing onto a pantomime horse with young Felicity Kendal, I was so myopic I nearly lost my foot as two bits of scenery clamped together.

'Yes, the periphery's fine.' I know what it is but I've never had to use it.

Of course, my 'periphery', fingers crossed, will suffice but will Brown Owl be up to the stunt? Or, to put it another way, will she want to wipe me out while she's got the chance? ('Oh, sorry, I slipped on a cable. He's not dead, is he?')

I'm not worried about the two and half pages of dialogue now, just whether the 'periphery' will be up to speed and quick enough to avoid the lethal blow? This is a dangerous moment.

'Action!'

The wedding ring business. I'm watching the eyes of my potential murderess, then I leap up – dialogue, dialogue – smash all the photos off the mantelpiece, storm across the Fowlers' lounge to the sideboard, more photo business: now the plate. Whoosh! And I avoid it, and fall out of shot.

'Cut!'

Did it! Did it! I give my 'periphery' a cuddle – well done, my dear friend!

Then...

'We're going to have to go again. Sorry.'

Shit!

It takes them ten minutes to put the set back together again. I'd rather be at the dentist having a root canal session.

'OK, stand by.'

I want to be at home watching *Deal or No Deal* or popping pimples – anything but this ... again!

'Action!'

Everything is going smoothly: the ring, a good sad look from me, photos flying with serious venom off the mantelpiece; now, full of cofindence, I launch myself at the sideboard with abandon. Maybe I wasn't focusing on the climax of the scene, getting too excited; whatever happened, the periphery wasn't in gear and clunk! I fell out of shot as if I'd been hit by a sledgehammer. I wasn't dead but it felt like it.

'Check it.' Not my head, naturally, just the shots.

'OK, good. Next scene.'

I didn't ask for a nurse or a doctor, or even an ambulance to rush me to *Holby City* – I thought anything would be better than Robert Powell tucking me into bed.

There was a dull ache. I must have a hard head. One more scene to do then I can go home. Brighton tomorrow.

Chat, chat, chat.

'Check it.'

As I walk back to my dressing room, the producer rushes over.

'You all right, Ray?'

'Well, if I'm rushed into hospital tonight I'll be suing you lot for a few million.'

A nervous laugh from the lady; they're all hanging on by their fingernails.

'Anyway,' she says, changing the subject, 'you've got some big stuff coming up.'

'What?'

'Oh, I can't tell you.'

What? What? Brain spinning. Oh, well, it doesn't really matter. That was my last run in with Mrs Pauline Fowler. Poor old Bill Treacher must still have nightmares and headaches: she hit him with a frying pan!

Driving back in the car, I couldn't help thinking what an amazing experience it had been. I suppose that all my years in this crazy business must have prepared me for the battering *EE* dished out. Just not the plate.

All this while feeling sorry for myself but in full employment – money every week, or nearly. Ninety-nine per cent of Equity members would break their legs (or anyone else's) just to get their noses round the door. Here's me, clogged up in traffic on the North Circular, wondering if it's time to apply for a bed in the Bill Treacher Home for Retired and Damaged Mr Fowlers.

What a mixed up prat I am! In The Greyhound pub I get talking to Laura, who works behind the bar. Her twenty-two-year-old brother, nearly five years in the army, having done one term in Northern Ireland, is about to start his second term in Iraq. Each term in Iraq lasts five months and twenty-nine days. Why? Because if they did six months they wouldn't have to pay tax. Shorten term by only a few days and they have to find £4,500 in tax. The American soldiers get their mortgages paid and pay no tax at all. Their base has a swimming pool, tennis courts and an ice hockey rink. The Brits have nothing.

There's me: make up put on, a dresser who puts my clothes in my room, and all I have to do is fanny around on the set trying to remember my lines. No bombs are going to blow me up, I'm not the target of any snipers. The only thing I can say in my defence is that they don't have to be a Mr Fowler. (Right, Bill?)

They tell me I've got a week off. Next thing, no I haven't. I'm needed Wednesday, Thursday and Friday.

Wednesday 25th October

There's a 'Goodbye' book for Brown Owl, MBE. Jackie, Help Desk ask me to sign it. Wrote: 'I wish you'd have learnt plate spinning instead.' I wonder if that'll be sussed. Maybe a bit too subtle.

Now she's going, there'll be a big hole here in terms of familiar faces. Natalie, James, Jessie Wallace, Shane Ritchie, Kacey Ainsworth, Nigel Harman, Letita Dean, Hilda Braid, my old mate Gerry Cowper – all have gone. That was a strong core.

There's certainly a feeling around the place that the show won't have the same impact any more. Of course, there's still June, John, Babs, Lacey, Pam, Charlie and Steve, but they can't be on screen all the time. The new people aren't bedded in yet, the audience don't really know them. Maybe the viewers will feel let down. Or since television is chewing gum for the eyes, perhaps it won't matter. 'The king is dead, long live the king'. Ena Sharples and Pat Phoenix left Corrie, but did it matter?

Glimpsed Brown Owl – flowers everywhere, her last day. I hoped all the gifts were genuine.

New scripts, here we go.

The crematorium ... three days! 'Mrs Fowler's final exit. A raven looks down on the unhappy mourners, it screeches and takes off into the darkening sky.' Four ravens are booked, and trainer.

The first raven does it in one take!

'Better than the fucking actors.'

And then the police arrive! You can't have a normal funeral, not in soap land. They take the body away for a post mortem. Screaming from Adam and James, breast beating all round.

'They're not cutting up my mum!'

June faints. Mo mutters something like 'It's all a bit fishy.'

In the next script Martin sees a wreath on 'Arfur's bench'. It's from me. Turns to Sonia: 'I know who murdered my mum.' Dum, dum, dum. But I was away at Christmas. (Joe, I mean, not me.) I've just

217

got back to the Square for the funeral. What does this mean? Oh, dear. I'm planning my alibi already.

This is becoming like an Agatha Christie plot. Who did this dastardly crime? I don't know. She just collapsed in the Square, in the snow, on Christmas night.

'I must insist, constable, that I was spending Christmas with my daughter. Remember? It was in the script. If you don't believe me, give her a call. She'll back me up.'

'No, Pauline wasn't very nice to me but I got the feeling that things might improve. I know she threw the ring back at me. That upset me, I must admit. I did get angry and smashed the place up. But when she bashed me with the plate, it knocked some sense into my thick old noddle.' (Sob.)

'Yes, the last time I saw her, constable, was that night and, as I turned to go, I said to her, "You broke my heart." Then I laughed but it wasn't a pub laugh, it was a sad laugh, ironic, I think you might call it. You can ask her if you like... Sorry, she's a gonner, isn't she? But, trust me, I felt "ironic" and sad, so sad that I said again, "You broke my heart." Then I left. That was the last time I saw her. Honest, constable.'

But will this boy in blue believe me? I don't know.

The three days at the crematorium are dismal. There seem to be hundreds there. Every extra that has appeared over the twenty odd years is kitted out for the mourning.

The troops were getting restless at some point and were herded into the chapel to chew their sandwiches and swig down their tea.

It was a miserable, moaning occasion. They seemed to have been hanging round for ages and although generally they don't mind – it's the nature of the job – they were uncomfortable in their ties and their unfamiliar frocks and all the waiting was getting tiresome.

So, there was grumbling and a general hubbub of discontent. In the midst of this is Adam (Ian), striding up and down, punching a fist in the palm of his hand, building himself up for the next scene: the confrontation with the police who are going to take 'auntie Pauline's body' to the mortuary! The discontented murmuring continues; Adam's concentrating, punching away, working up a real frenzy.

Suddenly, he stops, glares at the fed up extras and screams, 'Shut

218

up, you lot. I'm trying to concentrate. I've got an emotional scene to do. Shut up!' Very Actor's Studio. I'm glad now that I didn't get in. Much too tense for the likes of me.

Next morning it's raining. Barbara, having queued up for her breakfast in the drizzle, slips down the metal steps after collecting it from the hatch in the food wagon and takes a tumble. She is taken to hospital, having damaged her ankle and wrist.

I think, if she's not going to be able to film, as I'm sitting directly behind her in the congregation, they won't need me. I'm waiting to be sent home, very happy, though not for Babs, of course.

No chance. They stick someone else in Barbara's gear and a blonde wig and plonk her in front of me. The only problem is that she's about a foot taller than Babs. Does that stop them? Not on your life! They track up and down the aisle, do a wide shot of the congregation – 'It'll all come out in the edit.' I suppose it did because nobody said anything. But I didn't get my early doors.

The raven flew, Dot fainted, actors and extras in black grew more and more miserable and, finally, it was over.

The minibuses took us back to the studio. The ravens were returned to their cages. It's dark and dismal, the traffic is appalling and over the horizon are more histrionics. Then Sonia gets arrested.

'Another fucking funeral,' dear old John says, darkly.

27

'Not Another Funeral!'

Diederick Santer, our new executive producer, calls me up to the office.

'You killed Pauline.'

'Did I?' Nobody had told me.

'We don't see you do it, of course.'

'Oh.'

'Later, you fall out of a first floor window and die. We'll get you a stunt man.'

'Thanks.' I don't want to be in a wheelchair for the rest of my life.

'We didn't tell you earlier because we didn't want any Machiavellian acting.'

Diederick is obviously a very intelligent man if he uses phrases like 'Machiavellian acting'. I know he produced a classic series on BBC 1, probably adapted by Andrew Davies. Anything that Andrew writes is classic. If he wrote on a toilet wall the authorities would immediately 'list' the urinals. He has a reputation for 'loosening up' the text. If he wrote an episode of *EE* he'd have Dot stripping off and bonking Phil Mitchell. Now that *would* be a classic.

Diederick is also very tall. So was Kate Harwood who, incidentally, has moved on from *EE* to an enormously high-powered post within the BBC, so that's my television career over.

But, as the great Max Miller said when, having gone over his allotted twelve minute slot at The Royal Command Performance and Sir Bernard Delfont told him he'd never work for a Moss Empire theatre again, replied, 'You're £100,000 too late, Mr Delfont.' Similar with me, Kate.

In my experience, all producers are tall; it seems to give them psychologial power. All except Alan Yentob, who is quite small.

I left dear Diederick and crossed the car park back to my dressing room. Under normal circumstance, having been 'tipped the black spot', my chin would have been on the floor. But not this time. Bouncing and full of beans, I was going to be free. All my dreams had come true!

Dave Hill came up.

'What did he say?' (I must have told him about the meeting.)

'Oh, story lines, you know.'

Not a lie but I thought I'd better keep 'my good news' to myself as long as possible.

But not all TV deaths are 'good news'.

An example was be Geoffrey Palmer's demise in *Death of an Expert Witness*. The tragedy of this was that he was the only person in the cast I really got on with. Not that they were boring but they developed an arrangement whereby after the day's filming, the cast would assemble in the bar of the Nelson Hotel in Norwich, then decide where they would all go out to eat.

This corporate activity didn't appeal to Geoff and me. We stayed in our rooms until the coast was clear, then the two of us would shoot off for a curry. Terrific! But the script said that I had to kill him in the second episode and there were five more to go. Geoff went back to London and I was lumbered with meals on my own for the next ten weeks. It's no fun being a killer, particularly if you kill a friend who liked curry.

And now, Pauline Fowler, MBE. I suppose if I'd stayed round a bit longer I could have dispatched Betty. Poor little sausage, it's not her fault.

More scripts greet me. Now I know that I've killed her; the great writers have gone mad. First I'm found on my knees by Arfur's bench, which is festooned with tributes to Mrs Fowler. I read Dot's card and weep!

Then, at a New Year's party, I get pissed ('We can edit it, don't worry') and my final line is: 'The witch is dead!'

Then a scene in the Vic. I kick off. Martin, hearing about my slagging off Pauline, still tries to be mature and console me. He invites me to the funeral. (By this time, we've shot all that, but, when we did, I didn't have a clue about these scenes.) I say to him, 'The only reason I'll come is to make sure they've nailed down the lid!'

Nice old Joe has turned from a kind, sad and loving person into a screaming maniac. There's no subtlety in those quills upstairs.

Three weeks and one day to go. The one day is the stunt, falling out of the window. A few more days wandering around, then to Brighton.

There's a lot to do when I come back. Dot 'Miss Marple' Cotton has to wheedle the truth out of me over many interminable scenes.

Still, they are with June – what a glorious way to leave.

28

Winding Down – Nearly

A few days with the final scripts. The last waltz with June, then the exit out of the window. One last day, a week later, to shoot my collapse into Bridge Street outside my favourite pub, The Queen Vic. Dead as mutton.

It's a load of stuff to get into my head – the perennial problem – but I have got time.

Tuesday, Wednesday and Friday – just four days before they arrive with a bang.

Friday 24th October
Do usual stuff. A few drinks, sit down with my scripts. Try to snooze. Difficult, with lines whirling around in my head, unconnected like a nightmarish kaleidoscope.

Saturday 25th
Weekend shopping in Waitrose, jousting in the aisles with wheeled baskets driven by women with squabbling children. Very few of these women's husbands are ever there. Can they all be widows? Will phones: Fulham lost 1–0 at Reading. '...but tried hard.' Maybe I'll have that on my gravestone.

Evening. Script, script, script. Thirty-two scenes. Some like lightly scrambled eggs on hot buttered toast, simple and easily digestible, others like a bath full of octopus liver and bats' testicles stew, thick and gooey, through which June and I, with leaking wellies, wade manfully, waiting for the director to shout 'Cut!' and praying for him not to say, 'Let's try another one.' I go to bed with a headache.

Sunday 26th

Two days to go to my demise. At eight o'clock the Sunday papers crash through the letterbox onto the mat. A very Sunday-like hour. Get breakfast, flick through the papers; nothing's going into my noddle apart from Fulham's 'gutless defeat'!

Will and his rose-coloured spectacles!

Scripts, scripts, scripts, pub with Colly, scripts, scripts, scripts, snooze. Exhausted.

Watched *Cathy Come Home* on BBC 4 in the evening. It's part of the BBC's warm up for their updated *Cathy* which is to be on BBC 1. The original was shuffled off into the backwoods.

I do see the updated version – the conceit of this concept! Why did they have to connect it to the original? It could never match up; people's memories are too strong. It's place in history is assured.

I hadn't seen the original *Cathy* for ages. I was suprised – I was good. I had a similar experience many years ago when I seemed to be working solely in the theatre and I got an offer of a part in *Rumpole of the Bailey*. When I finally saw that I was equally suprised to find I was better than I thought I had been.

But all that was then; this is now. *Then*, on my first day I was in a blue funk about having to do eight lines and salsa dancing, but *now* I'm running a marathon with June 'Zatopec' Brown. When you're young you get fed up, so you go out and kick a ball around with your mates and you forget all about it. Later it's depression, so you go and get pissed, pass out and wake up with a banging head. You've forgotten about your depression, now you've just got a stinking hangover. Very much later, you just feel old – and there's no cure for that. In bed I resolve to take up philosophy when I dive out of *EE*.

Monday 27th

Last day of freedom. Miss Zatopec phones me. She's never phoned me before!

'We must talk tomorrow, Ray.'

I think I might have said, 'Right.' But I can't be sure.

When she phoned it was a shock and what she said worried me even more. I rushed to the scripts, searching for answers. I didn't find any.

Went to the pub with Dave. Pints and a few tinctures of Baji Rosa, back to Noel Edmunds' laughter and tears, then a snooze.

I knew my lines – of course I knew my lines. Nothing to worry about.

Tuesday 28th

June tells me why she phoned.

'I'm finding the lines difficult.'

She's finding them difficult! This is impossible, she's got a laser-like mind.

'I just say the odd word. You rabbit on and then I have to pop in for a word or two. I'm worried I'll say the wrong thing, come in at the wrong time. I find these scenes very difficult.'

I try to console her. 'You'll be fine.'

'I'm worried.'

'It'll be all right.' This is ridiculous. Me, trying to calm the great Brown. She worries because she wants to get things right. A lesson to us all: *Brown. 28. 06.*

Kellie Shirley collars me in the corridor. She saw *Cathy.* Her enthusiasm knows no bounds.

Just three 'scrambled eggs on hot buttered toast' scenes with June. Smooth as silk. No worries there.

Wednesday 29th

In very early. Mountains to climb. Eight scenes of enormous proportions and a load of regurgitation to be done. Regurgitation of lines, that is – repeating what you've taken in. I've learnt the lines, so I must be able to repeat them. That's how actors work. Ha!

After spending the morning recalling my lines, I was ready to have a lie down in my dressing room.

'Let's have lunch, Ray.'

June wanted to talk about the afternoon's scenes.

The canteen. Full of cameramen, props, dressers, all the miscreants who were saving themselves for the evening's boozing. June batted away those who wanted to join us.

The glorious June wanted to 'run the lines' between mouthfuls of her lunch. I survived on a cup of coffee, desperate to run out and have a fag, but my respect for her kept me 'regurgitating' the lines, my memory of which seemed to diminish the more we went over them.

Lunchtime over, we went back to the coal face. I was getting ever more weary but I attempted to stick to my task. I failed occasionally but desperation pulled me back on track. Tomorrow is a day off. I just hope we've got a couple of AA batteries to stick into my brainbox for Friday.

Thursday 30th

A headache day. The builders start on our roof so there's a lot of tea flying around. A lot of 'You're in...', 'Can I have a picture for my...', etc. The clock says 12.30. It's a bit early but I go to the pub. Nice. Wander home, men all over the roof. Need kip and also need to look at the script. Five scenes and not all easy by a long way. Sadie's out tonight, so I'm going to make a delicious curry. Sadie doesn't like my concoction and this is an opportunity to indulge myself. I won't give you my recipe it may not be entirely to your taste!

Anthony Worrall Thompson has a restaurant near us. I looked at the menu outside. 'Fresh diver caught scallop, guacamole, crème fraîche and a dribble of curry essence.' This is a starter at £7.99. I thought they must have left the 's' off scallop. So we decided to go in – I love scallops.

My starter arrives and it is *one* scallop! One scallop costs around 65p in Waitrose. Maybe it's not 'Fresh Diver caught' but you can't tell me that Anthony Worrall calls up a diver and says, 'Get us another scallop, Mr Walker (he's the famous diver who shored up Winchester Cathedral – bit of history for you), we've got another mug here.'

My curry was delicious, though I made too much, as always. Strong enough for the full taste but not such as to give us a dodgy tummy tomorrow. Have sweet dreams of my friend, Mr Patak.

Friday 1st of December

I get a car in. It's very early. Five scenes to do. Not as many as Wednesday but thicker and trickier. It's my last dialogue day – about eighteen months after my first. Time has flown. Mixed feelings: I'll miss some of them but there are others who don't deserve a flicker.

I must mention Laurie Brett (Jane), whom I've grown to admire over my time here. A vastly sentimental lady and an amazing drinker (though that's only what other people have told me. I've never tested the veracity of that rumour). But a terrific attitude towards her family. She sees her good fortune – getting a rôle in *EE* – as a way of helping them. I wish her as long a stay in *EE* as she needs, so that eventually she will be able to secure her own life too.

At last, June and I start rehearsing. Within ten minutes, the lights begin to flicker, so we are sent off for an early lunch. I don't need this.

Canteen. Run lines, between mouthfuls, looking at my watch. I've got bunches to remember and all this 'running' is not helping.

Eventually, they found a shilling for the meter and normality was restored.

Scene 1154/27. It's virtually all me for four pages, during which I have to quote Pauline – the things she says to me like: 'Stop snivelling. What kind of man are you? You don't know how pathetic you look. Face it – you don't want a wife, Joe, you never have. You don't even want a mother. You want an owner. You want me to feed you and tickle you under the chin. You want to curl up against me, like you're some sort of Betty, and it makes my skin crawl.'

You can hear her saying it, can't you? I certainly can because I've heard similar remarks.

Before we launch into this scene, June says, 'Do you want something?' She sounded just like Bernie the barber in Brighton, except without the addition of '...for the weekend?' What June is referring to, of course, is the famous Menthol crying stick. Every time I see anyone crying on television, I'm sure Mr Menthol has been at work.

During the last scene in the first series of *Big Deal*, having lost £10,000 in a poker game, I rush to the airport to try and get Sharon to change her mind, not go to Australia, and stay with me. I cried, she cried. Then I noticed that she was crying more than me. Lots more. When I asked her where all that fluid had come from, she produced the Menthol crying stick. I remembered this trick and, a few years later, having to turn on the waterworks in a scene, I called up the services of Mr Menthol. Unused to this product and with no instructions on the label, I ladled it on liberally. I thought my eyes were going to fry to a crisp. I had to go and stick my head in a bowl of water.

So, I said to June 'no', I'd do it my way. As most of the scene was quoting Pauline, I'd planned to try my hand doing a Rory Bremner. I'd been listening to her for over a year, and I have a reasonable ear for inflection and tone. The result was eerie; it sounded just like her! I was thrilled. That extra fag had done the trick! It was like Jonathan Price doing his Hamlet: instead of meeting his father's ghost, it welled up inside him and his father's voice came out of his own mouth. He seemed to be having a conversation with himself. He got great reviews. Everything else after that was a let down.

June and I finish one take. I get through it without too many hitches, so I'm quite pleased.

The producer, Tanya Nash, comes round.

'Ray, cut back the Pauline imitation. It doesn't really work.'

I didn't have the energy to argue. But why can't they take risks? Wouldn't a man in my position, in real life, twist and turn himself into knots in his hatred of somebody who was so cruel. His imitation might not be perfect, but in his desire to get his point across he would use all the means at his disposal. But I was vulnerable. How could I stand up and demand that it stayed in? It's too much of a gamble. So, I throw in the towel and settle for the odd, not too dangerous, inflection. Fowler fury stretched back from the *EE* grave. The power was still there.

During *Death of an Expert Witness*, sitting on a bench in a graveyard, with Roy Marsden looming over me, I had to give my confessional speech. During rehearsals, Roy had leaned closer to me and, keeping his voice low, said, 'Cut it back, Ray.'

Cut it back! That's something else I'll have on my gravestone.

The day went on in much the same way and then it was over. As I made my way back to the dressing room, I had a niggling feeling that I'd let myself down – 'A bad workman always blames his tools.' I should have been able to do more, I should have asserted myself, but that's not my way, and I'm too old to change. All that's left is regret.

Brighton is glorious. It seems to be smiling through the scaffolding embracing its seafront teeth. A week before I fall out of the window I sit in a shelter on the promenade. It might have been the same shelter that I sat in fifty years ago when Ann arrived with the telegram offering me my first job at The Nottingham Playhouse. It was raining then but not today.

The defunct West Pier, collapsing piece by piece into the sea, a metal spider on its last legs, was my favourite pier as a kid after the war. We'd flood onto it on our holidays and weekends and run straight to the ice hockey machine.

The hockey machine had character and it malfunctioned in our favour. Slip a penny onto the metal slider tray, push it about half way, listen for the balls to drop and away you go. You never spent that penny as long as you hung your coat over the half open slot – there were plenty of lurking Pier attendants in those days and they didn't trust little boys.

Another machine with character was the pinball machine in Sadie's coffee bar, the one with the cigarette hole in the plastic surface. I renamed it 'The Magic give us a Kiss Machine'. I realise that Sadie and I are now the only ones who remember that magic machine. It's sad. But at least our boys and little Joe can read about it here.

The third machine was of the drinks variety, and situated just outside The Playhouse Theatre at Butlins Holiday camp in Clacton. I was always short of money, having to pay for my digs up front. Once I had bought my packet of ten fags for the week, it was all too easy to gamble away the rest of my money in the amusement arcade on my way down to the camp.

It was a hot summer. (Weren't they all?) Consequently, I used to get very thirsty. A couple of swift bashes on the side of the drinks vending machine guaranteed a cardboard cup of ice-cold fizzing Seven Up.

Sitting here in the shelter on Brighton seafront, all these machines buzzing around in my head, I remembered Ron Pember, my embryonic playwriting pal in Clacton. I thought of the plays we planned to write, all about those 'lost' young men of the angry type, giving up everything, desperate, losing faith and the will to live and, in the end, going back home, back to the womb.

231

The irony of those scenarios is that, in a curious way, they mirror what I'm doing in Brighton – licking my wounds, but not giving up. I'm certainly angry. And, like Jimmy Porter, angry with the world but, unlike him, I'm also angry with myself.

'Stand up for yourself.'

So I do and walk along the seafront.

Alforno's, a pasta restaurant, juts out over the beach. Miss Tig and Abby are sitting on the veranda; I have a glass of wine with them. Life *is* good in the sunshine.

'Put some sun protection on your head, Dad!'

Joe and I sat here one evening during a holiday trip to the seaside.

'What was the war like, Grandad?'

I gave him the full blast. 'Barbed wire all along the beach, barrage balloons, the Germans were just across the sea in France.'

'We're you scared?'

'I used to think that if I ran up the hill, their tanks couldn't roll up there, so I'd be safe. I was only about three.'

'The Germans must have been horrible!'

'They were.'

Then we became aware that the people sitting at the next table were speaking in foreign accents.

'Germans!' Joe whispered.

We finished our pizzas double quick and flew.

'The West Pier,' I said as we made our way along the seafront. 'Look at that.' It was a glass-sided booth at the far end that seemed to have escaped the rigours of the elements. 'Isn't that someone sitting in there?'

There was a dark shape inside it.

'He could be a German spy!'

This game went on for months. The seagulls were the spies, who flew over Brighton, spotting places where the Germans could land. We even went so far as to buy a book about seagulls, with illustrations, so that we could identify the 'German' ones. What we would have done if we'd discovered a 'spy seagull' God knows. Fortunately, we never identified one.

I finished my wine with Tigs and Abby and continued my wander. Next to The Metropole Hotel is a pub called The Hole in Wall in which I had once taken refuge when caught in a severe and sudden downpour. I had pushed the door open and said, 'Do you serve drowned rats in here?'

A voice which could well have come from one of the cast of *Soldiers in Skirts* had answered, 'Don't worry, ducky, we serve anybody in here!'

Along the coast to my right is the Palace Pier, now for some reason called the Brighton Pier. At the end of that pier was a theatre, now turned into a fruit-machined, money-making paradise for fat men in suits puffing on cigars.

I first worked that theatre playing a boy who nearly has his head chopped off in an amateur production of *The Mikado*; then, much later, in the opening production of a company about to embark on a summer season in Ilfracombe.

Just before its demise, the theatre was also used for scenes from Pete Walker's *The Flesh and Blood Show*. When we thought we'd lost six-year-old Will to the cruel sea, panic set in and we went round screaming his name until he popped up from behind one of the fading plush seats in the auditorium, whereupon, as is common to all parents in a state, we proceeded to tell him off.

This was the part of town which Phil Daniels and his mods tried to trash when shooting the film *Quadrophenia*, which Steve ('Chip butties keep me fit') McFadden failed to get into because he didn't get out of bed in time.

Funnily enough, Denis Waterman wasn't in that film. You'd have thought he would have been, wouldn't you? He's been in almost everything else. His latest escapade is *New Tricks*, a gentle cops and robbers caper. Before *EE*, to try and keep my new agent Roger sweet, I went along to read for it. Three or four scenes that's all. I read my usual Max Miller nonsense. Did I get it? Of course I didn't. Four scenes in *New Tricks* and I couldn't pull it off.

Just past the Brighton Pier, in Manchester Street, is what used to be called *The Komedia*. A venue for stand up comedians and music.

A year or so ago, Barry and Terry Cryer were celebrating a wedding anniversary there and invited me along to watch their daughter, Jack, singing. What a singer she is! Stunning.

Later that evening, after a few scoops, I grabbed Barry by the shoulders and said, 'You know something, you're a genius.'

He merely laughed that dismissive laugh we've all heard on *I'm Sorry, I Haven't a Clue*.

I pass Redbrick Lodge, Ann's parents' house fifty years ago and, on the corner, the church where she married someone else. I decided not to go and see Paul; it was a nice day for a walk.

At the Marina there is the Walk of Fame. I've got a plaque. There's Max Miller, my audition companion, Olivier and other local notables. My plaque is positioned between Ballyreagan Bob, the champion greyhound, and the Brighton Tigers, the Canadian ice hockey team which packed up in the fifties.

Halfway between the Marina and Rottingdean is Roedean School for Girls. When I was a teenager, it was rumoured that there was an ancient tunnel, embedded in the cliffs, that led up to the school. My mates and I had many a whispered conversation in which plans were laid to try and discover this tunnel one night, get though it and ravish the hoity-toity girls slumbering on silk sheets. Kids have mucky minds.

Rottingdean is a small coastal village with a couple of pubs, some local shops and a mix of expensive properties and council houses. Two buses go from there through the country, up through Moulsecombe, further up to the racecourse and then down, down steep hills into the town. For Joe and me, upstairs, right at the front, it is our 'white knuckle ride'. Through the narrow streets and roads we go. The trees seem to have given up being knocked around; they have withdrawn their branches permanently to give the 2a and 2b room to swing and swerve around to their hearts' content. It is a great ride. I haven't done the Grand Canyon but it would have to go some to beat this.

It's funny that the plaques on either side of mine have connections with interests I had in the old days, the compliant ice hockey machine on The West Pier and Ballyreagan Bob, the greyhound.

I always take Joe to the Greyhound Stadium in Hove. I used to go with Michael and Will and Tom. Ian Botham was there on a charity night sitting on a table below me and the lively Mike.

'Ray, have you got a tip for the next race?' he asked.

Mike looked up from his dark rum and coke. 'How d'you earn a living now you're not doing Question of Sport, eh?'

Mr Botham stood up. He's a big bloke, and I thought he was

going to whack Mike. He might have seen the pained expression on my face, but he sat down again. He didn't ask me for a tip the rest of the evening.

Joe loves it there. 'Why don't they let you bet on the dog that comes last, Grandad?' Reasonable idea because the ones we back seem inevitably to end up in that position. Our ambition is to pay for the taxi to the track and another to The Regency where we spend the rest of our winnings on a fish-and-chip blowout.

'Go and see Charlie, Grandad.'

Charlie Miller is an on-track bookmaker. I've known him for years and I ask him to mark our card.

'I'll do the first four races and I'll catch up with you later.'

We won on the first four! Charlie turns up.

'Why don't you give up bookmaking and just bet, Charlie.'

Logic from Joe. A wry smile from Charlie.

''Cos I make more money on the losers than I do on the winners.'

So the winnings paid for everything.

'We've got enough money for a gut-buster breakfast at Billy's tomorrow before we go home.'

'How much have we got?'

'Twenty pounds.'

'Let's forget the breakfast and split it. I could do with the money.'

Shrewd boy.

Now I get the 2b on my own and rock-and-roll down to The Cricketers for a welcome couple of beers.

Saturday 9th December

Last day, no lines. I just have to lie down in Bridge Street, dead as a dodo. It'll be a strange day, so I decide to take Joe and Annie, his friend, and Tessa, her grandma, who will chaperone. Kids have to have chaperones up here, 'in case they fall over a cable'.

We get there at 2.30 to find they've shot all the stuff they had to shoot and all the actors have gone home. Disappointing for the kids.

They have to wait until it's dark to film the fall out of the window. So a bit of food for the little ones and then a tour round the studios, followed by a further trip around the Square. It's very bleak, like a ghost town.

The time has come for them to watch 'me' fall out of the window. I meet Tid, my stunt double. He looks pretty good in the sparse grey wig – all the right gear, but no treble chins or beer gut. They won't notice that when he comes flying out of the window.

He has to fall backwards through the first floor window, bounce on the overhang of the sitting room window, then twist and fall into the Square among the deserted stalls. Not easy and certainly dangerous. I wanted to ask him if he was scared but decided against it.

He did it in one! A lot of applause among the technicians. Quite right too. He told me he reckoned that he'd probably have a couple of bruises. I'm surprised he didn't have a couple of broken legs and a broken neck.

I asked the kids if they'd found it exciting. They nodded unenthusiastically. They'd seen more exciting stuff on digitally enhanced movies.

'He could have broken his neck.'

'Did you see *Pirates of The Caribbean*, Grandad?'

Now it was my turn.

'I want you to twist into your final position – that way it will cut in with Tid's fall – then I want you to keep your eyes open for a couple of seconds. I'll shout "Now!", then you close them. Give me room for the dum, dum, dums.'

I was thrilled to be getting a dum, dum, dum. I'd only had one and half all the time I'd been here. The one I had screwed up – it was all a rush and scramble – so I'd pulled a few faces. No time for a retake. The half was sharing one with my wife. She must have done more dum, dum, dums, than Gene Krupa on his bass drum. But now I was getting one and dying. No need for pulling faces, just die. Fabulous!

I did six takes! Tid fell out of the sky in one. I can't even die properly.

'OK, that'll do.'

I think they gave up on me.

Then the *EE* moment, like the champagne on your birthday.

Jane, the AD, steps out. 'That's Ray's last scene on *EastEnders*.'

There's applause. I wonder how many times they've been through this ritual. Tanya, the producer appears, carrying two presents.

'You know what this is.'

It was the *EastEnders* board that everyone gets signed by the cast.

'And this is from Diederick.'

It was the routine cufflinks bought in bulk from Aspreys.

JOE FALLS ONTO THE CLOSED UP TOY STALL. THE STALL CONCERTINAS IN AROUND HIM.

GO TO DOT AND JIM FROZEN IN SHOCK AT PAULINE'S BEDROOM WINDOW.

FROM THEIR POV, TAKE JOE. HIS BODY AT AN IMPOSSIBLE ANGLE, HIS EYES ARE OPEN, BLANK AND LOOKING UP TO THE HEAVENS.

JOE IS DEAD.

But I'm not really, am I?

We leave. Everybody seems to have gone, but John Bardon looms round the corner. Almost the first person I saw when I arrived eighteen months ago and now definitely the last. What a bookend situation. The great man ambles towards us.

'What a fucking time of night to start work!' Sees Joe and Annie. 'Sorry kids.' Gives me wink. 'Your last day, son?'

I introduce him to Joe, Annie and Tessa.

'All right, darlins? Nice to meet you.'

He turns and puts his arms round me.

'Good luck, son.' Then he kisses me on the cheek. I'm not exaggerating when I say that I love that man tons.

We get in the car and go home.

Next morning my shoulder aches from having six times twisted into a dead dum, dum, dum position. But it's over. No more five o'clock alarm clocks, no more going to bed at nine o'clock with a glass of wine and a fag, staring at tomorrow's script, not going to sleep in case the alarm doesn't go off. Back to normal.

But thank you, *EastEnders*, for allowing me to meet such people as Angie, Jackie and Karn, all of whom – particularly Karn – work their socks off and, of course, all the actors, most of whom I've talked about in these pages, whom I admire for their 'stickability' and good humour under fire.

I thank *EE* paypackets for the roller coaster ride, the ability to avoid the *Coronation Street* of 2008 of five episodes a week, though if it had been able to transport me back to 1962 I would probably have grabbed it with both hands. All the hopes – all encouraged by my naivety no doubt – all turned to dust. But isn't it the way with all actors' careers. Of course it is. Maybe it was only to be expected.

But *EE* opened my eyes and, whatever your age, that's no bad thing.

There's so much to cling on to. The family provides a lifeline. They might get pissed off with you (and they certainly do that, believe me) and you can get pissed off with them. But they're still the centre of your life.

And Sadie and I are right at that centre. Between us we have produced extraodinary children. Emma, a social worker, caring for people more than she cared about herself; Will, the entrepreneur, more ideas then a normal brainbox could hold, his latest being Myfootballclub.co.uk, an online company that has bought Ebbsfleet United; and Tom, the brain for organising business, making sandwiches and football commentary, now helping Will.

New arrivals: Joe, Emma and Nel's son, growing into a wonderful young man; and Anna, Tom's beautiful wife, who makes us very happy. And now a stork arrives bringing Maisy, a new Brooks to join the team.

Asleep at night, I dream of being very young again and I keep saying over and over, 'If I had the chance, I'd do everything all over again.'